Seth is a master at helping people discover the great success they yearn for. The roadmap that he provides within this book not only guides the reader through a journey of clarity, achievement, and goal realization; it helps lay a useful mental foundation that is necessary to tap the essential fuel and passion to keep you going year after year. This is a great guide to help anyone realize their true potential!

Dave "The Shef" Sheffield, Author and Professional Speaker

Seth has captured the essence of true leadership in this powerful work. To let go of control and be willing to surrender into the service of humanity, the earth, and the divine is to let our will be led by greater purpose and vision. Only then can our truest gifts flow though us into the world. Through this work, Seth has delivered such a gift. Keen learning, deep observation, and inspiration have culminated with soulful excellence in the concepts, strategies, and tools presented here for true and sustained breakthrough in a unique and powerful way.

Marilena Minucci, MS, CHHC, Creator, Quantum Coaching Method™

Indestructible Success is full of incredibly effective tools that take your life to a whole new level of consciousness in ways you'd never imagine! It is a book designed to help you live your life more powerfully by bringing to the surface profound knowledge that you already have inside you.

Stephen J. Hopson, Speaker and Best Selling Author of *Obstacle Illusion*

If keeping a sound mind while building your business seems hopeless, chances are you've never heard of Seth Braun.

Rose Payne, Founder, HighLevelWellnessOnline.com

I've found the book to be a treasure of incredible insights and tools. I jumped in and landed in the section of the inner game and was hooked. I will be using it as a manual and guide for a long time. I really think the book is a treasure for practitioners, and it's remarkable what you've synthesized and presented.

Nicole DiDio Johnson, founder, TheHealthyDesign.com

I am so grateful to have this book. I think that it is going to serve me until the end of my life…it brought me to a different dimension of work…it has helped me see obstacles as opportunities, which means less stress. I could not stop reading the "outer game" chapter! It's helping me a lot with the work I do with my clients.

Slavka Benova, Certified Health Coach

W9-ART-326

INDESTRUCTIBLE SUCCESS:

Creative Entrepreneurship and
The Art of Small Business

Seth Braun

HAVING FUN AND KEEPING IT REAL

Rhythm House
Rhythm House Publishing

Seth Braun provides practical tools to develop inner strength and outer actions to create happiness and prosperity, personally and professionally.

Joshua Rosenthal, Founder, Institute for Integrative Nutrition

Seth Braun's message is a professional and spiritual transmission. This book works on you from the inside out, evoking a new level of clarity, purpose and power. Lots of books provide skills and strategies… this one makes you want to wake up, stand up, and joyfully create the destiny that is yours alone.

Jeff Salzman, Founder of Career Track, Co-Founder, Boulder Integral

Seth is right on target with this comprehensive, multi-level approach to both inner and outer soul work. Based on his own deep exploration of both the shadows and the light, this book is a treasure trove of powerful tools that are immediately accessible at so many levels.

Tom Daly, PhD, Founder, 4 Gateways Coaching, Founder & Director of the Living Arts Foundation

Seth shares from personal experience, making the teachings and tools that much more effective.

Andrea Beaman, HHC, Chef, Author and host of Fed Up!

Seth Braun is a clear and intuitive teacher and coach. My work with Seth opened me up to a new way of eating and caring for my body that has allowed me to perform at high levels in my work and life. Indestructible Success will change the way you care for your small business or practice, allowing you to be fed by your work rather than being drained by it. This is a must read for anyone trying to grow their business in a holistic way.

Brian Gast, Executive Coach, founder of Quadrant International

Seth Braun has created a monumental resource for coaches wanting their own transformation. This book is about integrating all the different possibilities in one's life; from divorce and back, to growing a successful business, receiving money from known and unknown sources, walking your talk, and connecting with the divine. Seth is the coach's coach. This is an invaluable resource to sharpen your inner and outer game, and take the limits out of the sky.

Stacey Morgenstern, co-founder of Holistic MBA

INDESTRUCTIBLE SUCCESS:

Creative Entrepreneurship and
The Art of Small Business

Seth Braun

HAVING FUN AND KEEPING IT REAL

Rhythm House
Rhythm House Publishing

© 2011, Seth Braun

The Warrior Artist Project

ISBN: 978-0-9834446-0-2

Library of Congress: 2011904723

Publisher: Rhythm House, Fairfield, Iowa, USA
1. Personal Growth. 2. Small Business. 3. Creativity

Indestructible Success: Creativity, Enterpreneurship,
and the Art of Small Business / Seth Braun

Indestructible Success logo and name are ™ of Braun Co. LLC
Cover Design by Nicole Didio Johnson at Healthy Design
Layout by Sylvie Abecassis
Printed by InfoDistributors, www.InfoDistributors.com

This book is for educational purposes only. This book is not intended to be
legal, medical, financial, psychological, or any other professional counsel.
The information here is not a substitute for professional advice or care. If
you need or want or other expert assistance you should seek out the help of a
qualified expert. The author, the publisher, their employees, agents, and any
other parties involved in the production, editing, or review of this book are
not liable for any damages arising from or in connection with the use of or
dependence on any information contained in this book.

DEDICATION

To my wife AnaVictoria and my daughters, Paloma and Marisol;
Love is the hidden foundation of Indestructible Success.

TABLE OF CONTENTS

INDESTRUCTIBLE SUCCESS:

Creative Entrepreneurship and
The Art of Small Business

INTRODUCTION

We live in an age of overwhelm.

To live well in the age of overwhelm means having a compelling vision – taking meaningful action – cultivating courage – developing confidence.

Instead of getting stuck in hating the distractions and stresses of our time, we can get stronger by seeing the opportunity inherent in the problem. The opportunity is to step into the integral age and to develop more robust systems for inner and outer skillfulness.

You can meet the complexity of your life.

In meeting the world, you will become the change you wish to experience.

Creative Leaders, Leaders of the Creative

The material you will learn in this book came from what I learned going for my dreams as creator then helping other people go for their dreams as a coach. This has made me an entrepreneur and small business owner.

Working for smart creative leaders, I noticed themes emerge. There have been consistent and similar challenges on the road to making a dream a reality. Dreams that range from starting a private practice, recording a solo album, initiating a career as a professional actor or opening a restaurant.

My clients have taught me that the great problem of our time is not a lack of motivation, it is not a lack of great ideas, nor is it a dearth of ambition. The great problem of our time is distraction, overwhelm and complexity. (My editor has made it clear repeatedly that overwhelm is a verb, but in this book I use it to describe a state experience.)

And as this book demonstrates, this obstacle is your opportunity.

The Rise of The Right Brain

It occurs to me that successful creators, leaders and entrepreneurs need to develop the capacity to manage their internal state of mind and energy more precisely than ever before while also skillfully navigating the influx of information, opportunity, relationships and influence from others. You are being called on to hold multiple perspectives. You are asked to simultaneously tolerate ambiguity and generate determination. You are asked to relate to people along a wide spectrum of paradigm alignments.

Socially, you are just beginning to have the opportunity to transcend the culture wars between traditional, modern and post-modern paradigms, while including all of the wisdom from each.

In business, you are fully into the shift from managing things (the industrial age management model) to managing creativity, energy and information (the knowledge worker economy).

Technologically, you have the ability to connect to nearly anyone at anytime.

Therefore, I assert that what you need now more than ever is training in the internal and external foundations for success. You need to develop your capacity.

This is obvious to people in clearly creative fields but applies to broad industries as well.

Since automation can handle routine and recurring tasks and since much of the production work requiring repetitive work is being outsourced to Asia, your greatest asset is your creativity, innovation and leadership capacity. You need to develop tremendous agility with traits such as adaptability, emotional stamina, peak performance states, extended concentration, capacity for large amounts of data, ability to quiet the mind and skill in communicating abstract ideas while relating to diverse populations. And most importantly, you need to learn how to focus on key outcomes, develop your faith in your self and your ideas and get a grasp on knowing how and when to persist like a bull dog and when to flow like a river.

From Distracted and Overwhelmed to Confident, Focused and Productive

Since most of my clients are unconventional or post-conventional in orientation, they are dealing with this stuff in spades. Let me give you an example of a client that applied the principles of this book.

Marian Flaxman came to my weekend training and identified that she had six major projects that she was engaged in. She was passionate about all of them. They included:

1. Going back to university and studying with a mentor she admired in a business sector she loved, the hospitality industry
2. Teaching workshops at high schools on health and nutrition
3. Starting a food production company for healthy cultured beverages
4. Coaching people on health and nutrition
5. Playing music
6. Raising her four year old daughter

We spent time reviewing how much time it would take for her to successfully engage in each of these. We worked together to identify her "hell yeah" passions, skills and value creation opportunities. Here are a few of the tools we used:

• 4 Gateways coaching for clarity and the "Aha!" moment
• Mind mapping was the core process to capture the whole experience
• Journaling gave way to deeper insights
• Planning with calendars made it practical and triggered some hard choices
• Affirmative Invocation generated energy and confidence.

After three days of visioning with these tools plus peer-to-peer conversation, she decided to pursue one focused project, a retail food production business.

This naturally morphed into a restaurant concept. Today, she is the successful owner of Culture Shock, an innovative cafe in Ithaca, NY that serves what is probably the widest variety of non-alcoholic cultured and fermented beverages. Her success came by getting clear on what I call her "north star," and staying in the same direction. Now it is an entirely unique and exceptional place:

Culture Shock is a place where art, music, and food come together. Where cultured food meets cultured people, and menu choices are inspired by cuisine from distant cultures. The food is fresh and vibrant, and so is the atmosphere. Live cultures in the drinks, live music on the stage. Fresh food on your plate, fresh perspectives on the walls. When you walk through our doors, we invite you to Taste Live Culture, not just in your food, but through all of your senses. (www.tasteliveculture.com)

You will get the same experience from this book that Marian got from the weekend training.

You are going to get a system for results:

- Clear instruction on how to discover a compelling vision for your life
- A step-by-step guide for creating goals that bring that vision down to manageable chunks
- Methods for focusing your time, energy and attention to get consistent traction on your goals
- A regular rhythm and routine that you can use to persistently take the most relevant actions each week

You will be provided with tools and techniques for personal cultivation:

- The three-part process you can use to generate the confidence necessary to play big
- An understanding of how you can use 9 steps to turn fear into fuel and develop courage and compassion
- A perspective on how to be the change you wish to see by living according to your personal code of integrity

You'll learn processes for better outcomes with people:

- A process for coaching your team, colleagues, peers or employees for better results anywhere at anytime
- Tips on powerful and effective communication to share your creative or entrepreneurial endeavor
- Suggestions on how and why collaboration will take you farther in sharing and expanding your success

And you are going to get powerful practices for the fundamentals of achievement:

- Reminders on how to take back your time and increase your productivity
- The low-down on how to make relationships not only fulfilling and rich but also a bedrock for success in your projects
- Best practices for authentic selling and marketing of your ideas, products or services

A whole heck of lot of inspiring stories to light a fire in your heart and mind for the next greatest version of your life!

Taken as a whole, the book teaches you the Four Pillars of Indestructible Success: Vision, Action, Courage and Confidence.

So why am I so interested in all of these tools, techniques and strategies for success? Is it because I am really motivated, really organized and super focused?

I've immersed myself in this material because of the terrific effort it has taken to corral my life into order and functionality. I successfully used these practices to overcome significant setbacks, including tragedy, addiction, divorce, financial disaster and lot of dark places inside. And I used these practices to create the life of my dreams; I have enjoyed building tremendous health and vitality, recording original albums, producing and directing theatre, staring businesses, writing, publishing and selling a best-selling book series, and recovering my family.

You don't want to learn from someone pretending to have every aspect of their life totally buttoned up. How could you relate? You want to learn from a guide on the side, not a sage on the stage. We are all craving authenticity and transparency. You want a sense of depth from embracing the paradox of not always having an answer. I struggle with the challenges that I refer to in this book. But I also practice the tools. I think that makes me an effective teacher.

Indestructible Success is not about a perfect life. This book shares natural principles that work. It is really pretty simple. What makes it unique is the way I apply the principles of creative process to business and apply the results-oriented business models to creativity. And this is where I think we are going –creative entrepreneurship. While there are many books on success, this one explicitly outlines an integral approach to developing the internal and external qualities that knowledge workers, cultural creatives and next generation entrepreneurs want and need.

Indestructible Success means that you can meet an obstacle, learn from it, and grow stronger as a result. It is written to help you find a way to live your dreams, which is often through business or creative endeavor. I want to help you serve the world. My hope is that the result of your relating to this material is greater agency (*the state of being in action or exerting power*) in your own life.

Have fun and keep it real.

Seth Braun

SECTION A:

**Discover Your Dreams
and Make Them Real**

CHAPTER I

VISION = ENTHUSIASM

> *Where there is no vision, the people perish.*
> **Proverbs 29:18**

THE PURPOSE OF CHAPTER 1:

I want you to feel inspired about discovering a compelling vision, and I want you to have tools you can use to uncover that vision for the next greatest version of your life. You will learn how to get clear on your vision for your mission in life.

Have you seen the light?

James Brown, from The Blues Brothers

On a Mission From God

In the 1980 comedy *The Blues Brothers*, Jake and Elwood Blues (John Belushi and Dan Akroyd) have to find a way to pay the taxes on the orphanage they grew up in or the children there will lose their home.

In trying to figure out how to do it, their mentor and father figure Curtis (Cab Calloway) tells them to "get some churchin' up."

In the middle of a service at the church of Rev. Cleophus James (James Brown), a beam of light enters through the stained glass window and engulfs Jake. In that moment, Rev. James says, "Have you seen the light?!"

Jake, "I see it!"

Rev. James, "Have you seen the light?!"

Jake, "I see it!"

Rev. James, "Have you seen the light?!"

Jake, "I see it!"

And Jake turns to his brother Elwood and says, "The band Elwood, the band!," and thus begins their mission from God where providence moves to help them accomplish their goal.

Have you seen the light? Have you looked inside to find out what your mission is?

Vision Pulls You Forward

When you have an inspired vision, you are literally compelled to act on it each and every day. Some people have goals that are so compelling that they can't wait to get out of bed. Other folks have a dream of creating a new life for their family and kids and will find the energy to work tirelessly for years on end. This is having a vision. This is how vision pulls you forward.

But this idea confuses people.

Sometimes they think that since they don't have this experience, they must not have a vision, purpose, or a dream. Still others wonder why they are not inspired by a vision that they had a few years ago.

Having vision is not something that happened to you in the past. The gravity of a powerful vision is the result of spending time in that field. It is there. You need to encounter it.

Let me explain.

Everyone has a vision. You have a vision now, whether you feel connected to it or not. I have a powerful vision for my life, but sometimes I get lost or out of sorts. That doesn't mean my vision disappeared. It just means that maybe I am tired, overwhelmed, frustrated, or the like. When that happens, you have to reconnect. That is the trick.

Even if you haven't ever really had this connection, you still have a vision. It is like Michelangelo uncovering the sculpture in a block of marble. It is in there. You don't make it happen. You simply remove the stone around it and it emerges!

A Blind Vision

My good friend Brian Rocheleau, known to his friends and fans as "Rosh," came to me as a client. He had a dream. He wanted to create music that would impact people. He wanted to find a way to move people with his artistry so that they would be inspired to live their unique dreams.

To do this, he set a goal to record an album and continue touring Europe doing house concerts. He would be a messenger for cultural exchange through music. Rosh had already completed a house concert tour in Ireland and Norway as well as tours around the USA. As far as I know, no one had done what he wanted to do next—set up a house concert tour for an American folk musician in Iceland.

Well, Rosh raised the money to fund the production of the CD and the cost of the tour. With Herculean efforts, he enrolled total strangers in his vision, including the mayors of small villages. The tour was a great success. He made back the money for the investors and then some for his pocket. It was uncharted territory, a real adventure.

But not without fear.

You see, most of the tour necessitated hitchhiking in Iceland. Icelandic is not an easy language. Iceland is not an easy place to hitchhike. And get this…

One night, Rosh showed up at a church to prepare for another concert. The people who were supposed to host the concert must have bailed. No one was there. No one came. It was cold. He was hungry. He played the show for an empty church. And all of his worst fears came true. He was frustrated, disappointed, upset. Then he poured his emotions into a list of his greatest dreams. All of his fear, all of his upset, and all of his frustration at showing up to an empty venue were channeled creatively.

He got one hundred percent clear that he wanted to make music for an audience that would be devoted to the music and that the experience would be wildly inspiring for the audience as well. He wanted to create more than a concert. He wanted to produce an experience.

But that's not the point of my story.

Later in Rosh's trip, he walked into a pitch-black café. It was a "blind café."

The waiters are actually blind and they seat you, serve you, and escort you.

Hmmm...

Rosh was so moved by this that he thought, why not set up a blind café in Boulder, Colorado (his home at the time) and play a set of music in that atmosphere? People would have to really tune into their other senses and they would really feel the music.

Well, it has been two years since the first Boulder Blind Café opened for business. He has now produced the Portland Blind Café and the Boulder Blind Café a half dozen times, as well as the Austin and Cincinnati Blind Cafés. By the time this goes to print, there will have been more. By the time you read this, The Blind Café may have been in San Francisco, New York, Miami, and Boston.

Rosh had to use everything he learned from his previous entrepreneurial and creative experience to pull these off. Find investors, raise capital, and coordinate food, wait staff, venue, and musicians (including a full acoustic string section). Then, orchestrate the whole event as a masterful producer. This is Rosh's gold, his dream, his unique gift. When he brings it all together, magic happens. People weep, laugh, and are moved by the experience.

This is creative entrepreneurship. But it wouldn't have happened if Rosh hadn't learned how to use his fear instead of being used by it. You will learn more about that in Chapter Five.

Rosh and the Blind Cafe are inspiring examples of how a compelling vision can bring out the best in your life and the best in YOU. Rosh continues to develop skillfulness in harnessing a vision for what he can create and then make that vision a reality.

Dreams

I think dreams are given to us by God. They are a Divine Idea planted in our soul. We are created to discover this dream, act on this dream and bring it to fruition. In the process of doing this, we are destined to become the next greatest version of ourselves. And in the process, we help others too. I can't prove that this is true. But given the choice, I'd rather believe that this is how life works. It is more interesting to me this way.

I believe that you have a dream too. And I believe that your God Mission in life is to find and fulfill your dream.

Is a Vision the Same as a Dream?

Wow, great question. Yes and No. A vision comes forth from our dreams for our lives. If your goals are tangible and measurable, and your dreams are ephemeral, vision could be the intermediary, giving us a template from our dreams around which to build our goals, plans and actions.

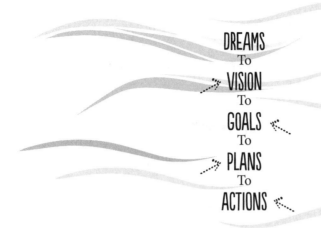

DREAMS
To
VISION
To
GOALS
To
PLANS
To
ACTIONS

Vision happens in your whole body. It is felt, seen, and experienced in the heart, in the gut, and in the mind.

I have a client, Ellie, an incredibly capable woman working as a health counselor in a large city. She was frantically running around, piles of papers on her desk, a list of phone calls to make, and a lot of fear about money. She had been very successful as broker, but now in this career, she was afraid that she was not good enough.

We worked together to address some of the core issues, to improve her daily use of time, and to generate positive states. But these would be lost without helping her reconnect to her sense of purpose, the experience of vision.

Always, there is a heart quality to this, and in this case, Ellie needed to reconnect with that energetic quality. Sure, she knew that she wanted to have her own space in an integrative medicine center. She knew she wanted twenty-five clients a week, that her target income was $7,500 a month. But her vision had become dry.

To bring life into it, I asked her why she wanted this. "Why" brings us back to the sovereign element of our being and helps us get a bigger perspective. She spent a few weeks regularly inquiring on "why," and the extrapolation on that, "What is my purpose?"

Once she did this, it became easy to stand in a powerful way. She remembered that her reason for doing this work was to help thousands of people live with more joy, more health, and more capacity. This connection to her vision gave her confidence. Her commitment to helping others became bigger than her fears because she had vision.

Ellie reconnected to the heart of service and contribution. Her clients felt this and her practice perked up.

What Stops Us From Living With Vision?

There are four main blocks that keep you from dreaming big and crafting a compelling vision.

1. **Distraction and Overwhelm**
2. **Fear**
3. **Comfort**
4. **What Will They Think?**

1. Distractions and Overwhelm

Distraction and overwhelm are the biggest obstacles to living with effectiveness.

It is not lack of ideas.

It is not lack of motivation.

For people like you and me, it is getting too many ideas stuck in the mind and not enough expression of those creative ideas. That is the root of overwhelm. It is fueled by the constant influx of media and information via technology (Internet, TV, movies, etc.).

For us, we get going on a project, and then some shiny object grabs our attention. This is distraction. It happens because we have so much opportunity!

As I write this, my four-year-old daughter, Marisol, bounces into my office. She reminds me of my vision and my purpose, which begins first and foremost in my home.

Marisol is showing me that even though her dancing and giggling in my office could be seen as an interruption of the important "work" of writing, she is the heart of my contribution. This reminds me to clarify that not all interruption is counter to vision or an obstacle to be overcome. Generally, the obstacles I see are smart phones, texting, e-mail, Facebook, Twitter, web surfing, and TV, in that order. I'll address these at length in Chapter 16.

Are there other interruptions?

Absolutely. Especially when you work in an office or group practice setting. The above examples are really about you working with your own experience. When you add in the social aspect of a clinic, center, or office space, you actually have less possibility of surfing the Net all day, but increased possibility of getting pulled out of productive focus by chitchat, gossip, and the potentially positive but often negative distraction of other people's goals.

2. Fear

The second major obstacle to experiencing a bright compelling vision is internal and boils down to a sap of fear.

As I mentioned, I think this is getting clearer and more defined collectively. We can agree that fear often stops us from taking action. Yet it is also an obstacle to dreaming up new possibilities. Sometimes the fear blocks us before our vision even gets articulated.

For you, a highly motivated and ambitious person, this is an automatic association. Vision is going to mean action. With my high achieving clients, I see that fear shows up as a block to even seeing the dream clearly.

When you are clear, you step up and take action. Fear of failure is pernicious. Since you are really smart, your automatic avoidance of hurt and pain mechanism kicks in and does the job of protecting you. That is when you get the experience of, *Hmmm...I guess I don't have a vision.*

Enter stage right, "The 9 Steps" process discussed in Chapter 5. The block to dreaming is fear of failure. We know that if we fall flat on our face, big time, it is going to hurt. Not to mention the hard time we give ourselves when we make a mistake. When our identity and self-worth is wrapped up in what we do, failing in our work becomes a devastating blow to our happiness.

Hence the 60 percent approach to being safe: you go for your dream with 60 percent of your potential; then if you fail, you can console myself with knowing that you could have done better. It protects the current identity. But with your biggest dreams, does 60 percent work to make them reality?

No.

So we need the courage to dream big. Chapter 5 describes techniques for dealing with fear.

3. Comfort

Do not confuse comfort with happiness. You can be uncomfortable and happy. And you can be comfortable and depressed. Living your dream means being uncomfortable. We can endure a huge amount of discomfort if there is meaning behind it. Take childbirth for instance. Women willingly endure a huge amount of discomfort because there is a compelling reason.

The way to beat comfort is to dig deep and discover a vision that is so inspiring and so connected to your values and your passion that you would do anything to make it happen. Here is something that you can write down and post up next to your computer as a reminder: *Don't ask for life to be easy, ask for it to be worth it!*

4. What Will They Think?

First of all, who are *they* and why are *they* so important?

They, in this case, represent the inner circle of imaginary people that you think are assessing your life. Everyone has this inner circle. It is often made of up of a mix of family members, people you went to high school or college with, people you have worked with, clients, or even ex-boyfriends.

Often times I hear the quote that people rank public speaking as the number one fear in the world. But the accurate statistic is that public humiliation is the number one fear in the world. Public speaking is just the most obvious way for many people to publicly humiliate themselves.

We have a deep mammalian drive to fit in to the group. It is a survival instinct. And it is at the root of all of the great mythic adventures. It is called the Hero's Journey. The Hero's Journey is what we all take whenever we want to create and live a compelling vision.

Hero's Journey

Knowing the stages of the Hero's Journey can be helpful to navigate potential obstacles.

The Condensed Hero's Journey:

1. The Call – you get inspired and naively see nothing but roses and rainbows on the path and set off eagerly.
2. The Separation – you leave the familiar town, village, tribe, way of thinking, way of acting, or the current paradigm; no turning back now.
3. The Descent – you realize that making this journey is full of challenges and trials, some are interesting and some just suck.
4. The Transformation – as a result of the sometimes cool, sometimes awful trials and tribulations, you have become a different person.
5. The Return – you come back to where you started a different person and you have gifts to give your community, your life, your creative work, etc.

Having a Vision

Question: *How do I tap into my vision?*

The question is well phrased. How do we "tap" into or draw out a vision? We're not inventing so much as discovering. Michelangelo revealed his sculptures from the stone. Great composers talk about music channeling through them. In a very real way, you are removing that material that keeps your vision hidden in stone.

I recently heard that Joseph Shabalala, the founder of Ladysmith Black Mambazo, started the sensational South African men's chorus as a result of a series of dreams. His dreams continued to guide him throughout the career of this globally recognized musical treasure.

I think our visions and dreams are seeds planted in us by the Divine. And like any creative act, persistent endeavor is the ground for emergence. You have to stick with the process of culling out all the non-vision material, the cutting away of the marble.

Having a buddy, friend, coach, or colleague work through this will help. You can encourage each other, check in, and stay focused.

Two Concrete Steps You Can Take

1. Morning Pages, *from The Artist's Way,* **by Julia Cameron**

Morning pages are three hand-written pages of stream of consciousness first thing upon waking up. After three to six months of this, you'll see trends and patterns emerge. A common sentiment expressed by students of *The Artist's Way*: "The line to my intuition has been re-wired. I am getting clear signals about the direction to take in my life."

Or, you can take it one step further and buy the book and do the 12-week *Artist's Way* program. Most cities have groups of people that meet and facilitate the process with each other. Please note that *The Artist's Way* is an open source platform and Julia Cameron does not "certify" anyone to facilitate. I know some groups that are facilitated by paid instructors and others that are peer run. Both seem to produce results.

2. *Purpose and Passion Journal*

Another surefire way to ignite the vision mechanism is to carry a "purpose and passion" journal around with you.

Purpose and Passion Process

Buy a small, pocket-sized notebook, like a moleskin journal.
   Each day, notice what excites and engages you.

Make notes about people, places, things, and circumstances that make you come alive.

- Take time each day to ask the questions:
- What am I designed for?
- What is my purpose?
- What legacy do I want to leave?
- What am I passionate about?

If I could do anything I wanted, without any concern for money or what other people think, what would I do?

After a few months, a definite pattern emerges. Review your notebook and see what obvious message appear.

Dreams

Yet another experiment is to do as Joseph Shabalala. Follow your literal dreams. I experimented with this for a theatrical production titled *Dream of Warrior Artist*. The process was an eighteen-month dream journal that influenced the rehearsals of a very powerful cast and culminated in a stunning performance of the relationships between the dreams of the night and dreams (aspirations) of the day.

What Do I Know for Sure?

Sometimes, though, it is as simple as asking, "What do I know for sure?"

I asked myself this question, or was asked this question, in a men's group in Boulder, Colorado, in November 2008. Since then, I have shifted massive amounts of my life focus and direction. Here is the list of five things:

- I need to be present for my daughters.
- I need to speak in front of people.
- I need to write books.
- I need to have my finances working.
- I need to coach people in groups.

Since then, I moved to Iowa, bought a house, remarried my ex-wife, and am having the time of my life with our two daughters.

I joined Toastmasters, began giving speeches regularly, and am now a paid professional speaker.

And, of course, I wrote this book.

My first book, *Healthy, Fast and Cheap* went on to sell over 30,000 copies. My career launched into delightful new opportunities. And I have the most amazing clients I could imagine.

All of this happened because I got clear about what I wanted. And it happened in literally two minutes.

This could be a life-changing moment for you. This question directly relates to the problem of distraction and overwhelm. So many are plagued with the burden of *so many good ideas*. With so much possibility, how do we know our right place?

What do I know for sure?

What do I know for sure helps us clear the debris and get to the gold!

O magazine always concludes with Oprah sharing *What I know for sure*. Did I get that imprint from her? I'm not sure, so I thought I'd open the little book *What I Know for Sure*, a collection of essays from 2000 to 2004. This one stood out:

> *If you don't know what your passion is,*
> *realize that one reason for your existence on Earth is to find out.*
> **Oprah Winfrey**

Here are a few nuggets from that article:
• All of us need a vision for our lives.
• Everyone has the power for greatness.
• God's dream for you is bigger than yours; surrender to it.
• If you want success, success cannot be your goal.
• Shift from success to service.
• The way to ultimate and real success is to honor your calling.
• Your life's work is to find your life's worth.
• Exercise discipline, tenacity, and hard work.

Uncovering a sense of purpose means listening for the dream and looking for the vision.

You can access the vision for your life by paying undistractible attention to stillness. It takes faith.

What if it's not there?

What if I hate it?

What if it is stupid?

The truth is that the intelligence that creates and sustains the implicit order in all of life probably knows what to manifest through you.

Take the time to listen.

Purpose and Vision

Visioning aligns you with your deeper life purpose. Rather than split these into two exercises, you will find that as you drop into a deep well of charisma for a vision that it is inextricably linked to a sense of purpose. Doing these exercises will bring you closer to living on purpose by showing you what that looks like. This could be defined as your charism. A power given you for the benefit of others.

A Contemplative Process for Purpose

Here is a step-by-step process that you can take immediately to connect to your purpose and a vision for a compelling future.

Set aside 20-30 minutes of your day. Take out a few blank sheets of paper. Then put yourself through a process of progressive relaxation. Breathe deeply into your belly; feel your body begin to relax and consciously choose to bring that relaxation to any tense place.

Next, tell your mind to relax, as you continue to breathe deeply.

Relax. Relax. Relax.

Finally, tell your emotions to relax. Allow any and all frantic, anxious, excited, or worried-ness to melt away as you relax, relax, relax. Imagine yourself in a warm, safe, comfortable place of great beauty. In this place, imagine a time when you felt connected and in the flow of life, and bring that feeling to a full expression in your experience.

From this place, ask yourself, "What am I created for?"

Then just listen.

Get supremely quiet and really listen with everything you've got. Take a minute to come up and out to make note of what you receive, and then return to the feeling of connection and flow.

Anchor it by establishing a strong memory of a time of powerful connection. Then ask, "What is wanting to emerge through me?" and listen with everything that you've got. Really listen, listen, listen. When you are ready to come up and out, make notes of any insight you've noticed while in the interior experience.

Then, bring yourself back into that relaxed, interior place and ask the question:

"If I were totally free to create anything and everything, what would I do?"

Stay with the process long enough to really soak up the question, and then come up and out to write down any thoughts and awareness.

There are more questions that you can use in this kind of process. I encourage you to repeat this regularly as you excavate your soul's deepest longing, the dream of your heart.

- What did I love as a child?
- What would I do whether I was paid or not?
- What do I absolutely love?
- At the end of my life, what would I regret not having done?
- What is the legacy that I am here to leave?
- What am I naturally gifted toward?
- When have I been most alive?
- What do I want to accomplish in the next 50 years?
- What do I want to accomplish in the next 25 years?
- What do I want to accomplish in the next 10 years?
- What do I want to contribute in the next 5 years?
- What can I create in the next 3 years?
- What can I bring to fruition in the next year?

When you do this kind of exercise, you are literally receiving the imprint from something that has not yet been created. You are opening to the unmanifest potential. You are allowing the unknown to become known to your conscious mind. This is visioning. It is removing the statue from the marble. Maybe it is a feeling, an image, or words.

Move through the film of uncertainty into the place of receptivity. The truth is that you don't know where your life will be going. But there is a place in you that can connect to intelligence that lives outside of time and space. That intelligence springs forth in vision.

True North and North Star

These expressions are used throughout the book and refer to heading in the right direction. You never know where life will take you, but you can have a sense of the direction. As you get a sense of your vision, this becomes your True North heading.

This inspiring vision or ideal is like a light that guides your feet. It becomes a lighthouse when you are getting tossed around on the waves of your own mental agitation.

There are many additional resources for connecting to your Divine Dream, your life's purpose. Here are a few:

Life Visioning, Rev. Dr. Michael Bernard-Beckwith

What Color Is Your Parachute, Richard N. Bolles

The Artist's Way, Julia Cameron

RECAP FROM CHAPTER 1:

- Vision literally compels you toward the future.
- Vision is part of the Dream of Your Heart.
- Vision is the template for goals.
- Outer distractions and inner fears are obstacles to vision.
- Contribution is at the heart of vision and life purpose.
- Dreams are inherent, not created; they are excavated.
- Connect to vision by asking, "What do I know for sure?"
- Dreams, life purpose, and vision are spiritual issues.
- To really dig into vision, meditate on it consistently.
- Use questions to hone your insight.

Your vision becomes a True North compass point you can use to guide your daily life or a North Star you can navigate by.

Stay in the process. Live in the questions. The greater your sense of desire to know, the more life will present you. Trust and look for synchronicities, coincidences, and inspiration.

Did you get inspired? Did you get some tools to help you uncover your vision?

SELF-STUDY EXERCISES:

1. Buy a small journal and keep track of what inspires you, excites you, or clicks inside of you on a daily basis. Do this for at least thirty days, and then review. What patterns emerge? What does this tell you?

2. Spend thirty minutes contemplating the questions that are listed in this chapter.

3. Ask trusted mentors and friends what they see as a vision for your life. Compare how their observations relate to your observations.

CHAPTER 2

PLANS = PEACE OF MIND

Most people plan their iPod playlists better than they plan their lives.
Seth Braun

THE PURPOSE OF CHAPTER 2:

In this chapter, you are going to get some useful tools on how to plan effectively. You'll learn how to turn your vision into smaller goals that you can realistically achieve monthly, weekly, and daily.

CHANGE MONSTER!

The big resistance I hear about plans is, *"What if things change?"* Then change your plans! In fact, they will change. Just by planning, you are in a higher state of consciousness. You can see more clearly. You can be more effective.

Plans and Goals

To have a goal, you need to have a plan. To have a plan, you need to have a goal.

Goals bring your dreams and visions into form. Your plan is the map to the destination of your goal.

They go hand in hand.

Mastering the Planning Process

The essentials of a plan are:
1. Actions
2. Time
3. Sequence
4. Outcome

You don't need to use the system that I use and offer here, but you do need a system that has the four elements mentioned here.

We are going to work with goals at macro and micro levels. The plan is a macro level, and actions are chunked down elements (micro). We'll deal with this in the next chapter.

You are going to take your vision from inside your heart and mind and make it real on the outside. This is creativity, and there is a real *art* to it. But it is the *science* of achieving goals that you'll use to make your dreams a reality.

Work Your Plan and Plan Your Work

You are now asked to specify the outcomes that emerged in the visioning process. When in doubt, return to "What do I know for sure?"

Do you squirm when you are asked to make definite plans? Are you concerned that you will lose spontaneity? Often the resistance to plunging in wholeheartedly comes from the fear, *What if I miss out?* The solution is simple: If an opportunity presents itself, take it! Then change your plans.

Overcoming Resistance to Commitment

The plunging-in phase is analogous to jumping into an icy mountain stream. At first, you have what we called in Outward Bound, the *anti-dip*. This is just avoiding discomfort. Once you make the plunge, whoo-hoo! It is enlivening, energizing, and chi invigorating!

For seventy-two days I ventured over land and sea on the Hurricane Island Outward Bound Wilderness Leadership Training. Jumping in icy waters was par for the course. But did that make it any easier on day sixty-two than it was on day one? No way!

With greater responsibility comes more freedom, and with more freedom, more responsibility. Plans free you from the spinning of ideas in your head. Once on paper, you can appreciate the opportunity to be less afraid and focus on action.

It is up to you to give your dreams everything you have!

The Indestructible Success Planning Process in Detail

Here is the basic idea for a three day planning process:

1. Brainstorm, mind-map, and work big. Get all of your ideas for your projects and goals out onto paper, everything that you think you need to do to make your vision real.
2. Then, take some time to organize your brainstorm. If it helps, you can use the goal setting guide in Appendix C.
3. Finally, move this into a twelve-month calendar, on big wall charts or big paper.

The funny thing about getting a really robust vision and plan out on paper is that it allows the mind to see the whole thing differently. If that seems frustrating, don't worry. Once all of the stuff rolling around your head is down on paper, a freedom emerges.

Here are some KEY concepts:

- Planning is supposed to be confusing.
- If you feel confused, congratulations.
- Planning is like wringing out the confusion.
- If you are overwhelmed, you are on the right track.
- Feeling lost means that you are about to synthesize a more coherent understanding.

Stay with the process and keep writing, mind-mapping, and…

GET THE IDEAS OUT OF YOUR HEAD.

Please don't force yourself to make your plan in bullet points. Use whatever program or method or system of planning works for you.

Three Day Process for Getting Clear

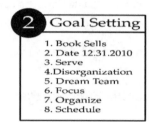

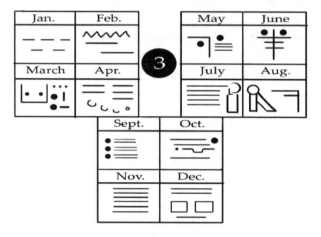

Day One

Start by working BIG! Get a flip chart, a roll of newsprint, or some other big paper. Grab a handful of markers. Do a little dance party and you are ready!

Stand up, draw with markers, write BIG, use space, have symbols, lines, squiggles. Feel free to doodle and design. These kinds of "games" and play move you through feeling stuck. It keeps you in the game and lets the *subconscious mind* work on the task at hand.

Okay, I know, we actually are still at the end of the visioning process and just into the planning process. There is always some overlap between the two. So here is my best version of *vision into plan*:

Keep working big, big, big. Use as much big flip chart paper as you want and mind-map the whole vision. Really spend some time with this and flesh out your vision into specific milestones, dates, times, people, places, and things. Get out everything that you possibly can think of and map it.

Mind-Map. What's That?

Mind-mapping is a liberating planning session. You organically allow the main ideas to show up on the page. Then you add circles, lines, dots, and flowers (or anything else that you want to symbolize connections and synergy). Most people begin with the main idea in the center of the document, add related ideas as they occur, and use lines and hatches to connect related concepts.

Day Two

Review your brainstorm/mind-map/vision document. Go ahead and add anything that POPS for you, but don't start another brainstorm session. Now is the time to move this into a framework. I do this on flip charts too, because I like to keep working big and creatively. You might find it helpful to use the goal-setting guide in Appendix C. Write down every step. Answer every question. Work the details.

Organize for each of the major life goals that you generated in the visioning process. Sometimes it is only one, but often there are many parts.

Day Three

Now it is time to put the whole thing into a calendar. (If you used the goal-setting guide in Appendix C, then this would be step nine.)

Once you have molded and shaped a plan for achieving your goals, pull out three flip charts and draw a line through the middle, top to bottom and from side to side, making four boxes on each sheet. Label each box with the month of the year, twelve in all. Using your best judgment, begin to map out your goals in a timeline over twelve months.

Jan.	Feb.	March	April	May	June
New Year, New You Programs	Interview Administrative Support	Train new assistant. Attend conference.	Begin referral program marketing	Organize new client intake process, One week hiking trip	Networking Press release about new technique

July	Aug.	Sept.	Oct.	Nov.	Dec.
Radio and TV interviews, Client appreciation day	Personal development retreat for 5 days	Begin promoting fall class series.	Class series begins, Record classes on video	Classes continue, Study video, improvements	Take one week off to review the year and rest

Get it out on a big calendar so you can see the whole twelve-month process.

*Purpose must be continually in your life to impassion you. Never catch up to your goals. Your **is** can never catch up with the **ought**.*

Dr. Viktor Frankl

I'd rather attempt to do something great and fail than attempt to nothing and succeed.

Rev. Dr. Robert H. Schuller

Why Should I Do Three Steps?

This process rocks! It's like doing a rough draft, outline, and final draft of a paper. You get to clarify and refine each step.

You can do this with rolls of newsprint or on corkboard five feet wide and ten feet long. Any way you do this, make your final draft something you can look at and see in your office or workspace. You can also buy a cheap office desk calendar for about five to ten dollars. Rip it apart. Pin it up, month by month, on your wall. And then use this for added granularity and specificity.

Now I know you can get a lot of tools to customize and support this process. There are planner companies that specialize in large dry erase boards. There are theatre production companies, teachers, and educators who use twelve- to twenty-four-month wall charts with dry erase markers. Feel free to explore. Try all sorts of ways to think outside the box.

What System of Organization Should I Use?

Do you find this process challenging? Is there a feeling of unease when taking a vision and turning it into a plan? By having a compelling reason for making your business or creative mark, you can learn to love this stage of creation.

There are hundreds of systems—iPhone, Android, iPad, laptop, cloud computing, Google calendar, and all sorts of project managing software— you can spend more time updating an outline of your projects than working on projects! Being organized for the sake of being organized is not the point. You go through this process of visioning and planning so that you can integrate the process and the intelligence for yourself. Then you have a reference point as you progress.

Study the work of Dr. Stephen Covey and David Allen. They have complementary systems for staying organized and effective.

Special Note: To supercharge your results, add in the inner game secrets to your tool kit (from chapters 5, 6, 7, and 8). Work these as you take action on your goals. Then your goals become the symbol of who you are becoming. This makes life rich, free, and beautiful! Upsets are welcomed and obstacles turn into opportunities, and every step of the journey is an outlet for you to generate joy and passion for life.

Now it is time to move into my favorite chapter.

RECAP CHAPTER 2:

- Plans = Time + Actions + Sequence + Outcome
- Plans free you up. Responsibility = Freedom
- You can make plans and still be spontaneous and responsive to opportunity.
- There is a foolproof system for achieving your goals.
- Work your plan through several versions; play and get BIG.
- Mind map.
- Plan a year minimum.
- Don't get overly absorbed in planning. It is a means to an end, not an end in itself.

SELF-STUDY EXERCISES:

- Make sure to take the time to do the mind mapping exercise. Try it out.
- Then take your ideas and organize them in a way that works for you.
- Once you have your ideas out on paper and organized, then plug them into a calendar with milestones.

Now, how do you make the plan actionable? How do you make it real? In Chapter 3, you will find out.

CHAPTER 3

ACTION = RESULTS

Knowledge without action is stale. Action without knowledge is frivolity.
Dream Seeker

Your actions are symbolic of your character. It is where your deepest notions are made visible to all around you. It is how you show what you really believe.

THE PURPOSE OF CHAPTER 3:

You are going to learn a habit and a tool that will allow you to consistently grow and achieve by chunking down large goals into small steps. This consolidates and focuses you on what is most important. It keeps you working your plan and planning your work. You'll have the tools for inquiring and learning more about yourself each and every week. The ability to accurately measure progress and success each week leads to self-reflection and inner growth.

Small Steps Are the Solution

As we move into the weekly and daily practice of taking meaningful action, a friendly reminder. The little things we do really do add up. Consistency over time is the KEY. The philosophy of small, sustainable, consistent steps is called Kaizen. Kaizen is summed up in the *Tao Te Ching*, "the journey of a thousand miles begins with one step". This philosophy is well documented in Dr. Robert Mauer's book *One Small Step Can Change Your Life.* The Indestructible Success action system revolves around these small steps. Each week, we identify the big goals that we have and then we take consistent action toward them. Simple as that.

Why Do We Focus on Seven-Day Cycles?

Any book on effectiveness has to point to Dr. Stephen Covey's contribution. Covey highlighted the trans-cultural emphasis on the week as the cornerstone of our effectiveness structure. Therefore, the Indestructible Success system revolves around the week as well.

A Consistent Weekly Practice

We call this the "Work Your Plan" practice, or WYP for short. This weekly/daily effectiveness technology is contained on one sheet of paper front and back. Although contained in a simple format, the practice integrates many powerful elements, including:

1. Focusing on your True North Goals. True North Goals represent the best idea you have of where you want to go. When you are bushwhacking through a thick forest, and you have a map and compass, you choose true north destinations rather than the mountain, which you may not be able to see. Your vision becomes the True North Goal. It is your compass.
2. Today's date, the date you will assess your progress and a measurement of your progress. This gives you a contained, defined period of work and you can learn about yourself by the metrics. What you measure tends to get better.
3. Each day you check a box when you start the day reviewing the practice sheet.
4. Use S.M.A.R.T. actions. This means that your action steps are going to be Specific, Measurable, Achievable, Relevant and Timely. It is common sense, but good to remember.
5. By writing down your goals in results based language you get clear on what you want to create, which helps your mind more efficiently create what you want. By writing down the purpose, or "why," you fuel the action item with emotion and meaning.
6. At the end of the day, write down one thing you learned and one thing you accomplished.

Work Your Plan

True North Goal:

Today's Date (/ /) to be completed by (/ /)
Last week's % of commitments = __

Outcomes: M[ ] T[ ] W[ ] Th[ ] F[ ] S[ ] Su[ ]

Lessons/Accomplishments: M[ ] T[ ] W[ ] Th[ ] F[ ] S[ ] Su[ ]

Accountability: S.M.A.R.T. goals (Specific, Measurable, Attainable, Relevant & Timely)

Goal	
Why?	
Action	

Goal	
Why?	
Action	

Goal	
Why?	
Action	

	What did I learn today?	What success did I have?
Monday		
Tuesday		
Wednesday		
Thursday		
Friday		
Saturday		
Sunday		

How to Use the Work Your Plan Sheets

Once a Week:
1. Write your top True North compass point goals. FOCUS
2. Write down today's date, and the date by which you will complete your commitments by (in one week). PERSIST
3. Celebrate your biggest learning and accomplishment each day. Yes! BELIEVE
4. Work the Action system by writing down your outcomes, purposes, and actions. PERSIST
5. Check in once a week with a buddy to celebrate your success and learn where you can improve. PERSIST

Every Day:

1. Review the W.Y.P. sheet every morning.
2. Read True North Goals.
3. Remind yourself of what you are learning and accomplishing.
4. Examine each of your goals, your actions, and your reason for acting.
5. Close your day by writing down one lesson learned and one or more accomplishments.

You want to be free to know that you are taking action on the important areas of your life and that you have priorities handled. This sheet serves two primary purposes:

1. To help you get really organized and efficient in setting and achieving goals
2. To show the surface mind how much it is accomplishing so that it can relax

You exist but as a part inherent in a greater whole. Do not live as though you had a thousand years before you. The common due impends; while you live, and while you may, be good.
Marcus Aurelius

Essential Practice

By tracking the percentage of follow-through on commitment, you also build the muscle of personal integrity.

It's a multi-layered practice. After three months, you can look back and see what you can learn about yourself. What is consistent? Are there recurring themes? Do you do well at certain phases, on certain projects? Do you take on too much or too little?

Making Progress? How To Measure Results

You must have measurement with action.

At the end of the week, you calculate your completion percentage. You check off each day that you reviewed your sheet in the morning and wrote down your accomplishments and lessons in the evening.

Outcomes: M ❏ T ❏ W❏ Th ❏ F ❏ S❏ Su ❏

Lessons/Accomplishments: M ❏ T ❏ W❏ Th ❏ F ❏ S❏ Su ❏

Each time you start your day reviewing this sheet, you'll have one more check on your sheet. Each time you write down a success and a lesson at the end of the day, you have another check on your sheet.

Clients have said to me, "Why do I get credit for such a small action?"

Because these small steps have powerful, whole system, organizing effects. Another client says, "This is too much to commit to every day; let me just focus on my to-do list."

Wrong approach! Consistently focusing on the <u>outcomes</u> is like having a compass. Otherwise, I guarantee that you will get distracted and you will lengthen the duration of your journey toward your dream. Focusing on outcomes keeps the wind in our sails. Momentum is built on fullness and fulfillment, not on constant striving.

A to-do list has no built-in metrics, no way of measuring your progress or identifying what you have learned. I still use a to-do list, but the WYP process is for the critical actions in my life that I MUST complete this week.

After you have tallied up the total number of days that you started your day reviewing your sheet (outcomes) and ended your day writing accomplishments and lessons, then you can determine how many goals have been completed.

Since we are using smart actions (specific, measurable, attainable, relevant, timely), you can quickly and easily determine whether you have met your commitment. There is absolutely no partial credit for one-half or three-fourth completions. This is part of the learning. How do you set realistic goals that are achievable but stretch you to your edge?

Here is an example:

I set a goal to exercise seven days this week. I exercise six days. I don't get six-sevenths of the credit. I get ZERO. My commitment was to exercise seven days. Lesson learned here is to set a realistic goal. Committing to do any task every single day is usually unrealistic.

Measuring the Goals in Review

I set eight goals. I achieve six. I reviewed my outcomes for the week six out of seven times in the morning. Every night I wrote down a lesson and an accomplishment.

6 out of 8

+

6 out of 7

+

7 out of 7

Of the total possible twenty-two, I completed nineteen, which gives me 86%.

We practice integrity by making commitments to ourselves and by following through with the best of our ability.

Are you trying to get 100 percent?

YES!

Is it a means to an end?

YES!

Is getting 100 percent the point in and of itself?

NO!

At the end of a week, it's easy to see what you have and have not done. After three months, it's easy to see the patterns emerge about what you commit to, follow through on, or avoid.

And as you learn to set goals that you can reach, you build integrity, which is invaluable.

Work Your Plan as Personal Inquiry

Working a weekly practice sheet can teach you a lot about yourself:

- How to successfully set goals that you can reach
- What it takes to set attainable goals
- How to handle fear and upset as a step toward fulfilling your goals
- How to translate actions into outcomes, obstacles into actions, or outcomes into opportunity
- Where your goals may be out of alignment with your values
- If you are setting goals and consistently avoiding action

This is an exceptionally helpful model because it:

- Keeps us focused on why we are doing what we do,
- Makes sure our vague desires get turned into action,
- Normalizes the concept that obstacles are always opportunities and opportunities often come with obstacles.

This third point is essential. You are never going to get to a place in your life that is problem free. If you are waiting to go for your dreams until you have done enough emotional process work, then you are stalling. Life is set up for you to go for your dreams. And when you go for your dreams, then you get just the right lessons for your growth. Emotional process work is great when you are in proper alignment with your purpose. Keep going for your dreams and use all the tools you can to keep yourself clear and grounded and taking action.

Is This For Slackers?

Although it seems as though this system is designed to get unorganized slackers from point A to point B, it is not. I found just as much or more value for the type A personality. The type A clients that are willing to do this find they relax more. At the end of the week, there is an objective record of accomplishments. It actually helps them measure their progress and they can rationalize stopping for family, rest and renewal.

There is also the headspace freedom from the constant mental spinning around projects. You can drop worrying and anxiety because you know you are taking consistent action on key points of your life each week. If you are not, add it in! If it's something big, like writing an e-book, then go through the three-step process of mind-mapping, organizing, and scheduling, and then chunk it down to a small action you can take this week.

This brings up a really important question:

When do I use the formula for setting and achieving goals and when do I write it in my weekly success sheets?

Knowing When to Plan Big or Small

You have a spectrum of goals.

Big > Medium > Small

BIG

Big goals absolutely need to be analyzed and planned with the formula. For example, earning $150K net in your small business is a clear goal that requires the formula.

MEDIUM

Writing an e-book is tricky. Is this something you do frequently? Is it under 50 pages? What is the content? Who is the audience? Have you written most of the content? This may be a big project or you may be able to complete it in a week.

SMALL

Making healthy meals would usually be just an action item. Unless you have some massive raw food experiment that requires gargantuan effort and planning, you simply make that an action item for the week.

How To Set Yourself Up for Success

As a musician, I have learned to make time commitments more often than product commitments for creative work.

Example: I commit to writing for two hours this week.

For more technical work I have learned to make product or project commitments.

Example: I commit to completing the bookkeeping for the second quarter this week.

Creativity and Goals

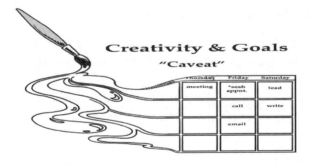

A caveat.

Books, songs, manuals, new projects, or programs that have a novel approach are often the result of inspiration, and try as we might, the creative work may not follow a cognitive timeline.

Creativity Demands Blissipline (The Discipline of Joy)

Being creative is not an excuse for flakiness. Do not confuse the two. I'll be the first to confess how challenging this is for me. Staying up until three or four o'clock in the morning each day writing the first eight chapters took a toll on my work and family life.

I could have done better at carving out the boundaries I needed. I admit that I fumbled through.

Nevertheless, the book emerged.

And I learned a powerful lesson. Creative work has its own set of rules.

What is another example?

If I am writing a book, I don't set a deadline on a chapter in the initial writing phase. That would create unhealthy rigidity. The creative flow wants to happen in its own way.

I would set a goal to write a set amount of time. This is especially true if the writing is technical. I once had to rewrite 250 recipes for a cookbook. This simply required that I show up and apply myself.

It is the same with practicing the piano. I can't set the goal to learn a specific skill in two weeks if I have limited time to practice. That might be unreasonable. Some weeks, I make leaps and bounds and others I barely inch along. This is the path of sharpening your skills. It takes time and commitment. That is why creative endeavor is best structured with time as the goal.

I can commit to writing for four hours a week. I can commit to practicing two hours a week. What happens in that time is up to me.

The Little Shoemaker

Jeff Salzman, founder of Boulder Integral, gave me some great advice on this. I was attending the Integral Incubator, working on my business and had asked Jeff's advice about my career as a professional speaker and author. He shared with me one of his favorite stories about creative genius and what it takes to leave a legacy of good work. It is from Igor Stravinsky, and is taken here from Stravinsky's Autobiography:

Tchaikovsky says in one of his letters: "Since I began to compose I have made it my object to be, in my craft, what the most illustrious masters were in theirs, that is to say, I wanted to be, like them, an artisan, just as a shoemaker is. ... (They) composed their immortal works exactly as a shoemaker makes shoes that is to say, day in, day out, and for the most part to order." How true that is.

So in a way, your creative work is simply a matter of showing up each day, at a prescribed period of time and making work. It is humble, simple and holy.

Creative Mastery

Fully addressing the pleasures and pitfalls of the creative life is beyond the scope of this work. I highly recommend following the program laid out in *The Artist's Way* by Julia Cameron. This is a must read if you intend to write books, create products or programs, or do any other creative work. *The War of Art* by Steven Pressfield also stands out as an excellent resource.

Whatever your creative endeavor, use the process here: Dreams > Vision > Goals > Plan > Action to make it a reality! It will be one of the most rewarding experiences of your life!

In the next chapter, you'll see how to integrate this weekly process into your daily flow in the section on morning practice.

RECAP OF CHAPTER 3:

- The week is the hub of your effectiveness practice.
- Take time each week to acknowledge your biggest learning and your biggest breakthrough.
- Always have your True North Goals in mind.
- Set SMART goals.
- Have a system for consistently measured results.
- Creativity caveat: sometimes creative work doesn't fit nicely into your plans. Be flexible, but not flaky.
- Have a list for quick reference while completing the weekly success sheet.
- There are Big > Medium > Small-scale goals. Use the best technique for each.

SELF-STUDY EXERCISES:

- Make a point to stop one day a week and reflect on the previous week.
- You don't have to use the Work Your Plan process I outlined but you can.
- Take inventory of your dreams, big goals, and projects.
- Then write up a list of the most important actions for the upcoming week. Schedule them into your calendar and treat them like gold.

CHAPTER 4

SHARPEN THE SAW

THE PURPOSE OF CHAPTER 4:

You will ignite a spark under your butt to do the things you probably know you need to do in both your personal and professional life! These are the habits and tools that make up a healthy rhythm and routine to life. Sharpening the saw means that you are developing habits that keep you at your best.

First: Morning Practice

The number one most significant place to sharpen is your morning practice.

Why?

Because it affects each of the tools in every part of this book in a major way. It is entirely actionable. And it is in your power to transform. Last, it has a powerful effect on the results you achieve each and every day.

Envisioning my own life's purpose, I received a stunningly clear image that brought this home to me.

I imagined my deathbed at a well-ripened old age. Friends and family were gathered around and from that place, I asked myself the question, *What would my regrets be?*

- Not giving my gifts to the world 100 percent.
- Not becoming a genuinely loving force.

- Not showing up for my family and my children.
- Not having a consistent and powerful morning practice.

It occurred to me in this vision that my morning practice was tied into giving gifts, being loving, and showing up for my family.

I still have a long way to go. But I have come SO FAR. At one time, I was the most "un-morning" person on the planet. But why is this so crucial for me and for you to cultivate?

1. How you start your day determines the quality of day you will have. Period.
2. It is difficult to shift out of the tone of the day beginning on a sour note. It can be done, but it is HARD.
3. A powerful morning practice frees you from self-consciousness throughout the day.

This third point means that if your morning practice is robust, then the day can be devoted to service, contribution, and presence for others. But if your morning practice is weak, you go through each day feeling like you missed something. You'll be wondering, "Should I be meditating, should I journal, or should I exercise?"

Start your day hitting the major self-care items and set yourself up for success. A typical morning could look like this:
6:00 wake up, breathe deeply, first thoughts are some form of dedication to the highest good.
6:10-6:30 meditation/prayer
6:30-7 review your success sheets; jot down actions that are relevant to the day, plus any other thoughts that arise in the morning
7-7:30 make your bed, brush your teeth, take a shower, get dressed
7:30-8 breakfast
8-8:30 brisk walk, yoga, or other forms of exercise
8:30-9 anything else that you need to feel ready for the day
9 a.m. begin workday

Or your day might look like this:
5:30-6:00 wake up and write morning pages
6:00-6:30 review weekly success sheets; jot down or transfer items from your success sheets into a small notebook if you need to have it throughout the day

6:30-7:00 make bed, put jogging clothes on, go for a run
7:40-8:00 shower, brush teeth get dressed
8-9:00 breakfast, clean up, attend to family
9 a.m. begin workday

You get the idea. There are many options, but each of us needs to determine what we need to do to start our day powerfully.

I think that it is absolutely necessary to have one or more of the following in the morning practice:

- Morning Pages: This is the technology that Julia Cameron advocates in *The Artist's Way, The Vein of Gold, Walking In This World,* and other works. Simply put, it is three pages of stream of consciousness writing, nonstop, whatever is on your mind, first thing in the morning.
- Silent meditation or prayer: It is agreed across traditions that five minutes of meditation in the morning is enough to center the mind for the day. A Course in Miracles suggests that five minutes in the A.M. is all that is needed to give the day over to the Holy Spirit, which is the Whole Spirit of Life, God, Divine Order, Love, or whatever your concept of Divine Guidance is.
- Affirmative Invocation: a couple of the phrases that I use in the morning are:

    ↗ I ignite a fire of Joy in my heart and soul today and build the flame of love in my family, my work, and my community.
    ↗ Good morning, Universe, I am willing to allow more Joy, more Good, more Fulfillment into my life than I have ever dreamed, experienced, or imagined.
    ↗ I build my self-esteem for the service of a Divine Idea. I am incredibly gifted and have tremendous value to contribute to the world.

- Power Questions:

    ↗ How good am I willing to have my day be?
    ↗ What could I be excited about today?
    ↗ What is the best thing that could happen today?
    ↗ What do I want to contribute to those around me?
    ↗ Who am I sure is important to me?

A morning practice, consistently followed, will lead to powerful results in your life because of the consistency of attention on the cultivation of self-love and care. This leads into the second practice, the rest and relaxation cycle.

You can see that the morning practice is built into your *Work Your Plan* sheet. It is an integrated system.

Now, you can't have a morning practice without an evening ritual that facilitates good sleep. The necessity of good sleep cannot be over-emphasized, but the modern era has a lot of issues. And one of the most significant is sleep.

Second: The Sleep Situation

Up until a couple of hundred years ago, we were, as a species, bound by the cycles of night and day. The advent of the light bulb is an entirely new phenomenon. The even more recent advent of phosphorus computer screens and televisions and fluorescent and LED lights used at night have consequences that we are just beginning to understand. What are some of the most significant negative influences on sleep?

- Artificial light is known to disrupt hormone production, including melatonin. Computer and TV screens seem to be especially detrimental.
- Studies have indicated excessive cell phone use is corollary to sleep disturbances.
- Use of stimulants throughout the day to compensate for fatigue interferes with sleep (creating a downward spiral).
- Mental or emotional stress from career, relationships, or financial strain impacts the endocrine system and can hamper sleep.

Chronic issues with sleep undermine personal and professional goals by zapping your energy, leading to:

- Decreased physical exercise (which compounds the problem)
- Increased cravings for sugar and caffeine (which compounds the problem)
- Difficulty meeting your work obligations, seeing your client load and patient roster, or being productive
- Feeling burnt out and disconnected from the work you love

Depending on your constitution, you may never really have a problem with sleep, or the slightest disturbance can set you back. There is a huge chasm in constitutional types.

Generally, you need to do the following for a good night of sleep:

- Stop using your computer, TV, and cell phone two hours before bed.
- Create calm in the house before bed. Reduce stimulation and let go of work.
- Create total darkness in the room you sleep in.
- Get regular exercise.

Additional suggestions include:

- A hot bath with magnesium sulfate (Epsom salts) can be very helpful.
- Playing relaxing music can be soothing. Personally, I am deeply relaxed by a little hand drumming, piano, or chanting.
- Listening to subdued music can also be soothing.

For more information on the importance of sleep, check out *Lights Out: Sleep, Sugar and Survival* by T.S. Wiley.

Third: Exercise!

My friend Nanda had a picture on his wall of The Dalai Lama (exiled leader of Tibet), on an exercise bike.

I said, "Nanda, what is up with that."

He said, "it is a reminder that everybody, absolutely everybody, needs to exercise."

Now, I expect that all of this is review for you and that you have this handled. But, just to be sure...

Exercise. It's crucial to sleep, to health, and to effectiveness. From rest to stress release, mental performance to mood enhancement, exercise is a must.

Who Is at the Forefront?

My favorite exercise guru right now is Paul Chek. I'd love to meet him and learn about what makes him tick. His body of work is thorough and impressive. His body is pretty thorough and impressive too! I love Chek's approach because it is about functionality. How do we exercise in a way that our body is designed to exercise?

For me, following Chek's principles has lead to less pain, less injury, and stronger, total body integration.

Chek's work is best sampled in his book *Eat, Move and Be Healthy*. I feel good about the integration of metabolic typing in the book and I've noticed that really great fitness professionals tend to use metabolic typing. That says a ton about the effectiveness of a program.

I've personally worked with a CHEK-certified trainer and highly recommend it. I learned to exercise in ways that actually reduce the possibility for stress rather than exacerbate it.

Check out his site at www.ChekInstitute.com.

Make It Easy. Walk.

Of course, it could be argued that the number one function of the human body is walking. I'm a big advocate. You don't need a permit. You don't need a fancy pair of shoes. No special clothes. No advanced training. You can get out just about anytime, anywhere, in any season.

Make It Super Charged

You can turn walking into a mind-body integration exercise with massive benefits. "How?" you might ask.

Darth Vader Breathing.

All credit goes to Dr. John Douillard for really bringing this to the next level through his research and practice.

OK, what is Darth Vader Breathing?

In yoga, it is called **Ujai Breathing.**

Here is how it works:

You breathe in deeply through your nose. You exhale forcefully like you want to polish a mirror or clean your glasses. Then, you take that same breathing pattern and breathe out through the nose as well. Still, like you are fogging a glass mirror, but out through your nose. What you end up with is a sound like Darth Vader. If you don't know what that sounds like, *where have you been?*

Next, you extend the breath duration to the edge of your comfort zone. And here, you add in the walking. You might start out walking, practicing D.V. breathing, with eight steps for the in breath and eight more steps for the out breath. Breathe in, one, two, three, four, five, six, seven, eight, breathe out, one, two, three, four, five six, seven, eight. Then, simply practice extending the number of steps that you can take during the inhale and the exhale phase.

Why Do Darth Vader (Nasal) Breathing?

Without going into great detail here I want to make sure that you are breathing right during exercise. Dr. John Douillard introduced me to nasal breathing, or Darth Vader Breathing. This simple, free, and powerful technique radically altered my experience of exercise. Check out his book *Mind, Body, and Sport.*

Basically, you get the following advantages:

- Deeper penetration of oxygen into the lungs
- More absorption through longer exhalation
- More resourceful brain wave states
- Maintained elasticity of the rib cage and enhanced lung capacity
- Increased vascular nitrous oxide, a vasodilator
- Expanded heart rate variability, a key marker in reduction of heart disease
- Improved spinal health
- Enhanced immune system

Some of the benefits are subtle and impact the energetic body.

Subtle Exercise

We have a subtle body. Our subtle body is made of things that are real but can't be seen, like emotions and thoughts.

I'm also a big fan of Qi Gong, which brings me to a significant point. When I'm talking about exercise, I like to get integral. Integral Life Practice, coined by the Integral Institute, addresses three-body practice. These can be described as:

- Gross body; we exercise the gross body through weight training, cardiovascular exercise, flexibility development.
- Subtle; we exercise the subtle or energy body through yoga, Qi gong, and Tai Chi, as well emotional and mental practices like healing core issues process and affirmative invocation.
- Causal body; we exercise functionality of the causal body through meditation and prayer.

Exercise is essential. And exercising all three bodies is optimal.

Basically, if you are doing some gym time, a little cardio, and then some breath work, yoga, and meditation, you are on track.

The Basics

I've had clients who want to process their issues constantly and never seem to feel well. And when I inquire about exercise, I find that it is non-existent. I support them to get back on track with movement, and then 60 to 70 percent of their perceived issues clear up.

It really is that simple sometimes. Why make it more complicated?

If you are not handling the basics…

- Food
- Exercise
- Sleep

…don't look to some esoteric heavy method for an answer to get you feeling well. Again, I hope this is all redundant.

Naturally, this leads to diet.

Fourth: Food. Nutrition. Diet.

"I will zealously inspect all things which enter my body, my mind, my soul and my heart. Never will I over indulge the requests of my flesh, rather I will cherish my body with cleanliness and moderation."

You may be thinking that this is a quote from a great naturopathic physician, nutritionist, or even one of the philosophers from ancient Greece.

But it is from Og Mandino's book *The Greatest Salesman in the World.*

Mandino reflects on the power of love in the marketplace, suggesting that when you have love in your heart, it opens the door to success. His recommendation is that love has to start with you first. And the first step in loving yourself is to *zealously inspect all things which enter my body, my mind, my soul and my heart.*

You are what you eat.

I know that some of the readers of this book are health counselors, nutritionists, chiropractors, etc. You probably have your diet dialed in. For the rest of you, you take the time to dial in your diet or you rob yourself of a vast untapped resource of energy and enjoyment. Contact us and we can put you in touch with the best people in the world for nutrition coaching.

At the very least, download the free Integral Nutrition PDF from SethBraun.com.

Fifth: The Dance Party

Dancing is life's great joy. Want to spontaneously express joy and fullness? Then get you some dance party!

I spend significant amounts of time, attention, and money on stellar music. My playlists are like therapeutic and medicinal herbs I use to imagine, to invoke, to relax, to focus, to celebrate, and to dance.

I learned early in my adult life the power of dance as embodied prayer, as a way into myself, and as a way to connect to that interior world and bring it out.

If you feel embarrassed when you put on music and shake a tail feather, that's great! That means the ego is on wobbly ground and the more outrageous version of you is emerging.

Music and movement are components of the affirmation-invocation process, which you can and will learn about in Chapter 6.

Music + Dancing + Voice + Affirmative Statement = Affirmative Invocation

If you get bogged down at your computer, then take a break, put on some music and move your body.

OK, those are the personal tools. Sure there are more. Here are the top picks for sharpening the *professional* tools this time round:

Professional Tools to Keep Sharp

First Point: Time Sculpting

Time sculpting means taking time out on a cyclical basis to actually craft the rhythm and routine of your:

1. Day
2. Week
3. Month
4. Year

In the retreat portions of our longer coaching programs, we always do a time sculpting exercise.

Here are some examples.

Ideal Day

6 AM	wake up, make bed, brush teeth, review WYP, morning pages
7 AM	shower, shave, breakfast with kids
8 AM	Outline work day
9 AM	Begin work day
10 AM	Gym
11 AM	Work flow
12 Noon	Lunch

1 PM Work flow

2 PM Work flow

3 PM Work flow

4 PM Time with kids after school

5 PM Family dinner

6 PM Garden Time

7 PM Evening Teleclass / Toastmasters / Writing project

8 PM Evening activity cont.

9 PM Wrap up day, review WYP, read kids bedtime story

10 PM Asleep

Ideal Week

Time	Mon	Tues	Wed	Thurs	Fri	Sat	Sun
06:00 AM							Up early
08:00 AM	Office Time	Office Time	Late wake	Office Time	Office Time	Garden time	Driving
10:00 AM	Gym + one client	Gym + one client	Morning off nature time	Gym + one client	Gym + one client	Clients	Speaking @ Church
12:00 AM	Lunch	Lunch	Lunch	Lunch	Lunch	Lunch	Lunch
02:00 PM	Office Time	Clients	Clients	Clients	Creative	Off	Drive / clients
04:00 PM	Dinner + Family	Dinner + Family	Dinner + Family	Dinner + Family	Dinner + Family	Dinner + Family	
06:00 PM	Chi Kung	Clients	Chi Kung + Gym	Clients	Chi Kung	Off	
08:00 PM	Kids Story	Toast-master	Kids Story	Teleclass	Kids Story	Date w Wife	Prep for week
10:00 PM	Bed	Writing	Bed	Writing	Bed	Bed	Bed

One of my clients got thousands of dollars in value from time sculpting. He worked for himself freelancing. In the past, he would spend his time like a kid spends an allowance. No plan. He would work really long days when a project deadline was approaching and then get burned out. After doing this exercise, he began to measure how long projects took and was able to give a better estimate to people on the length of time it would take, based on what his schedule would allow. Sure, he still has to work long days sometimes, but not as a rule. Sculpting his time gave him greater command of his life. A greater level of flow in his schedule gives rise to a more balanced state of mind, which makes him more effective and attracts more consistent business.

Ideal Month

Looking at each month and intentionally creating time for rest, recreation, fun, as well as creative and business milestones keeps you on point. Examples of items to add in to a monthly review of time are:

1. Kids recitals, games, and awards
2. Group events, church, clubs, networking
3. Work travel, family travel
4. Anything that you need to be prepared for ahead of time

Ideal Year

The ideal year is just like the day, week, and month. You can use a $5.00 desk calendar, rip off each month, and then sketch out your ideal year. This may not be how your year unfolds – in fact it rarely is – but it gives you a great grid from which to make informed choices.

A few items to consider scheduling into a year calendar:

1. Holidays
2. Retreats
3. Work trips
4. MasterMind meetings
5. Gardening tasks
6. Academic schedules
7. Professional Licensing requirements
8. Personal, Business, Property, and Investment taxes

Time Sculpting provides an opportunity to step back out of your current demands and get intentional, deliberate, and strategic about time, based on your best information.

Follow the Dreams into Action processes outlined earlier in the book. By adding in specific attention to how you spend each day and month, in addition to the week and year, you round out the whole experience.

What would it be like to have a sense of what the next twelve months entail at any given time?

Next, you can clarify how you want your days to be.

How can you squeeze the most out of each and every day?

What time do you want to exercise?

How can you eat three meals a day with your family?

Does Monday have a different flow than Friday?

Taking time to deliberately sculpt your life will make structure and flow much more enjoyable.

Second Point: Productivity in Daily Work

We addressed the foundation practice of the weekly focus on productivity. But you have to have some sharp tools for the daily dose of information and choices.

The book *Getting Things Done*, by David Allen, provides me with the "in the trenches" mindset that helps me keep my office clean and helps me stay on top of information.

The synopsis is:

- Get an Inbox (a place to put anything you're working on).
- Put everything there that needs to be handled.
- Pick one day a week to handle everything.

Allen then gives the reader a thorough system of action so that you only handle each item once.

- Have an easy-to-use file system for items you'll need regularly.
- Have a place for reference material that is accessible if you need it.
- Have a place for items that you have to save but don't need to access regularly.
- Take action on items that require two minutes or less.

That's my reader's digest version. Oh yeah, find a label maker for your files. That one step will get you more organized. I can vouch for that. If organization of your office and files is an issue, then get his book.

Third Practice: Productive Time

Let me introduce you to *The Pomodoro Technique* and The Hour of Power.

The Pomodoro Technique suggests working in 25-minute blocks and taking a short break.

The Hour of Power is a system I developed to help my clients tackle challenging tasks.

I keep a Pomodoro technique journal on my shelf for days that I need help staying focused. I write down what I want to do, do it for 25 minutes (without checking e-mail, cell phone, the score of the game, etc.), then take a short break and repeat.

This is one way to track your time and prevent wasted attention. I like the 25-minute work sessions and the enforced break. Time to take one now!

In the Hour of Power, I check in with my client, and they agree that they are going to do something challenging, for instance, calling potential employers. James was in his 20's, recently graduated with his MBA. He was working a marketing job that was good, but not great, for where he wanted to go. He knew he had a few leads but kept putting off making the calls. We set up an Hour of Power where he called me, committed to making the calls in the hour and then called me back. He was able to make the calls and move his career forward.

Fourth Practice: Sabbath

The concept of the Sabbath is embedded in all of the great cultures of the world. The basic idea is to have time where you can renew yourself. Now this can be weekly, like a Saturday or Sunday. It could be daily, by way of a meditation practice or long walk. Or it can be through annual holiday excursions.

Friend and colleague Charles Faris, founder of BodyOdyssey.com, taught me to use the term "holiday" in lieu of vacations. When we take a holiday, we are taking "holy days," for our rejuvenation. When we take a vacation, it literally means, *a suspension of work, study or other activity* (The Random House Dictionary, College Edition). Consider reframing your time off as a holiday, a term consistent with European ethos, where they tend to think four to five weeks of annual holiday is about right. In America, our average holiday time is about two weeks.

I know. It is hard to do when you are creative, inspired, and passionate about life. Remember that time off equals more energy when you are on. Find a rhythm and routine for your rest, renewal, activity and engagement cycle.

Devote Resources to Keeping the Tools Sharp

For you to keep these tools sharp, you need to include books, seminars, and coaching in your business budget. When you commit to two or three intelligent books on a topic of interest, and maybe one seminar each year, you guarantee consistent and sustainable education on business.

A lot of people are afraid to invest in themselves. If your work involves contributing value to the world (and whose doesn't?) then you are the most important part of that equation. Invest in yourself and commit to CANI – Constant And Never-ending Improvement.

As you read this book, if you resonate with what is written, you may be interested in the Indestructible Success Training. It consists of:

1. A powerful four-day personal and professional development retreat where you can dive into The Four Pillars of Indestructible Success: Vision, Action, Courage, and Confidence.
2. One-on-one coaching to lift the veils of confusion, distraction, and fear
3. A Twelve-Month Integration Course to propel your creative Vision (book, program, curriculum, workshop, album, body, etc.) into reality

You will reignite your life purpose and leave with your heart full, your mind awake and the presence to create a life that works.

RECAP OF CHAPTER 4:

- A consistent morning routine is the underpinning of a great day.
- Restful sleep is the basis for a thriving morning practice
- Everybody, absolutely everybody, needs regular exercise.
- Check out Paul Check's book, *Eat, Move and Be Healthy* and Dr. John Doulliard's book, *Body, Mind and Sport*
- Eat real food and dial in your diet for maximum energy.
- Dancing is a great way to feel happy for no reason. You will be more productive when you feel good.
- Take time out to sculpt your ideal day, week, month and year.
- Use best practices for productivity like *Getting Things Done* by David Allen.
- Bring into play the Pomodoro technique or other time tracking practice to make the most of your time.
- Find time for explicit rest and renewal.
- Keep spending time, money, energy and attention to keep the tools sharp.

SELF-STUDY EXERCISES:

- Use your weekly review process or your Work Your Plan sheet
- Add one "sharpen the saw" item each week
- Experiment with adding small steps, consistently
- Keep coming back to small improvements in each of these areas.
- Find a way to remind yourself of your commitment

SECTION B:

**Develop Your Capacity
for Higher Achievement**

CHAPTER 5

UNSTOPPABLE COURAGE: HANDLE FEAR AND TURN UPSETS INTO OPPORTUNITIES

THE PURPOSE OF CHAPTER 5:

The purpose of this chapter is to help you recognize and handle fear and upset. You will get a tool for dealing with intense emotional experiences. You will know it is working when you are aware of fear and can use it as fuel for growth. That is the essence of courage.

FEAR – Dream Killer or Door Opener?

If you can face your deepest fears and not shrink back, then you do not need this book. You are a demigod. But even Hercules or Achilles had bouts of massive fear.

Let's face it. Fear is not going anywhere. Call it the shadow, energy, or fuel. Call it working with core issues. Call it removing emotional resistance or getting your game face on. We mere mortals need tools to work with fear in its many forms.

You are going to learn to differentiate your experience of fear into three distinct categories. Then, you can more skillfully and productively work with fear. As a consequence of learning how to work with fear, you will gain the ability to more skillfully manage other intense emotions such as anger, resentment, frustration, etc.

Courage is not the absence of fear; it is wise action in the presence of fear.

The Three Faces of Fear

Face number one is "fear as the energy to do your best."

Face number two is "fear as wisdom to save your butt."

Face number three is "fear as psychological goo that stops you in tarpits of funk." This is also known as "irrational fear" or as "core issues."

This chapter will touch on these three faces and then outline a process you can use to handle the most difficult form of fear, face number three. In the process, you will become more connected to yourself and freer to live the life you want.

Courage, from the Old French root word, *cour,* literally means to take heart. When cultivating courage, you will feel fear in your body, your heart may ache, and belly may have butterflies. The choice that matters is what you do about it. If you are not feeling fear, you are in denial or you are not taking the risks necessary for growth.

As my Toastmasters mentor Tom Traynor says of fear and public speaking, *you won't ever lose your butterflies, but you can get them to fly in formation!*

Face Number One: The Energy To Do Your Best

More often than not, the solution to fear is action.

That is why the familiar phrase still rings so true.

Feel the Fear and Do It Anyway.

Personally, I've never seen this lesson more clearly taught than in a 72-Day Wilderness Leadership Training program at the Hurricane Island Outward Bound School. The 12-person cohort had to face huge fears each and every day. But one day in particular stands out.

Our task for the morning was to climb up the face of a granite wall, left over from an old quarry. I thought, "No problem. I am in a rock climbing harness; I am sure that my partner has me securely strapped in and has a keen eye on the tension in the rope."

But as the first person out on the course, I soon recognized the reason for my instructors' wry smile. Midway through, I had to wiggle out onto a tiny crack that could barely be called a ledge, then leap from that sliver of rock and catch a rope end that was hooked into the rock face.

I was struck with fear. I froze. This - Was - A - Huge - Jump. Intellectually, I could reason that I was strapped into a climbing harness, but my reptilian brain only saw 200 feet of pure hurt below.

And haven't you felt like this at times too?

You know that taking action is not going to kill you, but you are paralyzed with fear. What an awful feeling. Like being in a dream, chased by the boogie man, but unable to move because your feet are stuck in oatmeal.

So there I was, on a ½ inch of granite, sweating palms, dry mouth, stuck in oatmeal.

It had been a whole six and a half seconds.

My instructor then said, "Before you jump from here, you have to pass our test."

"OK," I replied hesitantly.

"You have to sing your loudest rendition of the most rocking song you know!" came the reply.

And then it happened. This is where the fear turned into energy and the misery became motivation.

Goose bumps rippled across my skin.

I took a deep breath and I went nuts with the words to the Steppenwolf hit *Born To Be Wild*.

"GET YOUR MOTOR RUNNIN'
HEAD OUT ON THE HIGHWAY
LOOKING FOR ADVENTURE
OR WHATEVER COMES OUR WAY!

YEAH DARLIN; GONNA MAKE IT HAPPEN
TAKE THE WORLD IN A LOVE EMBRACE
FIRE ALL OF OUR GUNS AT ONCE AND
EXPLODE INTO SPACE"

I was instantly in a peak state of flow and power!

I was oblivious to the height, to the ledge, to the wind. I OWNED that tiny piece of granite. This was my world and I was going to say how this jump was going down!

And after I sang the chorus, I fearlessly leapt out and caught a hold of the rope.

My cohorts went crazy! They cheered! They hollered! And it set the stage for a bunch of hilarious acts to follow.

What a great feeling. When have you broken through your fear to find ecstasy?

This is what I mean when I say that fear is energy. This is what it means to turn fear into fuel.

The Second Face of Fear: Wisdom To Save You (Remember Yoda)

The second face of fear is wisdom.

Remember in Star Wars where Luke says to Yoda,

"I can be a Jedi, I am not afraid!"

And Yoda looks with a scowl and says,

"You will be…you will be."

Can you distinguish between fear as energy and fear as wisdom?

Most recently, I had a client who was scared to quit her job and strike out on her own with her own business. She was highly qualified in her field, had experience with successful consulting and had several advanced degrees. She even had loyal clients!

While it would have been great to run some method to reduce psychological fear or to channel that fear into action, practically, she needed to set up her new business to thrive. Since her main fear was about paying her mortgage, I suggested that she capitalize her business with a line of credit through the Small Business Association. With her track record, she was likely to succeed in her business. (She had an incredible network.)

But realistically, as a business owner, she needed that capital to buffer her growth.

That was just a smart business move. Her fear contained wisdom.

On The Stage of Life: Energy, Wisdom, or Fear of Failure?

As a performer, speaker, and musician, I learned that I would always feel fear before I went on stage.

I don't stop every time I am about to speak and do an inner process to remove the fear. That fear is my ally. It is there to help me kick butt and bring incredible value to the audience. That fear is there to help me to do my best. It is the first face.

Life is a stage. And many times, our fear is nothing more than energy.

I recall waking up at 3 AM a few weeks ago, feeling afraid about some of the projects I was working on. I told my wife about this and she said, "why don't you get up and work on them?" Brilliant! I used that energy to work until my kids woke up around 7 AM. In that time, I rewrote the 40-page PDF for the Integral Institute on nutrition, which was due that afternoon.

That fear was the energy for me to meet my commitments. As stated, this is the most common form of fear and the solution is committed action.

But sometimes fear stops us from even committing to the Outward Bound course, stops us from booking the speaking engagement, and prevents us from setting up the house tour.

This is the third face of fear. And this third face of fear can be a real bugger.

The Third Face of Fear: Psychological Goo

OK, psychological goo – what does that mean? When I say psychological goo, I mean the sticky places inside where our fear of failure, fear of embarrassment, and fear of pain stop us in our tracks. The problem with handling this kind of fear is that it lurks in the shadows. Much of the time, we are not even aware of it. I am going to give you a handle on this. There is a term that I learned to deal with this type of fear, *automatic, unconscious avoidance of hurt and pain.* Once you can name a thing, then you begin to have the power to deal with it.

Let me give you an example.

The Doctor Patient Case Study: How Fear Stops Success

In this story we have two characters, Dr. Janet, a naturopath, and Desperelda, her patient. (Names have been changed to protect identity.)

A client and colleague of mine, Dr. Janet, had a patient, Desperelda, who came to her somewhat desperate. Desperelda remarked that meeting Dr. Janet was real serendipity. She went on and on about how perfect the timing was, how her friend had dropped Dr. Janet's business card on the floor and said, *"Oh, I have been meaning to tell you, you should really call her."*

Desperelda goes on and on about how this is so right for her. *"Then there was the cancellation today so I could get into see you right away. How wonderful you are, I love your office, I feel so good about this!"*

Desperelda began a twelve-week functional medicine weight-loss program with Dr. Janet.

The first week, Desperelda called two times.

Then weeks two, three, four, five, and six, she called more and more often, until at week six, it was daily phone or e-mail messages. Finally, in week seven, she came to Dr. Janet's office, demanded to see her, and was squeezed in between clients.

Dr. Janet, clearly concerned about Desperelda's state, maintained her composure, asked Desperelda how she could help, and listened as best as she could.

Desperelda practically threw the fat manual and a bag with some of the nutritional products from the course at Dr. Janet. She proceeded to verbally attack the doctor and the program.

The more Desperelda spoke, the more Dr. Janet resisted the communication.

D: This program is a complete waste of time. It is two months, and I haven't lost a pound.

Dr. J: Well, actually, it is only week seven, and we are only halfway through. I really think you need to…

D: [interrupts] Does this program even work? I mean, have you even seen actual results?

Dr. J: [becoming noticeably agitated, but trying to remain professional] Actually, yes! This is a clinically proven system that has been tested by…

D: [interrupts] You keep forcing me to stop eating everything I like! *Weight Watchers* lets me eat cookies and ice cream. I think you have control issues.

Dr. J: [about to blow her top, catches herself just in time] Our assistant will refund your program cost completely. Now, I've got another patient to see [showing D to the door]. I guess this program was not for you. Good-bye.

Desperelda, still irate, causes a scene in the waiting area. She harasses the office manager, who just sits there and takes it, which is what she is paid to do. Desperelda then stomps off.

Here is how it could have gone if Dr. Janet had learned to turn her upset into an opportunity:

D: This program is a complete waste of time. It is almost two months and I haven't lost a pound.

Dr. Janet: [sits quietly, waiting to hear if there is more]

D: And I spent all this money on these vitamin drink shake whatever things. Does this even work?

Dr. J: [sitting, listening attentively, speaks after a pregnant pause] Is there anything else?

D: Yes. You won't let me eat what I love. And I have no enjoyment.

Dr. J: [quiet, waiting a moment] It sounds like you are feeling frustrated and worried that you haven't lost any weight. That this program might not be working. And you are upset that you are missing out on enjoyment to boot. Is that right?

D: [a little less excited] Yes. I'm hating this program. That's three months of deprivation. What if it doesn't work?

Dr. J: [listening and nodding, waits a moment] You don't want to deprive yourself for three months, work really hard, and then fail. That would be really disappointing. I see what you mean.

D: [more relaxed] Oh, I just don't want to do the same thing again. I've done this SO MANY TIMES. I get my hopes up and then I end up right back where I started.

Dr. J: So staying with this program is really scary?

D: YES! Scary as hell! Wouldn't you be a little scared if every time you tried to do something, you failed?

Dr. J: WOW. I admire you for being willing to share this with me. You could have given up weeks ago. Why are you still going for it?

D: Because I don't want to have this run my life anymore. I have been dieting for years, up and down, up and down. I am sick of it!

Dr. J: Yes, I get that. How can we create a solution in the next few minutes to take this one day at a time?

D: [has an emotional release with tears, composes herself] I always feel so much better when I talk to you.

Desperelda leaves the office feeling re-inspired to keep taking action. Dr. Janet keeps her client, keeps her cool, and has referrals for the next few years from a very satisfied customer.

What was the difference?
Why was the second example dramatically more effective?

When there is nothing to protect, there is no resistance. There is nothing to take personally. You can be entirely committed to contribution and service.

The difference in the second example wasn't based on a technique. You can have the best communication, the best education in the world, a PhD in listening, but if the heart is not there, it doesn't fly.

The success of example number two is all about the inner game. Let's take a look at the thoughts and feelings running through Dr. Janet's head.

First example:

- Doesn't she know who I am?
- Who does she think she is?
- I hope she doesn't want a refund.
- Doesn't she know I have clients that rave about this program?
- I can't believe her nerve!

Second example:

- She is very upset.
- Wow, that doesn't feel good. But it is true; this program doesn't work for everyone all the time.
- And I am certainly not perfect.
- How can I support her?
- What's underneath this anger, for her?

In the first example, the doctor is resisting the communication. Why?

If we separate Dr. Janet from the situation, we can see that her feelings live only in her, not in the experience. Dr. Janet is defending herself by justifying her feelings, attacking her client's intelligence, and, finally, running away from the whole situation by giving her a refund.

Has anything like this ever happened to you?

Would you like to be able to handle even your toughest communication as it was handled in example number two?

Alright, here's the secret:

Remove Resistance = Remove Fear

When you are willing to feel anything, you have nothing to fear in communication!

In fact, every upset becomes the solution for your desire to be totally free. Hey, most folks go around cursing their luck when an upset happens. That's like cursing the sun or the moon. Upsets, like the seasons, are unavoidable. You decide what they mean. You decide how you experience them.

Anger and disappointment are the opportunity bells for you to turn any upset into an opportunity to clear yourself, to become more whole and to master your emotional state.

For Dr. Janet, it was about being "good enough." We don't need to know why that was her sore spot, just that it was. As long as you can't accept a part of yourself, you will get triggered. When Dr. Janet could say, "Yeah, I'm not perfect, so what?" she was free.

The most direct and effective way to be totally free is to follow this simple step-by-step process.

The 9 Steps To Turn Upsets Into Opportunities

1. Recognize that you are triggered. Attempt to identify the trigger.

2. Acknowledge the feeling in yourself. Do you feel angry? Irritated?

3. Determine what the situation might mean about you. What is the judgment you are avoiding?

4. Feel the deeper feeling under the judgment.

5. Be willing to feel that feeling totally.

6. Be willing to accept the thing you fear most. Not want it, not intend it, but remove the automatic unconscious avoidance by giving up attachment to the outcome.

7. Forgive yourself for not accepting yourself.

8. Open to spirit.

9. Take action.

Why You Want to Use The 9 Steps

When you practice this process, you end up experiencing more courage and more compassion. These are more resourceful states to be in than fear, anger, resentment, jealousy or whatever is getting triggered.

How do you use these 9 steps?

Let's take Dr. Janet's situation in example number one and assume that she was determined to be free. Here is what might occur.

Dr. Janet would feel tense for the next few hours. During a short drive home, she listens to this process explained on CD, and when she walks in, she decides to take some time to use it.

1. Recognize that you are triggered.
In Dr. J's case, she can tell that she was triggered because she has a knot in her stomach, because she cannot stop thinking about the interaction, and the tension in her shoulders is worse.

2. Acknowledge the feeling in yourself.
She knows that she feels angry, very angry. There is a sensation of heat and tingling in her arms, pressure on her heart, and an upward rising feeling in her chest.

3. Determine what it means about you that this happened.
Here, Dr. J's mind kicks in and starts to protect her by criticizing this process: "What are you doing processing? You need to get to work. You don't have time to sit here and look at this 'inner-game' baloney." This is a clue. It means that you are on the right track. Dr. J recognizes the voice and chooses to continue. A quick way to get an answer to this question is to ask, "If someone were watching me, what critical comment could they make about me?" Dr. J wrote these down:

- I was defensive.
- I was impatient.
- I was afraid of losing the client and the money.
- I wasn't a very good doctor.

She starts to get to the root as she works through it. All these criticisms, if they were true, would mean that she is *not good enough*. Hence the voice that drives her to overwork and *prove* she is good enough derails the inner process.

You will know when you have reached the core judgment or meaning, what some people call the *core issue*, when a feeling slams like a ton a bricks in your gut—a *yuck, that kind of sucks* feeling.

4. Feel the feeling under the judgment.

This is where the courage kicks in. We are coming to terms with our humanity and developing more self-honesty, awareness, and humility. Dr. J, for example, was taught by the world that it is not okay to be *not good enough*; that was her core issue. The truth is, sometimes we aren't perfect. But our evolutionary survival mechanism is programmed to get and to protect. Thus, a major source of our problems stem from the protection, which functions by avoiding our feelings.

You need to realize, as Dr. Janet did, that resisting feelings simply does not work.

- You have to feel it to heal it.
- What you resist persists.
- Hurt and pain embraced is healing; hurt and pain resisted is suffering.

The way Dr. J could take this from an intellectual process to a heart process is to say, "If it were entirely true that I was not good enough, how would I feel?"

This Process Is Natural.

We all do this naturally as children. When my daughter is upset, bumps her knee, or feels frustrated, she cries for a few minutes and then it's done. She moves on. Which leads us to number five.

5. Be willing to feel the feeling totally and completely.
Again, the voice of protection surfaces for Dr. J, telling her that this is crazy, to stop, that it is a sign of weakness to let yourself feel sad or hurt.

After a moment of wavering, Dr. J chooses again to stay with the process. Her palms are sweaty, her forehead is hot, and she feels chills. This is all normal when the emotional energy is getting unstuck.

She stays with it and begins to feel the tremendous sadness that has been walled up by years and years of trying to prove she was "good enough." As the weight is released, she begins to feel the self-love return. A gentleness and tenderness for herself moves through her like water returning to a dry riverbed. The tears become tears of gratitude as she lets go of the impossible task of being perfect.

6. Be willing to accept the thing you fear most.

This is where the rubber meets the road. This is the core of the great teachings of "the inner game" of success. Let's review the mechanism:

- Fear is projected, unresolved emotional energy of the present inton imagined future.
- Compulsive and addictive behavior covers the fear and theunresolved emotional energy. This can be called *unconscious, reflexive aversion of hurt and pain.*
- Many self-help techniques only serve to continue perpetuating the cycle of avoidance, for example, using affirmations to avoid the fear of failure. Debbie Ford, founder of The Shadow Process, calls this "putting ice cream on shit."
- Spiritual and self-help books talk about being *non-attached* to the outcome; the nuts and bolts of non-attachment is the willingness to have the thing that you fear happen to you.
- You are not intending it, creating it, or even wanting it. You are simply removing resistance; i.e., fear.
- When you remove fear, you are truly free to focus on what you want to create. The mind is free of compulsion and addiction. You free up energy previously spent on avoiding circumstances that would trigger fear.
- Paradoxically, you are then free to avoid the pain and hurt of making poor choices and you are free to experience the compelling nature of a pleasurable vision.
- You remove fear by facing the unresolved emotions in the present.

So, for Dr. J, this question causes her to pause. "Can I really accept the thing I fear the most?" "What if I lose all my clients and patients because I just don't have what it takes?" What this does is force Dr. J to really, fully, and completely accept the part of her that is *not good enough.* That is not the truth about her, but it is an aspect. The energy she uses to resist that aspect is actually the energy she needs to live her dreams.

It is a paradox.

It is also profound humility.

Dr. J. recognizes that no matter how hard she works, she is never going to solve how she feels inside by what she does outside. No matter how organized or professional she is, she is human. Sometimes she is tired.

Sometimes she is impatient. Accepting herself isn't easy, but she finds the place in herself to accept the things she fears (she removes the fear and the automatic avoidance of hurt and pain). Some tears come, then some more tears, and then a deep experience of openness. Step 6, being willing to accept the things you fear most, often puts us back to steps 3, 4, and 5.

7. Forgive yourself for not accepting yourself fully.

Dr. J, recognizing how hard she has pushed herself to avoid failure, hurt, pain, and her own humanity, takes a deep breath, puts one hand on her heart and one hand on her belly, and says, "I forgive myself for not accepting myself fully. I forgive myself for thinking I need to be perfect."

Frequently people think this process means they give up being excellent. Not so, young Jedi. We are still committed to excellence, but we are removing the constriction that comes from thinking that what we do and our career (the external world) determine how we feel about ourselves (the interior world of the human psyche).

8. Open to Spirit

Dr. Janet then takes a moment to connect to her spirit in a way that is meaningful to her. She asks God to help her accept herself more and to be more patient with clients and herself. She makes a declaration to be of service in her work, and to live in the experience of freedom and joy more consistently. She ends with a heartfelt statement of, "I am willing to be changed at depth."

9. Take action

This means to take action in the area that triggered the upset – in this case, the experience of a dissatisfied client. Processing without action leads to a progressive deterioration of effectiveness. This process is always in service of your life's purpose. It is not a self-perpetuating cycle of "working on my stuff." You have to turn the fear into fuel.

Dr. J decided that she needed to take the following actions:

- She had to improve how she prepared patients for the program.
- She could create a buddy program so people could check in with each other and call her less.
- She would have her office manager call everyone (seventeen people) in the twelve-week program each week, to check in between weekly meetings.

- She would create an e-mail auto-responder to send inspirational messages once a week that matched the steps of that week.
- Finally, she would call Desperelda to really take the time to listen and see what she could learn from the experience.

Because she is clear, she can now take the steps to prevent this breakdown in her program from happening in the future. Her willingness to accept the thing she fears gave her the freedom to see what she needed to do to actually avoid the same experience.

The most fundamental skill in the inner game of success is to be able to turn any upset into an opportunity to learn. What would life be like if you had no fear of failure? If you had no avoidance of conflict? If you were not worried about disappointment or upsets of any kind?

- Would you be more free or less free?
- Would you be more inspired or less inspired?
- Would your effectiveness increase or decrease?

Occasionally, positive people still question this aspect of the inner game of success. They say, "What you focus on expands, so I just focus on something else, something more positive."

My question is, "Is it working? Has it worked to eliminate the fears, worries, concerns or upsets?" If it has, then keep doing it.

But if there is a persistent area of life where you are getting triggered repeatedly, try this out.

My experience is that life is honorable and will keep giving us opportunities to grow in self-acceptance, self-awareness, humility, and wholeness. And in truth, this is the ULTIMATE means to shift focus. The willingness to accept your fear means that you drop any automatic unconscious tape loop of fear. It is gone.

Life then becomes a constant celebration of profound gratitude. When you are truly willing to lose everything, suddenly your appreciation for what you have explodes. This genuine gratitude attracts more good, more abundance, and more success. This is what is means to *go for your dreams, but don't be attached to the outcome.*

This is the functional "how to" of being non-attached.

Feeling Your Emotions = Freedom

Success in life depends on your ability to master your emotions. To get to mastery, you may have to learn to have emotional vastness. Having emotional vastness means that you can feel immense joy and deep sadness. Both take practice. Chapter 6 addresses feeling joy. Mastering your emotions requires that you address intense emotion and channel it into useful energy. Easier said than done!

Feeling our hurt and pain, letting it go, and accepting ourselves completely is hampered by seven layers of protection (that I have encountered in my experience), which energize the protective response and resistance:

1. Physical, survival-oriented vulnerability to attack
   a. When you really discharge the stuck emotion, you move out of fight or flight mode, and a very real physical vulnerability occurs.
   b. We are literally hardwired not to feel pain, especially men, as a way to survive.

2. If I feel the thing that is down there, I am going to get sucked into a black hole of negativity and depression and I will be stuck there.

If I feel these emotions totally and fully, it will mean that I really 3. am unlovable, fundamentally flawed, incapable, unworthy, or whatever the fear is.

3. Crying means that you are weak. To survive, you need to stop this. What are you doing? Get to work.
   a. This voice is a social convention that some people have learned to a greater degree than others.
   b. If your parents, peers, or family said things while you were growing up like, "I'll give you something to cry about!" or "Stop your crying right now. What is wrong with you?" then you are more likely to hear this in your mind now.

5. A sudden forgetfulness, haziness, cloudiness, and general disorientation. This happens when one of the above is operating in the other than conscious process of protection.

6. A conviction that "they are the problem" or feeling "if only I could change this situation."

a. This makes it impossible to look inside.

b. No matter what, your feelings live in you.

c. If we magically snapped our fingers and made this issue go away, you would immediately find yourself in another situation that triggered the same feelings.

7. Compulsive behavior, such as overeating, TV binges, excessive alcohol, or other obsessive adrenaline pumping activity, keeps us from even getting to the state of recognizing the surface emotions of anger and frustration. This includes all forms of addiction. You can't get anywhere with this process unless you first look at yourself without self-deception.

These are the seven layers of psychological self-protection. They are not inherently problematic. In fact, they are essentially helpful survival mechanisms. The more we can develop acceptance, the more we are free to get beyond our fear, compulsions, shields, and projections.

With the exception of some rare saints, everyone has a version of this thought pattern going on inside of them. Accepting our fallibility actually ends the cycle of compulsion, the habit of blaming someone or something else, the instinct of shutting down, the routine of rehashing outdated social convention, the sequence of avoiding the dark side of our emotions, and the tendency towards unnecessarily protecting ourselves from physical harm when it is not a real threat.

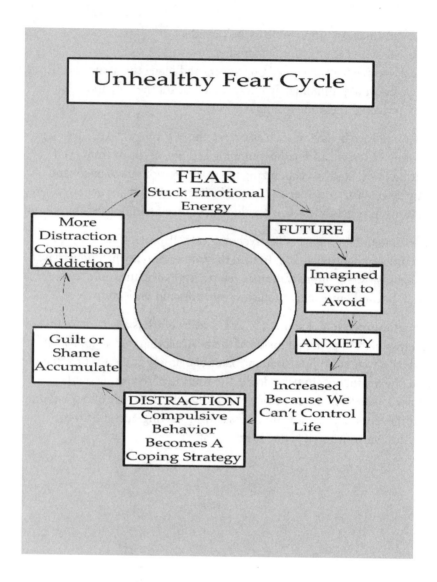

This form of acceptance and humility sets us free.

This process can seem <u>capital D Difficult</u>. And commitment to mastering your emotional state is the path of a warrior. It means a fierce love, a ferocious devotion to clarity. I honor you for this.

But this technology only works when you have the sister practice, which is coming right up.

RECAP OF CHAPTER 6:

- Irrational fear is a form of resistance.
- Compulsive behavior protects us from seeing, then addressing, the deeper fear.
- Trying to change the circumstances of life won't handle the fear.
- Upsetting emotions are not caused by circumstantial events but rather our reaction to those events.
- Fear keeps us from clearly and soberly seeing our lives and the solutions that we may need to seek.
- Feeling our emotions equals freedom, but there are layers of conditioning that protect us from feeling, which is part of a pattern of survival that may be outmoded.
- When you remove resistance, you remove fear.
- Practice looking within for the solution to disturbances. You can use the 9 steps here or one of the many other useful systems recommended in Appendix B.

Well, are you better able to recognize these patterns?

Are you ready to try this 9-step process?

SELF-STUDY EXERCISES:

1. What core fears come up for you related to your business or creative project? Take twenty minutes to identify.
2. Where might you be consistently procrastinating or what might you be avoiding? You will find fear at work.
3. Where are you afraid of failing? What possible failure could you have?
4. Practice going through the 9 steps on one of these areas of your life.

CHAPTER 6

UNSHAKABLE CONFIDENCE: GENERATING RESOURCEFUL STATES

Sow a thought and you reap an act; sow an act and you reap a habit; sow a habit and you reap a character; sow a character and you reap a destiny.

Samuel Smiles

THE PURPOSE OF CHAPTER 6:

The purpose of this chapter is to motivate you to establish a regular practice for cultivating unshakable confidence by generating resourceful states.

The Responsibility To Create Joy

In the last chapter, you were asked to make friends with fear and other intense emotions. There is a kind of balance to this practice relative to the practice of Handling Fear, Healing Emotions from Chapter 5. All practice serves the forward momentum of life's purpose. Handling our emotions is significant when it allows us to go further toward our dreams.

Generating resourceful states has value when we are working at the edge of making our contribution bigger than our fear of failure. Transforming fear and generating resourceful states are sibling practices, meaning they grow together.

But what exactly does *generating resourceful states* mean?

Generating Resourceful States Means:

The ability to synchronize physical, mental, and emotional experience for peak performance.

Taking responsibility for state of mind.

Choosing to be at cause in the world, not at effect.

I credit the term to Boulder Integral Co-Founder Jeff Salzman, who I first heard use this precise term. I am sure that there are other Integral teachers and communities that could also get credit here.

Emancipate Your Mind: Mind Training

We have an opportunity and a responsibility to express our total potential. When I was a student at Naropa University, this was referred to as "mind training." The metaphors of riding a horse that constantly needs to be brought back to the trail or the necessity of taming the "monkey mind" are useful concepts.

A Course in Miracles states in no uncertain terms that the human mind is undisciplined and quick to react according to the programming of the social structure. As the course states, "The purpose of these exercises is to train the mind to a different perception of everything in the world." This is mind training. *A Course In Miracles* outlines 365 days of focused training to deprogram and reprogram the mind to experience life from a spiritual perspective. The lessons on love and forgiveness are mind training.

The Happy Practice

When I was about twelve years old, my uncle had a small cartoon on his desk that said, "The Happy Practice: If you don't practice, you don't get happy."

YOU HAVE TO PRACTICE BEING HAPPY & JOY-FILLED!

Generally, people have done one or more of the following to shift state:
1. Affirmations
2. Focus on gratitude
3. Meditation
4. Reading religious literature (Bible, Bhagavad-Gita, Koran, Torah, etc.)
5. Reading inspirational daily devotions, like *Daily Word*
6. Exercise, especially dancing, yoga, and other mind-body synchronization

Generating resourceful states is essential. This partial list represents empowerment through consistent cultivation of daily practices. The practices are valuable when commitment and duration are involved.

The downside of these practices was mentioned in the previous chapter – are *you using them to avoid your fears?*

This is very common in the self-help/spiritual study world. Using a technique like affirmations can be great but not if you are avoiding the thing you fear most. That fear will still operate in the unconscious mind and run programs that affect your daily life. This is sometimes called *spiritual bypass.*

That is why I suggest having a practice to consciously work with fear and to actively generate resourceful states.

Inner Progress

Generating Resourceful States is about choosing to bring our best to life. It is helpful to remember the difference between states and stages. A state can come and go. A stage is lasting experience.

This is particularly relevant to contemplative, meditative, or spiritual practice, where an individual can experience a profound state such as Satori in Zen Buddhist tradition and not attain a lasting stage of enlightenment. Those who continue to generate that state through practice eventually attain a stage of higher consciousness.

If your intention is to develop Indestructible Success, the same wisdom applies. By consistently generating states, you eventually move into that stage. Let's take an example.

Og Mandino's book *The Greatest Salesman in the World* represents a genre of resourceful state-inducing material. You read a page of focused affirmative material three times a day for thirty days uninterrupted, or the process starts all over. There are ten such pages and the process lasts three hundred days. Note the significance of an uninterrupted series of habits. This is the key to taking a State into a Stage.

The ideas repeated daily guide the mind on principles that provide energy as a framework. In fact, Webster's definition of principle states: "Principles are forces of nature and guidelines." *The Greatest Salesman in the World* emphasizes love, persistence, service, commitment, contribution, kindness, compassion, and positive expectation. When we focus on cultivating principles through state change, we can grow into higher stages of being.

From the Inside Out

James Allen, in his classic *As a Man Thinketh*, writes that character develops:

- First in thought
- Next in action
- Then in habits
- And finally into identity and a belief about reality

We could call thoughts a *state* and identity a *stage* of development.

Identity and belief are self-reinforcing.

How We Learn To Generate Resourceful States

As a musician, this process is kind of obvious. If you wanted to learn to play guitar, you would discover what I did:

- Unconscious incompetence: I did not know how ignorant I was.
- Conscious incompetence: I realized how much harder than air guitar this would be.
- Conscious competence: I had to focus really hard on executing the technique.
- Unconscious competence: the guitar playing happened spontaneously.
- So too with our attitudes, emotions, and state of mind.

The take-away is that YOU can have your life work masterfully if you dedicate yourself to practicing mastery!

Every time We Learn, We Go Through Four Stages

Unconscious incompetence

We haven't experienced the state of mind of enhanced resourcefulness.

Conscious Incompetence

We realize a whole new dimension may be available to us if we would but choose to explore.

Conscious Competence

We require consistent, constant practice and application (affirmation, meditation, physical development, etc.).

Unconscious Competence

We establish an identity in confidence, joy, love, honesty, integrity, or whatever other principle we're committed to cultivating.

Modeling is the super-highway to the next level of cultivation. By modeling successful behavior, you put yourself into that state. Repeatedly modeling that state, as we saw in the above learning progression, leads to development at that stage.

Movement + Powerful Vocalization + Affirmative Language + Music = Power State Change

I've designed a process that I use in my seminars that combines dancing, powerful movement, inspiring music, plus targeted affirmative statements to invoke those qualities that we want to develop. I call this "Affirmative Invocation."

A note on affirmation:

Some people use affirmations as kind of a magic spell. They want to change reality in some way by getting something from life. Maybe they use an affirmation like: *Money comes to me easily and effortlessly.*

That affirmation is directed at changing the external world. This is fun, and maybe even true, but not what we are practicing here. In this context, we are using the process to create resourceful states so that who we become is more integrated, powerful, capable, and functional.

The way I see it, *who we become* is far more important than *what we get.*

What profiteth a man if he should gain the whole world, yet lose his soul?
Matthew, 16:26

Bring Out Your Best

Do you want excellence, style, and dignity? Affirmative Invocations can help you be more of your essence. That is the purpose. To bring your best to life means to be like Carlos Santana, churning out hits when his peers are dead, washed up, irrelevant, or uninspiring. How many other acts that played at Woodstock are still winning Grammy awards or making music videos for MTV? If you've been to his concerts, you know that fame and success are afterthoughts to his message of improvement, empowerment, and joy.

Make no mistake, man, if you are not into spiritual principles, you become a caricature of yourself real quick. You turn the switch on by getting quiet, getting your breathing, and your thinking together.
Carlos Santana

He is talking about generating a state.

By the way, can you generate unresourceful states? Of course, any time you get angry, stuck, cranky, complaining, bored, or uninspired. You can trace it back to a series of choices, behaviors, and patterns that put you right there.

State Change Creates Powerful Shifts

From age sixteen to eighteen, I was a high school dropout and drug addict, barely surviving a series of car accidents, drug overdoses, and high-risk behavior.

When I was nineteen, I began to read and follow the suggestions in the book *Three Magic Words* by U.S. Anderson.

Each morning and each evening I would rehearse the instructions.
- Put myself into a relaxed state.
- Plant the seed of positive autosuggestion into my subconscious mind.

I worked hard and went for my dreams too.

I started at Delta College, pursuing an associate's degree. I'll point out that I hadn't completed more than my freshman year of high school.

I also began to whole-heartedly study hand percussion.

And, I started a full-time job as a direct care worker for the Midland-Gladwin Community Mental Health System in collaboration with the Association for Retarded Citizens.

Three years later, I had achieved the following:

1. Full scholarship for Music Education degree at Central Michigan University for graduating from Delta College with Honor's Program highest recognition

2. Won three awards with the direct care work: 1998, Community Builder Award; 1999, Professional of The Year Award for The State of Michigan; 2000, Nomination for the John F. Kennedy Direct Care Work National Professional of The Year Award

3. Established myself as a professional hand drummer: a gig in a working band; running drum circles at music festivals; and facilitating drum circles for hundreds of youth programs, high schools, colleges, and universities, including Michigan State, Saginaw Valley State, Central Michigan, and Delta College

4. Innovated community drum circle *music therapy* sessions for the Association of Retarded Citizens. This was one of the most amazing experiences of my life.

5. Created innovative curriculum for the Art Smart $100,000 grant program for alcohol/tobacco cessation. Delivered four keynote addresses. Taught three dozen youth how to build hand drums from scratch, then delivered a course on how to play them, culminating with performances in parades, festivals, and community gatherings. And, this was LIFE-CHANGING for many of the youth. To this day, they tell me how powerful it was.

6. Worked three jobs in the summer of 1997 (full-time groundskeeper at Northwood University, half-time direct care work with the Association of Retarded Citizens, and my own landscape company on the weekend)

to pay for a 72-day Hurricane Island Outward Bound Wilderness Leadership Training Course

7. Fall of 1997, attended the 72-day semester program with Outward Bound and learned more in three months than I had ever learned in a year of school.

8. Paid for the hernia surgery from said course, as well as paid **cash** for my own dental surgery, tooth replacement, and orthodontics (braces) to correct a skateboarding accident.

I went from being a drug addicted, high school dropout to living my dreams because of these practices.

This was the season of powerful statements. I used the power of words to activate strength, enthusiasm, and energy. As I worked, I would tell myself over and over again:

> "I like to work hard. I have energy to work hard. I am rolling all the time."
> "Thy will be done. Thy will be done."
> "I am renewed, refreshed, recharged, and rejuvenated."
> "Every action I take brings me one step closer to my dream; I am on fire with passion for my life!"

By changing the subconscious messages running in my mind, I changed the script of my future.

The Formula To Create a Resourceful State

Question: OK, Seth, what can I do right now to change my state?

First, put on the theme from *Rocky*, "Gonna Fly Now," by Bill Conti.

Second, dance around like you're the main attraction at a hot Miami Beach club.

Ooh yeah, get busy.

Third, affirm out loud in a powerful voice a quality you want to have more of right now. "I'm resourceful, inspired, and energized, and I take effective action on the key areas of my life."

Fourth, create a distinct, powerful, physical gesture to accompany the statement. This can be the way that you stand, pumping your fist, clapping your hands, or raising your arms overhead.

Repeat, while really letting your body be free. Have fun! Feel joy! Release the life force energy and let the synchronized voice, body language, and feelings magnify each other until you feel super, ecstatic, and ready to take on anything that comes your way.

You have to be outrageous and you can't let your fears of looking stupid, being embarrassed, or feeling foolish derail you. Feel the fear and do it anyway.

Make It Right for You

First, select a statement that *feels* powerful to you. Don't use something that you think you should like or isn't genuine in any way.

For example, one man came up with "I am now wealthy, powerful, and effective in my career. I have everything I want and need." It was a good start, but he wasn't really flipping the switch. Part of the problem was that he was referring to the circumstance and not to the character. We worked his statement into: "I claim the power to create wealth, I claim personal effectiveness, and I am open to accept a mentally, emotionally, and physically fulfilling life."

The second step is to repeat the phrase with a powerful positive posture in a powerful voice with an embodied series of movements. Basically, you want to stand tall and speak this as if your life depended on it, as if it were the legacy for your children or your one chance to make a lasting impression on the world. You want to feel it in every cell of your body and let that feeling be totally embodied.

Third, add music that makes you energized, inspired, and gets your heart, your soul, your genitals, your belly, your backside, and your feet on board with the train. Get your booty on the floor. You want to stack up a powerfully positive statement with powerful music. Thus, an invocation of your best self emerges.

Question: *OK, I'm on board with this. What do I use for an Affirmative Invocation statement?*

Well, I'll include some of my favorites. I've adapted the best of the best from the teachers, coaches, and change-makers with whom I've studied. Modeling successful people is a fundamental technique for accelerated growth.

I now invoke the power of my subconscious mind to bring forth enthusiasm, confidence, heart, and passion, whatever it takes to help as many people as possible to live their dreams.

or

I am powerful. On this day, I walk with power, I speak with power, and I use this power to enrich the lives of those around me. I bring tremendous value to all who I meet, all that I do, and all that I am. Life rewards me generously for the value I create.

or

I am clear and decisive about my career. I am clear of intent and I work diligently toward my goals. I clear myself of all self-deception and act according to the good that I now know.

and

Today I step up to live my dreams, and I now decree and claim integration of my gross, subtle, and causal body, my emotions, my thoughts, and my actions, to bring forth the power to serve my heart's deepest longing to be a source of strength for my family, to do good in my community, and to build a legacy of health and human potential.

With these as the launch point, you can create your own. Here are the criteria:
• It must be a statement that invokes character, qualities, and attributes.
• You are not trying to change the way things are, so don't make up something like *A bunch of money is now coming to me.*
• You are enlivening the potential within you: *I am now realizing a new consciousness.*

It must connect your heart, head, and body.

Here are a few more examples of Affirmative Invocations that fit the criteria, which you can use or adapt.

I call forth my resourcefulness, patience, connection, skillfulness, faith, confidence, and intelligence to arise in my consciousness to meet the challenges in my life with a smile and genuine gladness for the opportunity to be alive and exercise my divine potential.

I am clear about my purpose in life. I have a clear path of mastery. I am clear of intent and take action consistently.

On this day I release the past completely and forever, and I step up into the next greatest version of my life. I now decree, I now command my subconscious mind, my emotions, my subtle, causal, and gross body to align in the service of my heart's deepest longing to be a leader in my life, a servant to the world, and a source of strength for my family. I now decree total fulfillment of my potential. I am a channel for God in maximum expression of contribution.

You have to look around. Find inspiration. There are a lot of ways to craft language to invoke the best.

By the way, I have to reiterate that there are MANY ways to practice generating resourceful states, including but not limited to:

- Affirmation prayer
- Morning practice
- Singing
- Exercise

Please, find the techniques that work to make you feel alive.

But you have to practice regularly in whatever you do.

It is like nutrition. There is no one diet for everyone, but there are universal principles that you need to apply. You have to eat right. This is soul food. And you've got to feed your soul.

And in this case, it's even more important than food in the sense that your character and self-identity determine even how you choose to feed yourself. When you are in a resourceful state, you naturally and effortlessly choose nourishing food, exercise, and habits.

RECAP OF CHAPTER 6:

- You need to take responsibility for your state of mind.
- Balance Generating Resourceful States with Handling Fear/ Healing Emotions. Use both.
- Every time we learn something new, we have to go through four phases: Unconscious Incompetence, Conscious Incompetence, Conscious Competence, Unconscious Competence.
- Use your Words, Movement, and Music to change your state.
- Make the Generating Resourceful States practice work for you by making it unique and relevant. Make it hit the heart and the head.
- Don't try to change the world around you with magical thinking. Use the practice to change yourself.

SELF-STUDY EXERCISES:

1. Identify an area of your life where you feel stuck. Write it down.
2. Write down your thoughts about this area for about ten minutes.
3. Now write down how you want to be in this area: confident, clear, powerful, effective, etc.
4. Create a positive, empowering, present-moment statement to practice with the Affirmative Invocation practice.
5. Put on inspiring music and move your body.
6. Repeat your declaration out loud until you feel it in all the cells of your body.

CHAPTER 7

LIVING IN FREEDOM

THE PURPOSE OF CHAPTER 7:

The purpose of this chapter is to show how you can create an inner experience of freedom while you are simultaneously engaged in challenging external circumstances associated with making your creative or business dreams come true.

When you feel free, you are able to go for your dreams with more passion, joy, and enthusiasm. Freedom is what we all want; yet how often do we live in the experience of freedom?

To develop freedom, study the habits and thoughts of those who exemplified freedom. In this chapter, we do just that. By studying how to be free inside, you will be more effective at creating a life that works.

Freedom: (from the American Heritage College Dictionary, 4th Ed.)
The condition of being free from restraint
Liberty of the person from slavery, detention, oppression
The capacity to exercise choice; free will
Ease or facility of movement

What Does Freedom Mean To You?

Health

For me, living in a state of health means I am free to express my potential.

Opportunity

Freedom means that I have access to circumstances that allow me to express my potential.

Creative Expression

Freedom means that I can bring something to the world in a new way.

Ultimately, for me, freedom means having the experience of awe, wonder, gratitude, and acknowledgment at the inherent opportunity in human birth. It means saying "Yes" to life as it is. When I know how remarkable it is that of the billion-to-one odds that one particular sperm and egg should meet at just the right time, between these two people, in this planet that is perched just the right distance from a fiery ball of gas and light to sustain life, I have to laugh out loud!

I'm really interested in practicality. I'm going to propose that spirituality is the bedrock of freedom, but I don't want to bullshit anyone with flowery words. I want hard-hitting, pragmatic evidence.

Learning Freedom

So what is the practical understanding of freedom? What does it mean? How can you develop the experience?

In answering this question, I turned towards study of Reverend Dr. Martin Luther King, Jr. It is safe to say that he was an expert at freedom. Breathed it, lived it, taught it, and made it real in the lives of every American.

Here's how Dr. King defined freedom:
"The capacity to deliberate or to weigh alternatives."
"Freedom expresses itself in decision."
"A third expression of freedom is responsibility."

Make It Practical, Relevant, and Actionable in my Life

I recently learned that Warren Buffet, the financial phenomenon, was so moved by Rev. Dr. King at an address at Grinnell College in Grinnell, Iowa that Buffet took up the position of trustee at the college.

Now this struck me. Of course, Dr. King has done more incredible acts, more heroic deeds, and made more impressive speeches. But I am interested in the most practical, business-relevant material, so this talk at Grinnell stood out.

My understanding is that Warren Buffet had little if any civic engagement at Grinnell during this phase of life. He recognized and analyzed investment opportunities. That was what he did, who he was, what he was about. Buffet is arguably the most successful, pragmatic, practical, and reality-based investment giant of all time.

Dr. King awoke in Warren Buffet a desire to be part of a solution. The principles that Dr. King demonstrated impacted the pragmatic mind. And these same principles impact you and me every day in very practical ways. Let's use them. As Dr. King stated: "The non-violent approach does not immediately change the heart of the oppressor. It first does something to the hearts and souls of those committed to it. It gives them a new self-respect; it calls up resources of strength and courage that they did not know they had. Finally, it reaches the opponent and so stirs his conscience that reconciliation becomes a reality."

The Principles of Nonviolence

Rev. Dr. Martin Luther King, Jr. led the freedom movement in America on an epic scale that will stand out through history. What were his foundations? What can we learn from him?

First and foremost, the idea of nonviolent resistance is directly linked to Mohandas K. Gandhi. Mahatma ("The Great Soul") Gandhi used politics rooted in the great spiritual techniques of Christianity, Hinduism, and Islam. According to the rules of the world, it makes no sense to "turn the other cheek," yet Gandhi took this quite literally, stating, "When you are willing to stand up to your enemy, without shrinking down, but without striking back, something powerful happens. His respect for you increases and his contempt for you decreases."

Freedom Formula

To live in freedom, live by this simple precept. When someone treats you poorly, you treat them well. When you become independent of the need for others to do good by you, when you choose to be loving and kind, *no matter what*, then you live in freedom. Period.

I can hear the response. *"Do I just let people trample on me?"* No. Gandhi made it very clear that there was no room for cowardice in his philosophy. In that way, it was not for everyone. You always stand up and submit to the reaction from people who may not like what you have to say, but you do not react with hostility to their reaction.

Making the Social Lesson a Personal Strength

It is not without purpose that I choose to illustrate freedom for the Indestructible Success project by involving the issues of these great leaders. Their message is not limited to the realm of great social action on a national and international scale. Their call to nonviolence is not for great political change only. The call to freedom through nonviolence is at the very core of human endeavor, from family to career, from finance to recreation.

We are fortunate to live in a time and place of tremendous freedom. These freedoms, however, can be seen to turn in on humanity if the internal state of freedom is absent.
- Freedom of speech turns into narcissistic rhetoric, hate messages, and debasement such as child pornography.
- Entire populations are killing themselves with diseases of excess.
- Anxiety and stress rage through the over-stimulated body and mind.

It may seem odd to think that nonviolence applies directly to modern personal problems, but it isn't, as I will demonstrate later. But first, where are you feeling trapped?

The Opposite of Freedom: Feeling Trapped

Based on my research, the main areas where people don't feel free are:
- Relationship
- Money
- Time
- Health (sleep, diet, symptoms, etc.)
- Confidence

Take a minute to identify the areas where you are stuck in your life.

The principles of nonviolence are the underpinnings of freedom in those areas too. As promised, I'll demonstrate.

If you are reading this book, you are in some way dedicated to serving the world, and for that I applaud, celebrate, and validate your heart and soul.

We are brothers and sisters on the path. Fundamentally, you know that love, validation, care, kindness, compassion, and qualities that support life are essential to our personal and professional effectiveness. Have you ever seen the effect of aggression, blame, attack, abuse, name-calling, and manipulation work in your favor with people or with circumstances?

Yet how many of us are committed to 100 percent nonviolence with our employees, clients, spouses, family, friends, children, or even the cashier at the supermarket?

How many of us can say that in the last week, I did not:
- Lie, hide the truth, distort, modify, and enlarge
- Manipulate, cajole, push, and nag
- Play the victim, became passive, sulk, run away
- Get annoyed, bothered, resistant
- Criticize, condemn, and complain
- Judge, blame, speak harshly

A Course in Miracles says that there is no real distinction between annoyance and rage. Every act of aggression is an act of "missing the mark" (the original meaning of sin) and the solution is the same in every case. Seek the truth. Every upset is an opportunity to become more whole, healed, and loving.

"You will become increasingly aware that a slight twinge of annoyance is nothing but a veil drawn over intense fury" (A Course In Miracles, lesson 21).

Free of Attachment

None of us are saints yet, but freedom is the freedom to choose, and as long as we have aggression, we are not really free to choose because we are preoccupied with defending and obtaining. But what could we be defending, and what are we trying to get with these subtle acts of violence?

We've all heard, "Resentment is like taking poison and hoping the other person gets sick."

Every act of aggression is a way to try for fulfillment, in the form of praise, adulation, status, pleasure, comfort, power, and safety. The way to transcend the acts of aggression is to live in fulfillment. The experience of love is the ultimate fulfillment and frees us from the never-ending cycle of manipulating the world.

The Resolution of Freedom in Your Life

This brings me back to the start of the chapter, to Dr. King and Mahatma Gandhi. If I have a hard time not becoming angry when my daughter is rude or my wife is curt with me, how did these men stay loving when they were physically, emotionally, and psychologically threatened day after day?

And thus, we arrive at the supreme practicality of spirituality. Spiritual orientation tends to fill the aspirant with fullness independent of the circumstance of life. This is the power of love promised in the great religious and spiritual traditions.

Gandhi described it as becoming a zero, and then discovering fearlessness. He was a devout student of the teachings of Christ, and of his own cultural lineage. He was raised in a temple that drew on the spiritual base of traditions and teachings of the Bhagavad-Gita and the Koran. He wanted to bring the pulse of India into solidarity, thus liberating the Indian people from Colonial rule.

Jesus the Christ referred to this as "Whoever seeks to keep his life will lose it, and whoever loses his life will preserve it" (the Gospel of St. Luke 17:33).

Ram Dass, in his modern classic *Be Here Now,* summed it up with, "The most exquisite paradox…as soon as you give it all up, you can have it all. As long as you want power, you can't have it. The minute you don't want power, you'll have more than you ever dreamed possible."

All of these point to the act of lowering defenses.

Spirituality as the Practical Path of Freedom

Spiritual endeavor consistently demonstrates practicality in the lives of great men and women throughout history. The consistent application of this endeavor fills you up, and you realize what it means to "be in the world, but not of it" or "to wear the world like a loose garment."

Often people fear that they will lose the drive to achieve and succeed if they no longer come from the "kick butt and take names" consciousness.

History doesn't suggest that, but you might save years of your life attempting to achieve a dream that is only the result of a desire to prove something to the world. Proving something to the world is very different than living the dream of your heart.

That leads us back to applying the tools in Chapters 5 and 6, especially on handling upsets. When you are really willing to have the thing you fear most happen, you cease to spend thought energy projecting into the future and you become free to choose without the "tunnel vision" that fear locks down.

Spirituality looks at this as *surrender.*

So we have the psychological principles used in the *9 Steps to Turn Fear Into Fuel and Upsets Into Opportunities* process and the spiritual law of surrender that overlap. From the spirit-based perspective, this is summed up in twelve-step program axiom *I admit that of myself, I am powerless to control my life, I need help.*

Consciousness Research

Significant exploration on the topic of practical spirituality comes from Dr. David Hawkins' eight books and countless hours of DVD and audio.

Simply put, Dr. Hawkins establishes that consciousness is stratified in human experience. He has created a mathematical scale to represent these stratifications. This scale can be likened to a thermometer or the scales of sound, light, or radio frequency. Acting principles such as love, surrender, willingness, faith, kindness, compassion, determination, and self-honesty (all classically termed "spiritual qualities") actually bring a more integrated level of energy and power to the individual.

This continues the common sense approach of the "Golden Rule" as well as the principles expressed by the majority of the successful "self-help" teachers through the last century.

As Dr. Hawkins describes it, we actually align with a "dominant attracter field," which, by its own energizing force, begins to align our life experience. Thus the experience of Grace and the significance of truly great spiritual and world leaders are validated as beneficial by the results produced by those who inhabit the field of the practices and teachings.

> *By their fruits, ye shall know them.*
> **Matthew 7:16**

Why Our Freedom Means Practicing Nonviolence

Nonviolence means practicing unconditional positive regard and acceptance. It does not mean passivity. The great leaders have demonstrated that we have to believe that underneath the behavior of oppression, there is goodness in the so-called enemy. We have to know the light in the person while persisting in understanding that the behavior is wrong.

How do you love fully, while holding boundaries, having standards, speaking your truth, and saying "NO" when needed, without stooping to manipulate, attack, abandon, or hate someone else? This leads naturally to Chapter 8.

RECAP OF CHAPTER 7:

- Freedom is the power to determine action, thought, or decision without inner or outer constraint.
- The principles of nonviolence show us the direct path to freedom.
- Ultimately, spirituality is the gateway to freedom.
- Spiritual endeavor facilitates an alignment with progressively more potentiating fields of consciousness, which gives you more energy and more power.
- There is a pragmatic effect from spiritual development.
- We use subtle acts of violence regularly to get imitation love (praise, power, pleasure, predictability).
- Fear is the root of unloving behavior. By removing the psychological underpinnings of fear, we can access the experience of surrender.
- Integrate Affirmative Invocation and Handling Fear/Healing Intense Emotions with spiritual cultivation.

So, can you see how the principles of nonviolence can help you live with more freedom in your life?

SELF-STUDY EXERCISES:

- Write down where you feel trapped.
- Use prayer and contemplation to gain understanding and strength in this area.
- Identify your fears and surrender the resistance.
- Use this as an opportunity to use the *9 Step to Turn Upsets Into Opportunities*.
- Practice returning loving kindness to apparent acts of aggression.
- What are some of your daily aggravations? Can you change the situation? If not, can you find a way to embrace them?
- Can you generate compassion for your own and others' flaws?

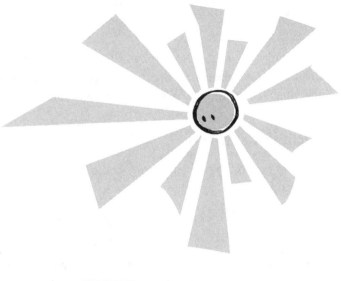

CHAPTER 8

BE EXEMPLARY

*Whenever you set out to build a creative temple, whatever it may be,
you must face the fact that there is a tension...a Mr. Hyde and a Dr. Jekyll
in us... And whenever we set out to dream our dreams and to build
our temples, we must be honest enough to recognize it.*
Rev. Dr. Martin Luther King Jr.

THE PURPOSE OF CHAPTER 8:

The purpose of this chapter is to give you examples of how and why
character and integrity lead to long lasting success and to inspire you to
continue to develop character for its own reward. You will develop the
warrior's practice of a personal code of integrity and honor.

Mental Prison

Drawing directly from the previous chapter, you see how we create mental
prisons from the inside out. Greed, wantonness, and self-absorption
confine those who seem externally free. We live in a place and time of
incredible wealth, opportunity, and freedom. Nevertheless, much of the
fabric of integrity is crumbling around us.

Viktor Frankl describes finding freedom in the most degrading
circumstances – the Nazi work camp. This is the polar opposite end of the
spectrum from our current social and external freedom. Amidst torture,
abuse, depravation experiments, and grueling physical labor, Frankl
discovered that no one could take away his inner freedom. Frankl became

exemplary and went on to inspire millions to choose the life of love and inspiration. As leaders, we are called to be exemplary and to practice what the integral community calls "transcend and include."

Socrates Knew This

Socrates nailed the problem we are contending with in the postmodern age thousands of years ago:

All men seek only the good but do not know how to consistently differentiate the helpful (good) from the detrimental (bad).

When you understand this, you will begin to better relate to the people around you, especially if they are vastly different.

There are three major paradigms, or world-views, pushing against each other in most of the world, traditional, modern and post-modern.

One of the tricky balance beams of social construction teeters between "traditional" and "progressive" values. Often, we seem to be left wondering if we need to choose between rigid authoritative tradition for the sake of tradition or an intellectual superiority complex that suggests abandoning any foundation of consistent moral, ethical, or value-based conduct, other than its own relativism.

You can see this with academia, religion, and politics. Some say that this is the push and pull between liberal and conservative, but that is just not an accurate way to describe the split. The split in consciousness is really between modern values, postmodern values, and traditional values; each has merits and each has blind spots. Great social movements sprang up around each of these paradigms.

Postmodern thought is particularly interesting when applied to art, music, and creativity. But when applied to intellectual rigor, politics, and industry, it can be disastrous.

What is disastrous about it?

Postmodern thought pushes the idea that all thoughts have equal value, that all cultures have equal value. It throws out hierarchy. The up side of this is the introduction of gender equality and racial and ethnic understanding. The dilemma is the loss of a substantial hierarchy of values, morals, and a clearly defined "right" and "wrong." While it is phenomenal for Miles Davis to exhort that "there are no wrong notes" it is detrimental to say that adults have equal rights to view child pornography as an expression of free speech.

For a much more intelligent assessment of this split, check out the writing of American philosopher Ken Wilber, including but no limited to *Boomeritis, The Marriage of Sense and Soul, A Brief History of Everything* or check out *Reality, Spirituality and Modern Man* by Dr. David Hawkins.

Regardless of the social climate, the value of character cannot be argued. The next greatest version of America and the world requires that we turn crisis into opportunity. You can build that by developing your character.

Building Character Means Taking Heat

Character is built on the application of the qualities laid out in the first three chapters.

In the film *12 Angry Men*, Henry Fonda's character is the lone dissenting voice on jury duty in what appears to be an open and shut case. As he deals with harassment from other jurors for wasting their time, Fonda's character holds to his conviction. There is some question—what if the guilty verdict cannot be assumed and the boy is innocent?

Fonda has to face the truth regardless of the heat, the fatigue, and the nagging. In the end (spoiler alert!), after a slow and agonizing process, the group reconsiders the evidence and, one by one, they change their position until all of them stand on integrity, rather than convenience.

> *The ultimate measure of a man is not where he stands in the moments of comfort and convenience, but where he stands in times of challenge and controversy.*
> **Rev. Dr. Martin Luther King, Jr.**

Why Exemplary Character Builds Success

But what does this have to do with Indestructible Success?

> *If the sun and moon should doubt, they would soon go out.*
> **William Blake**

But the sun and moon do not doubt, in the great cosmic sense. They are part of a natural rhythm. When you act with character and integrity, you walk with that same power.

Simply put, this means:
- You do what you say you are going to do.
- You follow through on what you start.
- You tell the truth.
- You persist even when you "don't feel like it."

Second, character, like integrity, is its own reward. When you walk your talk, it shows. Not only that, it lasts! Bernie Madoff was able to pull off a Ponzi scheme for a long time, but eventually, all things must run their course. When you walk with character—honesty, willingness, helpfulness, kindness, chivalry, purity, orderliness, etc.—then that too will run its course.

Third, paradoxically, when you totally commit yourself to being your best for an act of service and selfless contribution, suddenly your life gets a heck of a lot better. The first time I really grasped this, I was about twenty years old reading a book by Zig Ziglar, in which he says, "If you want your dreams to come true, help someone else make theirs come true." And when you dedicate yourself to something bigger, you find:
- A greater ability to live in integrity
- A shift in focus away from your problems
- More focus on solutions
- Life begins to support you

Archbishop Desmond Tutu put it this way: "You know when you are in the presence of someone who is good." Mother Teresa, Nelson Mandela— these people command attention because of who they are. By cultivating character, you begin to build the personal containment for excellence that your work will need from you. And let's face it; you get the reward of looking in the mirror and seeing a face that you respect.

When you cultivate character, you cannot lose. It may not get you rich quick, or garner immediate respect, but it's just like nonviolence; it will eventually produce results. And in fact, nonviolence is a fruit of great character.

Character Is Built on Mission and Purpose

Carlos Santana, in *Performing Songwriter,* challenged the reader to play music for something higher than money, fame, or pleasure. "You can become rich like Martha Stewart and still screw people over, famous like Joe Namath and use it to sell beer…Look at Elvis…if you are not into spiritual principles, you become a caricature of yourself real quick."

And later, in the Spring 2005 Issue of *What Is Enlightenment* magazine, Santana said, "Everyone is destined to prosperity, to progress, and the keys that humans need to find are intention, motives, and purpose, because that is who you really, **really** are….I invite you to crystallize your intention, motives, and purpose, because if you don't do that, you're always going to blame somebody else for what you didn't get to do."

It seems that what Carlos is getting at is that you can be a great guitar player, businessperson, or coach, but you have to get your purpose lined up with character.

The truth is, you can develop a lot of personal power using the inner/ outer game technologies. Many techniques that we teach and use in this book, trainings, and coaching can be used for selfish goals. But to harness the greatness of your biggest dreams, we surrender our small wants for our greatest desire.

Our biggest dreams, like a good yoga class, take us right to the edge of our ability. They challenge us to be more ourselves.

This leads us directly to one of the most powerful motivators for developing character. When you get a powerful vision for your life, align with spiritual principles, and have definite purpose, then you will be willing to do or be whatever you need to bring forth your heart's deepest longing.

Few men are willing to brave the disapproval of their fellows, the censure of their colleagues, the wrath of their society. Moral courage is a rarer commodity than bravery in battle or great intelligence. Yet it is the one essential, vital quality for those who seek to change a world, which yields most painfully to change.

Robert F. Kennedy

Transcend and Include

I'd like to think that, professionally speaking, we can "transcend and include" traditional values of honoring our elders, acting courteously, speaking encouragingly, restraining our sexual desire, and committing to relationship. I'd like to think that we could "transcend and include" the postmodern academic values that investigate the validity of all traditional values, oftentimes simply supplanting a new set of values based on their own code of intellectual superiority, yet based on a good intent to equalize and clarify positions of power.

I'd like to think that we can have a system of natural order or hierarchy that acknowledges the developmental phases of all aspects of life, from atom to molecule to proteins to organelle to cell to tissue to organ to organism; from infant to toddler to walking to talking to individuation, maturation, etc.

So, too, character development follows a developmental model, much like Maslow's hierarchy of needs.

If you are with me so far, then what exactly is character and how do you develop it?

What Are the Foundations of Character?

Common sense wisdom suggests the character traits that are helpful to be cultivated include:
- Honesty: not out to deceive anyone or yourself
- Integrity: will follow through on your word
- Acceptance: has room for human fallibility
- Willingness: ready to participate
- Intelligence: can think through a course of action
- Moderation: not too extreme
- Consideration: aware and responsive to others
- Health: steward of the body-mind
- Hard work: capable of accepting difficulty when needed
- Responsibility: maintains the boundaries
- Gratitude: expresses positive regard
- Humility: quick to accept responsibility for mistakes; quick to credit others with success
- Patience: shows restraint with emotions
- Persistence: not easily dissuaded
- Rationality: not prone to sentimentality or rash decisions

Benjamin Franklin had a system for cultivating "virtues" that consisted of a rotating set of qualities that he would practice daily. These included thirteen simple virtues, paraphrased from the *Autobiography of Benjamin Franklin*:

1. Temperance: Don't overeat and do not drink too much alcohol.
2. Silence: If you speak, make sure it is true, helpful, and necessary. Avoid gossip.
3. Order: Keep your space and time organized. Life has a rhythm; find it and keep it.
4. Resolution: Resolve to act in accord with your values, standards, and expectations. Act to maintain your resolve.
5. Frugality: Don't waste your money on nonsense. Use your resources for good.
6. Industry: Cut out time wasting. Engage in productive or restorative pursuits but beware of idle or distracting behavior.
7. Sincerity: Don't exaggerate or knowingly lie. Keep your mind and your communication free of corruption.
8. Justice: Don't harm anyone by commission or omission (by what you do or do not do).
9. Moderation: Beware of all excessiveness. Reduce the perceived need to retaliate for wrongs against you. Forgive.
10. Cleanliness: Keep your body, clothes, home, office, car, and property clean and ordered.
11. Chastity: Sexual expression for enjoyment, health, well-being, or children. Be responsible for your own and others' reputations and honor, and avoid unnecessary troubles.
12. Tranquility: Don't sweat the small stuff. Life happens.
13. Humility: Deep, honest assessment of character strengths and weaknesses; nothing to prove.

Franklin goes on to say that his major obstacle was number three, *order*, especially in keeping his day on track due to meetings and travel.

If he thought it was hard then, how much more so now with TV, cell phones, e-mail, Twitter, Facebook, BlackBerry, iPhone, and the constant voice of marketing? If you have not noticed yet, this is one of the KEY concepts to consider. Modern challenge is directly related to the experience of distraction and overwhelm. I address this at length in Chapter 13. You must develop habits of thought and action that counter these forces.

How Can I Cultivate Character?

First, look to role models. What qualities do they posses that you admire? How can you cultivate these traits?

Second, look to your own lineage and ancestry. I think about some of the experiences that my grandparents and great-grandparents endured and overcame, and I think about what it must have taken to overcome the obstacles they met. You can learn about character from mistakes that parents or grandparents may have made. What character traits were missing? How can I cultivate that?

Finally, I think the simplest, most effective way to refine your character is by choosing to spend time with people who reinforce the qualities that you want to develop.

If you are committed to honesty, but your buddy wants to brag to you about how he cheated on his taxes, that will not reinforce the qualities you want to develop. You can talk to your friend and stay in the relationship, talk to him or her and go, or just accept it as the way it is and choose to stay or to move on. It is not a cut-and-dry decision. Relationships are more complicated than that. But as a rule, if a person in your social circle does not have a lot of integrity or follow-through, or complains a lot, then be aware of the effect.

When you play big, supportive social circles celebrate. And remember at the end of the day, when you decided to play big, you are going to get more heat, more projection, and more people trying to get your time, attention, and money. Make sure your friends are a source of grounding, support, and reality.

> *Be exemplary. The world needs the light.*
> Marianne Williamson

Character Is Your Life Preserver for Surviving Success

Why is character so important to successful people?

Developing these qualities is preparatory. If you decide to play big, prepare to be laughed at, criticized, attacked, and belittled. When you know **you,** it doesn't matter what people say.

Integrity is its own reward. But when you blow up your career to a "big time" level, the spotlight will be on you with a magnifying glass. That is not the time to clean up your life. Now is the time.

Broad is the path that leads to destruction and many are the individuals who have "fallen from grace," through misuse of power, sex, and money after they reached the pinnacle of their career. Don't take the easy way. Be exemplary, because integrity cannot fail.

> *If you shape your life according to nature, you will never be poor; if according to people's opinions, you will never be rich.*
>
> **Seneca**

Two Feet on the Ground

Be exemplary. Be powerful. Embrace the necessary discomforts. Spirituality is the base for freedom, nonviolence, and character, but all too often, it becomes an excuse to avoid life. That's called "spiritual bypass." You see this as the "Eternal Youth" archetype, the Peter Pan/Neverland of play, superpowers, and imagination.

Now all of these are necessary, fun parts of living, but left unchecked, they do not support the character that provides stability and grounding.

> *If you have built your castles in the air, your work need not be lost; that is where they should be. Now put the foundation under them.*
>
> **Henry David Thoreau**

Be exemplary by accepting responsibility. Remember these two statements:
1. The buck stops here.
2. Take the high road.

The Buck Stops Here

The buck stops here. Great leaders always take responsibility for poor results and always point to those around them for success. That isn't false humility; it is a way of living. This position assures that "the buck stops here." You become a clearing ground for mediocrity, a nullifying agent for excuses. You become "the salt of the earth." You become exemplary.

This principle hasn't been better illustrated than in Jim Collins' book *Good To Great*. Collins does thorough research on extremely successful companies over long periods of time. These companies have several key traits. One of them is having what Collins calls "Level 5 Leaders." The traits of level five leaders include:

- Taking responsibility when things go wrong
- Giving credit to those around them when things go well
- Genuine humility
- Passion about the work they do
- Absolute commitment to serve the company

Take The High Road

Take the high road. Every interaction you have imprints on others. The simple mandate "Do unto others as you would have them do unto you," if consistently practiced, will assure your success with business, clients, and patients. People want to be treated well, and they inherently respect those of us who choose to take the high road no matter what.

Have you ever had clients, like our example of Desperelda in Chapter 5, who were at your throat? Sometimes you bite the hook and attack back, but if you are committed to the practice of *the high road,* you will develop a quiet power. Intellectually, you know their anger is not about you. But it is your self-restraint, which requires practice over and over again in these situations, which teaches your heart and your soul that what your intellect knows is correct. It is not about you.

The Warrior's Code

In many cultures, in many times, a warrior code of conduct developed that emphasized skillfulness, chivalry, right action and honor.

Today, you may be challenged to adopt your own code of conduct while simultaneously respecting and appreciating that there may be others with different values. This does not mean that you have to agree, or pretend that you are not aligned.

Sticking to a code of conduct that is true for you in your belly may mean that others criticize you. Standing in your power will definitely upset people. In fact, the more successful you are, the more personal power you have, the more insult and attack you will have to endure.

One of the greatest gifts I have been given in this lifetime is the training I received as a Warrior Artist at Naropa University. Professor Barbara Dilley and other performing arts faculty translated the wisdom tradition of Tibetan Buddhism, as taught by Chogyam Trungpa Rinpoche, into the language of the creative process. This translation featured one poignant credo from The Tibetan Sage-Warrior-King, Gesar of Ling; Heart Open, Mind Awake, Body Firm. That is to say we develop our ability to stay open hearted, with a fresh mind and presence in our body. Every time I heard the credo, heart open, mind awake, body firm, I felt like sitting up a little straighter and breathing a little deeper.

Martial arts teach a code of honor. So do many of the civic clubs in the world, including Rotarty, Kiwanis and Lions among others. Certainly some aspects of military training emphasize a code of honor. There are many fraternal organizations that help their members to develop and live by a code of honor.

For some, a mission statement captures this quality of wanting to sit up straighter.

I got the same jolt of dignity from our Outward Bound motto, *to serve, to strive and not to yield.* And this quote from the founder of Outward Bound Kurt Hahn really captures the spirit for educators: "I regard it as the foremost task of education to insure the survival of these qualities: an enterprising curiosity, an undefeatable spirit, tenacity in pursuit, readiness for sensible self-denial, and above all, compassion."

RECAP OF CHAPTER 8:

- Find ways to follow wisdom traditions to avoid the traps of human fallibility.
- Find what you stand for, and then keep standing for it.
- Remember that exemplary character leads to Indestructible Success.
- Remember that Mission and Purpose ignite Character.
- Integrate traditional and postmodern values into a "transcend and include" paradigm.
- Common sense qualities such as honesty, discipline, and integrity define character. It is not complicated.
- Surround yourself with people of character.
- Know that character is the life preserver for surviving success.
- Remember that the buck stops with you.
- Always do your best to take the high road.
- Be curious about what it means to be a warrior and see what would be in your personal code of integrity.

Well, were you able to see why developing your character supports building, strengthening, and sustaining success?

SELF-STUDY EXERCISES:

1. What values and qualities are most important to you? Which of these do you want to strengthen?
2. Does your social circle reflect shared values and standards?
3. Journal about where you have given your word and broken your commitments.
4. Then take action this week on one or two areas to clean up those commitments.
5. Pay attention to the commitments that you want to make this week. Make sure your yes is a YES and your no is a NO.
6. Where can you take the high road? Where can you take responsibility for your experience? Take action in one area this week.
7. Begin to write down a list of traits for your own warrior's code.

SECTION C:

**Bring Your Gifts
To The World**

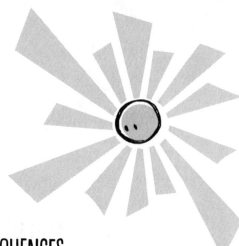

CHAPTER 9

COACH POWER: QUESTIONS, SEQUENCES, AND SYSTEMS

Questions are the master switch for shifting focus and shifting states.
Tony Robbins

THE PURPOSE OF CHAPTER 9:

The purpose of this chapter is to learn advanced skills in coaching yourself and others. You'll learn to break through being stuck and get into taking action on creating the life you want.

You Are a Coach

Everyone is a coach. You are either a good coach or a bad coach.
It is up to you.

You can help anyone by asking a few simple questions. You don't need a PhD. You don't need a prestigious coach-training certification. You don't need a guru or an esoteric practice. All you need is genuine interest and a couple of questions.

Of course, we are using questions all the time, but so often, they're the wrong questions.

- Why does this always happen to me?
- Why can't I get over this?
- Why is he such a jerk?

And of course, the mind will answer the question!

Q: Why does this always happen to me?
A: Because you're destined to fail.

Q: Why can't I get over this?
A: Because I can't.

Much worse, the way the mind works brings us behavior and subsequently experience that reinforces the question. Good news though: the life experience of asking the right questions will compound an upward spiral.

Questions are the foundation for teaching and facilitating change for clients, patients, employees, team members, or anyone else you care about.

Here are some of the questions that I've become familiar with in my work:
- Are you willing to have a breakthrough in this area of your life?
- What would you do if you knew you couldn't fail?
- What is the risk of making a change?
- How do you feel?
- If you did know the solution, what would it be?
- How does this serve you?

Questions are incredibly effective in communicating. Just check it out with children. You can spend a half an hour telling kids to clean up their toys, or ask them, "Honey, where do these toys belong, great, and who do you think is going to put them away? And when would be the best time?" It's amazing how kids, when given the chance to think independently, demonstrate intelligence, problem solving, and initiative.

When anyone, child or adult, answers a question, they are much more likely to follow the words than if you tell them what to do.

Tony Robbins is a master of questions. I've heard him say in seminars that he could make clients change with some techniques, but *he* got stronger from it, not them. And questions were the key to teaching.

But you have to know the right questions to ask.

Essentially, they are:	They are not:
Opening	Closing
Solution oriented	Problem oriented
Responsible	Blaming
Empowering	Disempowering

Question Block Sequences

Having a series of questions compounds the power.

One of my favorite question blocks for working with challenges is:
- First, what about this is working?
- Second, what about this is not ideal yet?
- Third, what am I willing to do or be to improve things?
- Fourth, what am I choosing not to do?

Focused inquiry to change states is yet another permutation of questions. This could be in the generating resourceful states section!
- What am I truly grateful for?
- What could I be grateful for if I let myself?
- What am I passionate about?
- What could I be passionate about if I let myself?
- What am I excited about?
- Whom do I love and care about?
- Who loves and cares about me?

The next step after question blocks would be organizing questions into a system to create more directed results. In the next section, you will learn a powerful and effective system for organized coaching.

A System of Inquiry

I must have taken a wrong turn in Albuquerque.
Bugs Bunny, upon finding himself on Mars

In Chapter 2, we experienced the importance of *The Plan*. In Chapter 4, we reinforced the idea of direction. It helps to have a map to get from point A to point B. Without a map it is easy to end up on Mars.

You're about to learn a powerful system for organizing questions. You'll use this to literally "coach anyone, anywhere, anytime." I'm going to share the fundamentals of 4 Gateways Coaching. This is one of the most powerful tools for coaching anyone, anywhere, anytime, and I am stoked to share it with YOU!

I have explicit permission to teach you this from the founder of 4 Gateways, Dr. Tom Daly.

4 Gateways Coaching sits on a powerhouse set of fundamental beliefs:
• All problems are opportunities.
    • All parts of you are important.
    • We get the perfect lesson for us.
    • You can change your outer experience by changing the inner • experience.

Now, the 4 Gateways are really, simply put, four fundamental ways of experiencing life. It is what defines human existence. It is our soul. Webster's definition of "soul" includes the ability to:
• Think
• Feel
• Be
• Act

4 Gateways associates an archetypal quality to each of the four:

Think-Magician

Be-Sovereign   **Act**-Warrior

Feel-Lover

And even though one Gateway has "feeling" as a quality or primary characteristic, there is an emotion associated with each of the gateways.

Thinking
Magician
Fear

Being   **Action**
Sovereign   Warrior
Joy   Anger

Feeling
Lover
Sadness

What makes this simple four-quadrant model exciting and versatile is its plug and play form. Any inquiry system plugs right in. When you access the four fundamental aspects of human nature, you have a system for effective coaching. It literally does work to coach anyone, anywhere, anytime.

Archetypes

The growth of archetypal psychology roots down to Carl Jung. Jung, a student of Freud, diverged from his teacher and developed the first transpersonal approach to psychology.

Archetypes are personality energy circuits common to everyone. Just as the brain develops neural patterns of speech, thought, and action, so too, morphogenic fields hold the collective patterns of human experience. Nowhere can we see these more clearly articulated than in our stories, movies, myths, and fairy tales.

Putting It All Together

Combine question, quadrants (perspectives), and movement into a reliable system of inquiry. Then, move through the sequence until the client experiences an "aha!" moment, and finish with an integrative round.

The questions you use live in each quadrant. Each time you pass through that gateway, you add another perspective and your insight deepens. By physically moving, you engage the somatic-kinesthetic intelligence. The result? A playful experience and a meaningful coaching session! How cool is that?

Begin and End Powerfully No Matter What System You Use

Like any good coaching session, you want a strong beginning to:
1. Create a clear time agreement.
2. Create a safe space, contained and controlled.
3. Ask the client what their ideal outcome is.

Once you establish a clear issue and outcome, you proceed through the sequence of questions and then finish up with a strong ending.
1. Ask the client, "What insights have occurred?"
2. Ask the client, "What action do you want to take?"
3. Visualize success (guide the client through this).
   1. Confirm accountability and support.

These opening and closing question sequences are useful no matter what coaching form you use. Here is the entire sequence of a condensed 4 Gateways Coaching session.

The Beginning of 4 Gateways Coaching

1. Create a contained space.
2. Check in, update, and establish rapport.
3. Come to a clear focus for this session, i.e., identify an area where the client would like to have a breakthrough.
4. Get a clear verbal confirmation: "Are you ready to have a breakthrough in this area?" (Client says, "Yes, I am ready.")
5. Note that if the client says, "Well, yes, I guess so," don't proceed. Stop and find out what could support them in getting to a yes. Ask them: "Sounds like there is a risk in having a breakthrough." (Client nods in affirmation.)
6. What is that risk? (Client says, "I may have to feel more.")
7. Yes, that may be true. Is that a risk you want to take? (Client contemplates and says yes.)
8. All right, are you ready to have a breakthrough? (Yes.)
9. Write down the issue on a piece of paper or choose an object to represent the issue. The process is usually done while engaging the body in movement, but it is not absolute. Some clients don't like it, or it just doesn't serve them. For me, about five percent of my total client base are not into moving around.
10. The client begins by standing at the three o'clock position, looking at the issue in the center of an imagined clock. In each quadrant, a variation on the question is asked.

The First Round of 4 Gateways Coaching

Now, there are four steps that you take to complete one round. There are classically three rounds to complete in one session. In the first round you elaborate on the issue and get more information, including mental, emotional, physical, and energetic clues and data.

Here is the first round sequence:

1. The first question you ask in the three o'clock position is, "What are your judgments about yourself or about the situation?"

1. The client moves to the six o'clock position. Ask the question, "What is the payoff of these judgments?"
2. The client moves to the nine o'clock position. "How do you feel right now looking at this issue in your life?"
3. The client moves to the twelve o'clock position. "Can you bless/accept/honor each of these places?"

These are general questions, and usually need to be contextualized to the situation. An example may be:

1. What are your judgments about yourself as a person, who has this situation with *your* health?
2. What is the payoff of keeping this situation going?
3. How does it feel to be addressing these situations?
   Where do you feel that?
   Can you name the sensations?
   How big?
   Coming up or down, etc.
4. Can you accept that this is where you are right now?

Another example:

1. What judgments would you have about a person who is stuck in the habit of eating when sad or anxious?
2. What is the payoff of that judgment?
3. How do you feel inside when you look at this situation in Jane's life (third person perspective)? Can you give yourself permission to feel that more completely?
4. Can you bless the part of you that criticizes you? Can you bless the part of you that looks for comfort from food? Can you bless the part of you that feels sad?

Two comments here:

Giving the client the opportunity to speak in the third person as they go around the circle allows for the archetypal, universal nature of human experience to arise. This makes working with human fallibility more easeful and compassionate, and reduces resistance.

What we can bless, we can accept. Use a language that the client can connect to. Essentially, resistance in one form or another is at the core of the issue, tangled in with several energy dynamics. You serve the client by helping them to be 100 percent accepting of where they are. Then they can make change with integrity.

4 GATEWAYS
BASIC

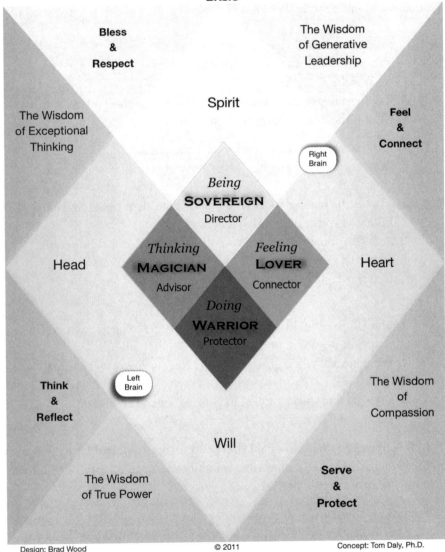

Bless
&
Respect

The Wisdom
of Generative
Leadership

Spirit

The Wisdom
of Exceptional
Thinking

Feel
&
Connect

Right
Brain

Being
SOVEREIGN
Director

Thinking
MAGICIAN
Advisor

Feeling
LOVER
Connector

Head

Heart

Doing
WARRIOR
Protector

Think
&
Reflect

Left
Brain

The Wisdom
of
Compassion

Will

Serve
&
Protect

The Wisdom
of True Power

Design: Brad Wood   © 2011   Concept: Tom Daly, Ph.D.

The Second Round of 4 Gateways Coaching

Repeat another round, moving though three, six, nine, and twelve o'clock. (The clock is an arbitrary map that everyone is familiar with and quickly grasps with little thought or effort.)

The questions you use in round two are:
1. Is there another way to see this situation?
2. What is the risk in changing?
3. To whom might this connect me? (Where was this pattern familiar?)
4. What is the deeper purpose of this issue?

Examples/variations of second round questions:
1. If this issue were a chapter in the story of your life, what would you call it?
2. What is the risk for your family if you considered changing jobs? Is this a risk you really think is worth it?
3. Does this situation remind you of any time in your childhood?
4. Why is this issue happening now, not a year ago, not a year from now?

Or,
1. Can you see that this issue is an opportunity to become freer in your life?
2. What kind of risk comes with more freedom? Are you ready to take that risk?
3. Does staying stuck connect to your parents in any way?
4. What is the Divine purpose of this issue?

In this round you want to establish a new perspective, identify the real risks in changing, make the connection to family and/or relationships, and focus on the deeper purpose of the issue.

For trained therapists, this is the round where you could do some family systems-oriented work. The third question (the Lover quadrant) addresses the connection to family of origin. I name this, acknowledge it, and move on. Maybe people make a connection, maybe not. I'm not a therapist.

The Final Round of 4 Gateways Coaching

In the final round, you continue with four questions, but aim them at closing the container, letting the soul/psyche integrate the shifts, claim the lesson, commit to action, and have a clear support team.

Here are the basic questions:

1. What insights do you want to take away?
2. What actions are you called to commit to? Can I hold you accountable?
3. Can you visualize yourself successfully integrating these actions, changes, or accomplishments?
4. Who can support you with this?

Of course, in this final round, you want to make sure that the actions are S.M.A.R.T. (Specific, Measurable, Attainable, Relevant, Timely) goals. I want to make sure the client ends up with clear "take-away" points written down as well as the names of the support people.

Here is an example of integration round sequence:

1. So, what key learning happened for you today?
2. How can you take powerful action on this issue?
3. Guided visualization process.
4. Who in your life supports you in having more freedom?

For number three, I use a process of progressive relaxation, into enhanced state suggestion, and positive rehearsal of successful integration, action, and experience.

Example:

OK, we are going to give you an opportunity to focus on success for a few minutes. I invite you to relax, let your arms drop down by your side, take a deep breath, and relax your body. If you notice any tension in your body, send it the message that it can relax, relax, relax. Notice your mind move from the tip of your head down through your neck, through the shoulders, back, chest, torso, organs, pelvic floor, hips, buttocks, thighs, legs, knees, calves, ankles, feet to the tips of your toes. Relax, relax, relax. Now scan back up the body (reverse sequence).

Now, allow your mind to relax, relax, relax, and imagine yourself successfully integrating this change into your life.

You are taking action; you are free, empowered, and kind to yourself. How does this feel?

Imagine this week, this month, three months. You are consistently taking action. You have integrated this change. How does it feel to be successful? Who is congratulating you? Who is encouraging you, celebrating your success? How does it feel to be totally integrated and on purpose in your life?

I invite you to imagine that a volume knob, like an old guitar amp, is connected to this feeling of success. And imagine that right now, it is at four, and I want you to imagine turning this up to a six or seven. How does that feel now?

Now, how about turning it up to twice the volume, to an eight, how does that feel? Allow your cells to be saturated with the vibration of success. Now, if you want, you can turn it up to nine or even ten if you would like, and imagine a wave of fullness soaking every cell, every fiber, and every part of you with the feeling of success and gratitude.

Keep the feeling flowing and as I count back from ten to one, you are going to let go of this feeling and it will slip into your subconscious to become part of you. You are effortlessly, totally letting go of any attachment; it just becomes who you are. Ten, you are integrating this new self, nine, eight, seven, allowing the feeling to gently move into the, six, files of who you are, five, you are easily coming back to this place, four, the feeling becomes part of you, three, now integrated, two, you are coming back, one, you are present in this place.

Shake your fingers, toes, eyes open, and we are going to move into the final quadrant.

Here is another example of the integration round:

1. So, what did you appreciate about our session today?
2. It sounds like you are ready to make some changes in your diet. Let me see if I heard you correctly. (Reflect back the commitments that you heard them say in the process, confirm them, and write them down.)
3. Guided Visualization Process.
4. Who is your support team in taking action on these food changes?

Ending the Session

You ask the client to remove the item in the middle that they had represent their issue: "This is not your issue." Then, you can have a seat and ask, "So, what did you enjoy about the process?" Even if you already asked that question, or something similar during the 4 G's process, you are now specifically getting a perspective on how that process went.

Here is a trick. Don't identify the process as the session. The session holds the process, but your work is bigger than any technique. Reconnect with this person heart to heart, outside of the form. But, find out how the form worked; did it match them? Get feedback if appropriate, but especially, get clear on what they liked.

Appreciation is really helpful for you. We need to constantly reinforce the work that we are doing. We give, give, give, give, and often wonder if we are making a difference! Absolutely we are! And we need to hear it. It is really healthy.

There you have a condensed version of the 4 Gateways Coaching process.

The Full Method

If you are interested in a slightly deeper version of this coaching method, then check out www.4GatewaysCoaching.com for more details, free downloads, videos and hire one of the coaches.

The method I teach here in *indestructible Success* is really the condensed version that I developed to use in 15-30 minute "power-coaching" sessions, when I had multiple clients in group calls, many clients a day or a short time with a client. Truth be told, if you want to be a great coach, you have to practice, practice, practice and get coached regularly too.

The Basics

We often compare learning the form to learning to play an instrument. It is helpful to learn the chords and scales really well before you improvise!

The best way to master the form is to study directly with Tom Daly in his annual coach training. Space is extremely limited due to small class size, and you need to spend some time working with a certified 4 Gateways coach first.

There are other systems of inquiry to learn, and I suggest that you find what resonates with you. Among them are:

- Integral Coaching, AQAL Map
- The Work, Byron Katie
- The Sedona Method, Hale Dwoskin
- Mastery of Life, Bill Ferguson
- Empowerment Process, Janet Swartz
- Transcending the Levels of Consciousness, Dr. David Hawkins
- 12-Step Processes
- Neuro-Linguistic Programming

RECAP OF CHAPTER 9:

- Questions can be used by anyone.
- Questions either create openings or make you close down.
- With questions, you bypass resistance.
- Series of questions compound power.

SELF-STUDY EXERCISES:

1. Practice asking yourself different questions when you feel stuck. How do these new questions help you open to solutions?
2. Ask a coaching buddy to be a guinea pig for you to practice a 4 Gateways coaching session. Just follow the questions exactly as the book states.
3. If you like what you read, buy the 4 Gateways Workbook at www.4GatewaysCoaching.com.
4. Integrate power questions into your morning practice (see Chapter 3 for more details on the weekly Work Your Plan suggestions).
5. Ask more questions from everyone in your life—clients, family, and friends—and really listen. How does this change your experience?

CHAPTER 10

COMMUNICATION POWER: SPEAK, LISTEN, AND TEACH

THE PURPOSE OF CHAPTER 10:

This chapter will help you authentically express yourself in the world so that you can take your plans and projects to other people and find the folks that you want to work with, serve and learn from.

Communication Is the Expression of the Vision

Once you have a dream, a vision, and a goal, and a plan to achieve that goal consisting of projects and action steps, then you are ready to connect and communicate. What does it look like to embody and express your vision? It always looks like some form of communication. Every time.

What Is Communication?

What do you think communication is? Sure, it is speaking, one person to another. Communication is the way we use words in front of a loved one, a friend, a group, a class, a client, or a prospect.

But communication is also body language, the way we dress, the style we have, and the lifestyle we lead.

Art is a form of communication. Art is the inner vision of the artist, expressed. When we enjoy music, architecture, design, or visual art we are listening to the artist. Science is a form of communication. Science is listening to nature. When we say that there is an art and a science to healing, we mean that we study and we express. Both are forms of communication. Every book that you read is a dialogue between you and the author.

As Chogyam Trungpa Rinpoche taught in his book *Dharma Art*, the way we live our lives is an artistic expression. We are our most wonderful works of art.

Authenticity

One of my teachers, Paul Ortell, taught a class called "Presence: Voice and Sound." I learned about my authentic voice. Authentic voice is not always singing, though that is what I did in the class. Voice is how we express ourselves. It could be design, poetry, business, ideas or written word. I learned that our voice is most powerful when it's authentic.

I was performing for the class one day and getting a mediocre reaction. Paul helped me to see, by polling the class, that I was hiding. He did this in a skillful way so as not to awaken resistance or defensiveness. I learned to express more raw emotion in my songs. People responded to this because it was real. I took off the mask.

Our authentic voice is usually hidden to some extent; hidden out of fear, desire to fit in or simply out of habit. World changers like Oprah Winfrey and Steve jobs found ways to honor their authentic voice, risk making mistakes and express their ideas in innovative ways. The result is global impact.

Joy and Sorrow

It was not always comfortable, but the audience was moved. I learned to take an audience through an emotional experience. I did this by being sincere. I did this by getting past the facade I wore and by expressing emotional vastness. Over the years, I've powerfully moved people with my music and later with my speaking. So if you want to be powerful in your communication, whatever your business, be authentic.

An authentic voice means expressing the totality of human emotional vastness.

Communication and Effectiveness

If you are a leader, if you serve, or if you aspire to create meaningful work, communication is essential. You must develop this area of your life.

You need to develop your ability to communicate through:
1. Your interpersonal communication: Are you a listener?
2. Your public speaking ability and the way you express your message
3. The way you present yourself nonverbally: is it congruent with your message?
4. The way you speak to yourself
5. The way you write your message
6. How you handle conflict

Of all of these, the personal development with the largest impact on your effectiveness is the ability to speak and to listen.

Public Speaking

Take two people with the same services or products. Tom is dedicated to developing his communication by going out and speaking in front of groups, and Jerry is dedicated to developing confidence by reading books about personal growth.

After one year, Tom has actively learned from his experience of speaking. He spoke to groups ranging from one to fifty people. He has bombed and killed. He sought out mentors and learned about basic principles that enrich his experience.

Jerry has read almost fifty books about personal growth and development. He has learned a tremendous amount about confidence. He understands a great deal more about life, about himself, and about others.

After one year, who has actually gained in confidence the most?

The fact is, it is important to do both: educate yourself constantly while getting out there in front of people. But the final analysis would find Tom has developed more confidence. He went through the fire. And that always tempers the soul.

Joshua Rosenthal, master teacher and the founder of **The Institute for Integrative Nutrition**, drove this point home when he said, "The number one way for you to build confidence is through public speaking." He also stated, "The number one way for you to build your business is through public speaking."

When you get in front of people, you are forced to get clear on what you are about. It pushes you back into the inner work of discovering exactly what is your vision? What is important to you? What do you stand for?

When you are out in front of a group, you're quickly focused into the present moment. You have to be on your toes and you need to know your topic. It is exciting and you become excited about your work.

Toastmasters

I joined Toastmasters in the spring of 2009. I wished I had joined seven years ago. What an amazing organization.

I am fortunate to be a member of the number one club in the state of Iowa as well as an advanced Toastmasters club. And I am fortunate to serve as an officer in two clubs.

The opportunities for personal growth and development are constantly surprising. Of course, this depends on the people in the club and the person joining the club.

Toastmasters clubs are all volunteer run. There are officers who keep the meetings going, and all members play a role in the meetings. This includes people who observe grammar and filler words, and a timer to help everyone communicate with respect to time boundaries. There is the Toastmaster. She runs the meeting. Evaluators help each speaker and role player with appreciative and constructive feedback.

When you join Toastmasters, you work through a series of ten speech projects that develop the fundamental qualities of great presenters. This includes, but is not limited to, vocal variety, gestures, movement, eye contact, wordsmithing, organization, and more.

To find a Toastmasters club near you, check out:
http://reports.toastmasters.org/findaclub/

Seven Ways to Maximize Your Presentation

 Keep it super simple.

I've been the worst offender of the overstuffed talk. Thanks to my peers, I have learned to do better. Get clear about your point. State it. Tell a story to support it. Give some compelling reasons to listen. Hit your point again. Then wrap up with a recap of the stories and compelling reason, and hit the point one last time.

Make eye contact.

Do this with one person on each idea that you communicate. This works out to three to five seconds. Then move on to another point, and make eye contact with another person. Continue doing this with people throughout the room. Focus on the happy people with whom you connect.

Use the space.

Don't just stand behind the lectern. Get out and deliberately use the space to accentuate the points in your speech. If you want to share some cool inside information, get right up close to the audience. If you want to show fear, then move away from the audience. Move from the left to the right to engage your whole crew.

Keep it simple.

You know about your subject matter. Chances are that your audience does not. Follow this simple rule. First, tell them what you are going to tell them. Then, tell them. Finally, tell them what you told them. Create a clear beginning, middle and end. Repetition helps your audience.

Tell stories.

Introduce your topics and main points with a story. Make a point, tell a story. Make another point and tell another story. Maybe make another point and relate a story. Then, wrap up by telling a related story that ties your main points into a conclusion.

Get experience.

Nothing teaches you to be a better speaker than experience. Toastmasters is a great resource, but you can start with any group. Just do it.

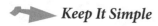 *Keep It Simple*

Why am I telling you this three times? I want you to hear it. Let it sink in. Your audience wants you to make a few salient points backed up with stories and examples. You may be an expert, but they are not. Chances are that you going to try and put too much into your presentation. Keep it simple. Got it? Good.

Practice these steps. Don't just read through and forget it. Run through your presentation and decide where you are going to make your main points in space. Set up some chairs and pretend there are people in them. Make eye contact on one point and move to another chair.

Most of all, get out there! And while you are at it, go see other people speak. Watch what they do, take notes, and choose one thing to incorporate.

And finally, if you can, join a Toastmasters club!

Just Do It

I can't emphasize enough the importance of public speaking on your career. If you are called to make an impact on a large scale, there is no better vehicle than public speaking. You will grow by leaps and bounds. Just by speaking, your confidence will grow. When your confidence grows, you inspire others to confidence. You really do well to take the leap.

The Other Side of Communication: Listening

Big egos have little ears.
Rev. Robert Schuller

Recall the social leaders you personally know in your life, the person you remember as being able to talk to anybody. What you will probably observe in your mind is that this person was not really "talking" to everyone, but rather *listening* to everyone.

The person who can listen without the need to respond is the person who can lead.

So simple, yet how often do you really, intently listen?

Your clients, patients, and colleagues speak to you every day. How often do you bite your lip to hold back your response? Or how often do you really register and consider the full effect of the speaker's words?

Most of what ails a person improves when they are simply listened to. Most people can solve their own problems when someone hears them out. Your employees and colleagues will find solutions when you ask questions and listen.

High Achievers Need to Listen

There is a myth of the entrepreneur conquering life's challenges on a solo mission. But the fact is that true leaders and change makers know their purpose is to listen to everyone around them.

I learned this most poignantly during a 72-day Wilderness Leadership Training Program.

I enrolled in the Hurricane Island Outward Bound Semester in 1997. I worked my butt off at three jobs to raise the money. I was twenty-one.

The course began on August 29, 1997. The course ended on November 11, 1997. Twelve college kids got on a boat at a dock in the town of Rockland, Maine. We headed out that night. An open ketch boat, we slept on the oars like sardines, afraid of bumping into each other. By the end of the course, we would be huddled together under tarps in the snow-covered White Mountains, practically groping each other to retain all the body heat we could.

I've never learned more in such a short period of time. I experienced a great deal of hardship and physical pain. And I learned how to listen.

Everybody had to take every role in the group of twelve, from latrine duty to leader. When my time came up for leader, I cherished the opportunity to practice. The trick was always staying in the middle.

If we were sailing, the trick was to stay in the center of the communication of the boat. The rudder team, the sails team, the navigator, the cooks, everyone needed to be updated and heard from constantly.

If we were hiking, the group stretched on a long way up and back. I had to stay in the center. When hiking with a group of twelve, all breaks need to be orchestrated. Otherwise, you would never get anywhere! That's why potty time, food time, map time, and rest time had to be considered with everyone's needs in mind.

After 72 days, I found my groove. It was like being invisible, yet the essential center of everything. It is an exhilarating thing. To be successful, I had to dissolve all ideas of what I thought needed to happen and respond entirely to what the appointed role suggested. The map team, the cooks, the tarp team, and the leave-no-trace crew all had their roles. The key to success was to do your role impeccably and trust that the other members did theirs.

The hard lessons came when a leader allowed the team to make mistakes, and the natural consequence forced the individual responsible to face eleven hungry, cold, and tired fellow teammates at the end of the day.

Because every day ended with an hour or two of dialogue, we spent a lot of time learning how to listen.

The bottom line is that we were able to overcome tremendous challenges as a team: sailing around the granite coast of Maine, canoeing in the snow, mountaineering in a blizzard. We did this because we built up the listening muscle, not the commanding muscle.

> *A leader is best*
> *When people barely know that he exists,*
> *Not so good when people obey and acclaim him.*
> *Worst when they despise him.*
> *'Fail to honor people, they fail to honor you;'*
> *But of a good leader, who talks little*
> *When his work is done, his aim fulfilled,*
> *They will say, 'We did this ourselves.'*
> Lao Tzu, *The Tao Te Ching* (**The Witter Bynner translation**)

The Right Mix

> *We have two ears and one mouth and should use them in that proportion.*
> **Epictetus**

Great coaches listen more, talk less. A great coach delivers penetrating and insightful lessons to clients. This comes only after years of consistent coaching. You can't deliver golden feedback to your clients, employees, managers, without listening.

If you are wondering, *how do I know how much to listen*, follow the advice of the ancient Greek philosopher Epictetus. Make sure that sixty-six percent of your time is spent in listening.

For the doctor with ten minutes for a patient, listen for six minutes, forty seconds.

Salespeople, take the time to understand what your prospect needs before you sell. If you have thirty minutes, listen for twenty.

If you are a coach, then ask questions. If your session is fifty minutes, then thirty-three and a third needs to be listening.

How Do You Listen?

Seek first to understand, then to be understood. Most people do not listen with the intent to understand; they listen with the intent to reply. They are either speaking or preparing to speak.

Stephen Covey

During long Outward Bound programs, they teach a simple yet powerful technique called *active listening*. We would form two circles and take turns going from one person to the next, taking two minutes to genuinely share what we appreciated about each team member. We would then repeat the process and give feedback on what we would like to see improved during the next expedition.

The person sitting there would simply listen. No comments, for the entire two minutes, and at the end, they'd say, "Thank you."

That is the most powerful exercise I have had in listening. Since our lives were literally on the line with each other, we *had* to step up and be as honest as possible. I did not like everyone on the course. I still had to find things I appreciated, which helped me immensely to create a bond of friendship. And the people I did like, I had to risk offending with feedback that I thought necessary for our betterment.

When you are with a client, employee, or staff member, turn off the talk dial and tune in to the ear dial. Make it meditation. When you notice yourself wanting to respond, simply come back to the sound coming in your ear.

Nonverbal Communication

Does your body tell the same message as your words? When you present your message, is your style of dress appropriate, i.e., is it congruent with your message?

I recently watched a History Channel DVD titled *Secrets of Body Language*. It summed up everything I've learned along the way. The words you speak can be twisted to make you look good. But the body won't lie. The quickest way to avoid this problem is to live in integrity!

When world leaders are on the spot, and they've lied, you can see it in the nonverbal cues. When Nixon showed up for a media blitz, he responded with powerful words, but he had his hands behind his back. That was not a clue per se, but the rubbing of his wrists betrayed his concern.

The body doesn't know how to tell a lie. The mouth does.

The moment you see a person, you make a split second choice about doing business with them, about spending time with them, and about whether you trust them. How you show up in your life is a powerful communication decision. Actions speak louder than words.

Dress for Success

I thought I'd been dressing right. I thought that a pressed button-down shirt and a sport coat worked well. I had three suits. I was pleased with how I presented myself in professional speaking engagements. Then a fellow Toastmaster lent me the book *Dress For Success*.

Although written in the late eighties, It was a real eye opener for me. I learned that my loud colors and pastels were not going to help me win over the trust of most audiences. I come off big, a little brash, and powerful. Therefore, I want my clothing to be understated. If I am dressing in a white suit with a flashy purple shirt underneath, it decreases my authority with the audience.

There is a time and place for loud clothes. It can be part of a message, a presentation theme, or a match for some audiences. In this phase of my career, I want to dress in a way that plays neutral to the powerful message I am delivering with my words, gestures, and body language. I am wearing navy blue and charcoal gray suits with blue or white fitted shirts.

The Right Costume

When I studied theatre with Lee Worley at Naropa University, she told me, "Every day, you wake up in the morning and you decide the role you want to play. You get up and you choose the costume that fits that role. You go out into the world and play the role, but it is not who you are. It is whom you are playing. You get to be anyone that you decide to be."

There are costumes for every profession. Some are for safety and are designed to be ninety-nine percent functional. But there is always style. There is always unique expression.

This brings us back to the idea of life as art. Our lives express an idea.

So dharma art is not about showmanship, or having some talent that nobody had before, having an idea that nobody's done before. Instead, the main point of dharma art is discovering elegance. And that is a question of state of mind, according to the Buddhist tradition.

Chogyam Trungpa Rinpoche

Trungpa Rinpoche is saying we have to live our message. We come back to walking our talk. We need to work the inner game. We need to work the outer game. We need to keep our house in order, our checkbook balanced, and our bodies fit and healthy.

When we live with a congruent set of values, our work and our message on the platform have a quality of solidity. That is the expression of greatness. That is when our dress, our gestures, our movements, and our message naturally come together.

Communicating With Yourself

We need to listen and speak to ourselves. This forms and transforms our beliefs, values, standards, and our overarching paradigm, or the way we see the world.

We listen to ourselves with meditation, journaling, reflection, contemplation, and creative expression.

We speak to ourselves with internal dialogue, with the media we ingest, and the people we choose to listen to (if we have that choice!).

The two practices that I would most recommend are *morning pages* and *meditation*.

In Chapter 6, I outlined a practice for *generating resourceful states*. I do not need to repeat that here.

I've referred to *morning pages*. It is essentially thirty minutes of stream of consciousness writing. It happens first thing in the morning when you wake up. You write about anything and everything. You do not stop.

This siphons up the creative flow. It clears the cobwebs and gets the intuition up in the morning. It is one way to get to the real you.

Dr. Win Wenger, in his audio program *Brain Booster*, recommends twenty minutes of nonstop writing to access deeper levels of intelligence. His assertion about the practice is right on track with Julia Cameron, author of *The Artist's Way* and the creator of the *morning pages* practice. When you write without stopping, you get past the censor. You can see what you really think, feel, and know. Get rid of self-deception and start where you are.

In terms of meditation, there are many forms, types, and styles. Look for trusted lineages from established disciplines.

Written Communication

Here are a few tips to help you get your ideas across.

For educational or informative writing and writing in general:
1. Generate a thesis or main idea. Get clear on the purpose of your communication.
2. Organize it into an Introduction, Body, and Conclusion.
3. Practically understand and apply grammatical rules like gerund agreement, singular-plural agreement, passive voice, etc.

For copywriting in your marketing:
1. Use more short sentences.
2. Get to the point.

3. Keep asking "so what?" and narrow down the benefits of your product and service for your client / customer.

When communicating ideas in any channel.:
1. Keep things concise.
2. Try not to make the message complicated if it can be simple.

The bottom line is that if you want to write, then write. And keep writing. You will find your authentic voice.

Effectively Handling Conflict

Remember that success comes when you seek first to understand, then to be understood. When it is your turn to speak, be skillful. Here is a great four-step approach that you can use to help navigate heated situations. You want to share your feelings, your observations and/or interpretations, what you want to have happen, and a specific request.

Here is an example:
1. I am feeling angry.
2. The story I am telling myself is that you are trying to steal my apples.
3. What I want here is for us to both have apples.
4. And my specific request is that you tell me whether you were taking my apples and, if so, if we can share them instead of you taking them.

Or
1. It seems to me that you are trying to take my apples.
2. And I feel angry.
3. Because I want to have apples.
4. And my specific request is that you let me know if you were trying to take them, and if so, lets share them instead.

It is really that simple. Fill in the blanks and use the four-step process to more effectively handle intense conversations.

RECAP OF CHAPTER 10:

- Communication Is the Expression of the Vision; it is always a bridge between your inner and outer world.
- To be effective in the world, you need to develop as a communicator.
- Public speaking is the most powerful way to build confidence and is often the best way to build your business.
- Listening is sixty-six percent of your communication. Leaders and high achievers listen.
- Your message is defined by what you say and by HOW you say it. Body language never lies, so live with integrity.
- Take the time to discover how you need to dress at this phase of your career. Dress for success based on what you discover.
- All of the communication principles apply to your relationship with you. Give yourself empowering messages and take time to listen to yourself.
- Practice the basics to get a solid written message out there.
- Use a simple four-part model when handling intense communication and remember to seek first to understand, then to be understood.

SELF-STUDY EXERCISES:

- To develop your speaking ability, visit a Toastmasters club near you. http://reports.toastmasters.org/findaclub/
- One of the best ways to improve your listening is to visit a Toastmasters club near you, http://reports.toastmasters.org/findaclub/
- Even if you want to develop your written communication skills, check out a Toastmasters club, http://reports.toastmasters.org/findaclub/
- I think I made my point, but just in case –you can attend a Toastmasters club for less than $2 a meeting and if you apply yourself in a strong club, it is the best dollar for dollar personal growth investment you will make.

CHAPTER 11

COLLABORATION POWER: ALL-SYSTEMS WIN

THE PURPOSE OF CHAPTER 11:

This chapter not only highlights the rapid change in business organization but also celebrates and highlights the ways and means for effective collaboration in your work.

The Game Changer

In the 1980's, The Encyclopedia Britannica had a well-paid staff of experts in their fields writing content for hard copy books. By 1990, Britannica revenue hit $650 million. Then it almost died. Why? Wikipedia. Instead of a well-paid staff of PhD's, 300,000 volunteers from around the world built Wikipedia.

The world economy is entering into a period of increased productivity the likes of which we haven't seen since the Industrial Revolution. We will again see a fifty fold increase in human productivity. Collaboration is at the heart of this evolution.

Driven by social media, open source software, cloud computing, global outsourcing, and drastic lowering of overhead, many companies are innovating new organizational structures. Gen Now (Generation X &Y) wants to work in the experience of freedom of place. They want to travel. They want to work in teams of 6-10 people. These teams are agile and effective, even in a company with thousands.

The workforce in the west is increasingly geared towards egalitarian corporate structures. No more are Gen Now knowledge workers willing to hear, "because I said so," as the compelling motivation for high-level performance. Social media fueled social change is outpacing the evolution of the corporation. In corporate culture 2.0, leaders will need to demonstrate authentic, fair, transparent, and honest engagement with the company, the teams, and the world.

In This Together

Ricardo Semlar made waves by completely dropping convention at Semco, a billion dollar business in Brazil. Semco has been profitable, agile, and adaptable in up and down markets. There are no titles; all employees are associates. Employees set their own salaries based on what the company makes, and have taken cuts at times to weather a financial crisis. They also set their own hours. People choose their managers, and then publicly share their evaluation of the management.

There Is No Right Way

Derek Sivers founded CD Baby as a way to sell his CD online. People asked him to sell their CD's. He never tried to build a business. He focused on serving people and people kept coming to him. Eventually, his website morphed into an online store. Why? Because someone asked for it. He shunned the MBAs and lawyers when it wasn't necessary to make his business complicated. And, Sivers sold CD Baby for twenty-two million dollars.

Sivers suggests that your business is something you can create as an ideal place to be. Business is a place to make yours and others' dreams come true. Your primary reason for being in business is to enjoy life and serve a client.

Paradigm Change

Ultimately, we are embracing another revolution. The industrial revolution began in the 18th century and increased human productivity by fifty times. The energy-information revolution will again substantially change the capacity for human productivity. Even though Peter Drucker coined the term "knowledge worker" in 1959, we are just beginning to fully grasp the management of the knowledge worker economy.

We used to manage things, but now we manage creativity. And this is an intangible part of human capacity. So we are now learning how to maximize the capacity of human innovation and generative productivity. Interpersonal competence becomes even more important. Intrapersonal aptitude is more central than ever. But we are still trailblazing.

So how can you work with others more effectively?

Example: Strengthen Localized Economies

It seems as though collaborative models are about to flood the marketplace. A great example of building collaborative models into a new business is *my*Local Cooperative, a startup from Fairfield, Iowa. *my*Local got started with a working group around the idea of complementary currencies. The group wanted to do something to help the community thrive despite the large economic shifts. They wanted the community to thrive. Could they apply many of the key lessons from the sustainability ethic? Could they create a collaborative model in a capital system? They called their project *Hero Rewards*.

Without charging anyone a dime, they ran a 14-week pilot. Volunteers worked alongside social organizations; Rotary International, Sierra Club, Downtown Artwalk, the Maharishi University of Management, among others. Volunteers earned themselves units of reward called the "Merit", which they exchanged for deals at local businesses. The local pizzeria offered a large pizza for the price of a small, cafes honored Merits with buy-one-get-one-free coffee, and the local theater group offered a similar deal on tickets.

The *Hero Rewards Program* kept over $2850 in the local economy and contributed to an estimated $8500 of additional local economic exchange and generated around $1700 of unique purchasing power while adding value to the community.

After the pilot, *my*Local created a model for more stakeholders in a community to collaborate on shared values and goals. It includes mobile devices and an innovative community financial transaction service called *Dwolla*. This has the potential to reduce fees, keep money circulating locally and build layers of community engagement. They want to take this to communities around the country and world, so check out their contact in **Appendix B: Money Resources**

Essentials of Collaboration

Everyone has strengths to which they play. When you play to your strengths and collaborate with people who compliment your weaknesses with their strengths, then you succeed as a team.

You might call these people boss, employee, partner, contractor, collaborator, pupil, teacher, or team. No matter what you name it, it is collaboration. You are moving into a new paradigm of power sharing. I call this "All Systems Win." When your team or organization operates from this platform, each individual is invested in the success of the whole and you can implement constant and never ending-improvement, or kai-zen, the philosophy of continuous small adjustments.

To quote Ricardo Semlar of Semco, "To survive in modern times, a company must have an organizational structure that accepts change as its basic premise, lets tribal customs thrive, and fosters a power that is derived from respect, not rules."

Practical Model for Collaboration

It is helpful to know your general strengths, to be working with those strengths, and then to know the other people you are working with. The Adizes Method, or PAEI Model, created by Ichak Adizes, features an elegant four-quadrant model for organizational development that can facilitate successful collaboration. From Chapter 10, you can see I love a good four-quadrant model!

The model is based on two continuums, effectiveness to efficiency and short term to long term. It stands for Producer, Administrator, Entrepreneur and Integrator, each standing in a primary quadrant along the continuum. Here is a diagram, which includes an overlay as to how I use this within the context of 4 Gateways Coaching.

4 Gateways Coaching and the PAEI Adizes Management Model

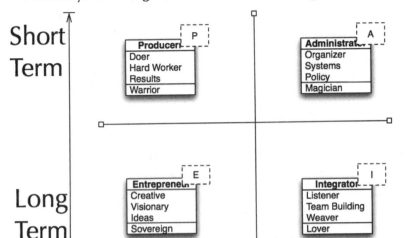

Producer: These people make things happen. They are the sales staff, the machinist, and the contractor. They are workhorses. They are prone to sacrifice relationships and therefore long-term results with their "shoot, ready, aim," style of working. They don't burn out easily, but they can hit a wall eventually, and when they do, it is messy.

Administrators: These people are focused on the "how" not the what. They want to know what the steps are going to be, what to do if something goes wrong and what the routines will be. They act more slowly than most of the others as they like to think things through to make sure it is the best course of action.

Entrepreneur: These folks can mentally download an entire business plan in a 45-minute brainstorming session. They can also easily miss deadlines on project reports because they have too many plates in the air.

Integrator: These folks make sure the whole system is working. They are people oriented and help the producer, administrator and the entrepreneur to relate to one another, or at least to tolerate each other for the sake of the larger organization.

It is believed that:
- You have primary, almost constitutional capacity in one of these areas.
- You will have learned to operate in a second area by necessity or choice.
- You can learn to function fairly well in a third quadrant.
- You can even learn to function from your weak quadrant with support.

Anytime you collaborate with a team, organization, or business, it is helpful to have references for the differences that are required in every successful collective outcome. Are you one of these? Does your business or team have each role filled? If not, you could have problems.

The Obstacles to Collaboration

1. I know everything.
2. I will lose my idea.
3. I will end up working harder than my team and not get credit.

These are all forms of fear. It is hard to collaborate when fear is present. To get past the fear, go through it. Speak your fears to the group. It can be uncomfortable. You are not sharing your fears to indulge them; you are sharing the thoughts that are getting in the way of your inspired vision.

Get Your Fear Out of Your Head

Here is an example:

I have the thought that we are going to repeat the same mistakes we made last year in our sales implementation. I want to know that we are being efficient, and I am concerned the sales team isn't listening to the feedback they got. What I would like to see is the sales team attacking these emerging markets that appear to be more apt to buy in quantity. I want us all to benefit from the research that we have.

You want to be able to share the default vision (your fear) so you can exorcise that ghost and then make psychic space for the vision of what you really want to happen.

It can be hard to do, because it often upsets someone else. In this example, the sales team may be offended. It gives the sales team the opportunity to share any fears, resentment, or concerns they may have. They can share their default future too, and thus make even more space for a new vision.

For this to work, each party has to practice listening without defending their position.

This simple technique, if implemented will transform the quality of the performance in your team.

Why Collaborate? The Deepest Level

I went to visit the Findhorn Foundation community a couple of times. Findhorn is a cutting-edge experimental community in Northern Scotland that pioneers innovation in human living. They have just as many problems as the rest of the world, but they are willing to try out new ways to handle them. In the process, the community has discovered a lot to teach.

My big take-away from my time there was this: *work can be the vehicle for human unity.* That means that the theory of unity can be experienced in human form most effectively when we share work together. It can be lowly and humble work like cleaning the bathroom, doing laundry, or other chores. This makes me remember to appreciate the chores with my family. Or, this can mean the most rarified co-creative work. When you build a skyscraper, produce a film, or run a hospital, you endeavor to cooperate with others at the highest level. Any time you team up, you have the opportunity to create a felt experience of unity. This is the soul of collaboration.

Collaboration In The Broadest Sense

Practically speaking, the Findhorn EcoVillage program as well as their overall ecological awareness extends the idea of collaboration to include the entire biosphere and all natural systems.

As the sustainability ethic increases and expands, we will see it fueled less by angry environmentalists and more by individuals and organizations that recognize the beauty, simplicity and power of nature. Through biomimicry, permaculture and living machines, we are learning to celebrate ecological balance because it is a better way.

The "living machine," at Findhorn is a great example. They treat raw sewage and wastewater with a series of living organisms from bacteria to plants. The water is then used for irrigation in the community.

Inevitably, we are heading in this direction. How can you apply the principles of Indestructible Success to innovate and implement higher order natural systems efficiencies that meet the needs of the planet?

Collaboration in Service

Naturally, you double the soul's goodness when you collaborate in service. Service to an idea, a principle, a person, or a mission allows you to realize more of yourself. Not only do you have the opportunity to realize more of your humanity, but you also have the opportunity to make things happen.

My friend Luke did this.

Being the Cause for No More Electrocution

Luke and I have been going to the Nicoya Peninsula in the province of Guanacaste in Costa Rica since 2006. But Luke goes more often than I... lucky guy!

On a recent trip, he walked back to the bungalow with his surfboard and saw a monkey jump on to a power line. Half of the power lines are insulated and half aren't. The confused monkey jumped on a bare wire and was shocked.

Luke watched as the howler shook with electric current, unable to let go because the shock contracted the muscles in his hands around the wire.

Finally, the monkey passed out and fell on his back. Luke walked over and sat with the monkey. He felt anguish, anger, and dizziness witnessing the meaningless electrocution.

Surprisingly, the monkey opened his eyes. Luke said, "He looked at me and asked, '*Why? Why did this happen?*'"

Luke found someone to get a local monkey expert and stayed with the monkey for forty-five minutes. Slowly, the monkey began to move his fingers and then his arms and legs. The question remained, *"Why?"*

It's unlikely that the monkey survived. The experience thrust Luke into a powerful commitment to be the cause of no more human-caused electrocutions in this region of Costa Rica. He decided that there were enough health coaches, yogis/yoginis, developers, surfers, health nuts, and beach-o-files coming to this area with enough money to simply and efficiently insulate all of the power lines in the region.

That commitment was huge.

As a result, Luke used his wisdom to collaborate with health counselors to create a retreat, run by health counselors, for health counselors. The retreat gives health counselors the opportunity to learn to lead a retreat. It gives health counselors the opportunity to have a retreat for R&R. It gives health counselors the opportunity to learn business and coaching skills in paradise.

All of this is in service of the contribution. Collaboration benefits the ecology and the economy. Howler monkeys are a significant part of the Costa Rica experience. And, it benefits Luke on the soul level as he realizes unity, develops character, and feels accomplished in service.

Who benefits from this collaboration?
1. Luke gets the experience of contributing, so he benefits.
2. Other health coaches learn how to run a retreat.
3. Other health coaches attend the retreats.
4. More people benefit from health coaches running their own retreats.
5. The non-profit animal rescue of Nosara benefits from money raised.
6. The wildlife refuge for rehabilitating monkeys benefits.
7. Tourists benefit by having monkeys in the jungle to enjoy.
8. The local economy benefits from tourist dollars from people who love nature.

By the way, if you want to support this amazing program and get an opportunity to hang out in paradise while learning and growing, then check out:
MonkeyBusinessRetreats.com

The Success of Web-Based and E-mail Marketing

A whole new wave of businesses are being built on collaboration. By sharing platforms, individuals with information products (teleclasses, books, online programs, video downloads, etc.) have been able to build and share e-mail lists that they then market to in a very organized and deliberate manner. Their marketing plans fit together with collaborating partners so as not to compete for the attention of their lists at the same time or with similar products.

Entire web-based businesses are built quickly and efficiently on very simple principles of collaboration. Find a complimentary service or product and find ways to promote each other's goods and services to existing customer base.

How can you collaborate and build your business at the same time?

To Succeed, Help Someone Else

The old adage remains true in a new era. The fastest way to succeed is to help someone meet his or her goals.

Did you think of a way that you can help someone else achieve success? Can you think of someone right now that can help your business or creative pursuit get traction?

RECAP OF CHAPTER 11:

- There is a significant paradigm shift going from industrial age to energy-information age.
- We are now managing individual creativity and group communication as much as or more than we manage things and systems.
- Collaboration is an opportunity to have fun and enjoy life.
- Working together is an opportunity to experience human unity.
- You can create powerful service and contribution through collaborating on a mission or an ideal.
- Collaboration is practical, leading to better results.
- To succeed, find ways to help someone else.

SELF-STUDY EXERCISES:

- Ask yourself how you can collaborate on your current projects.
- Ask other people in your life what they think about collaboration.
- Identify an area of strength and see how you can use that to help someone else or some other project.
- Identify an area of weakness and ask someone for their help with your project.
- When collaborating, be willing to share your fears and then replace them with the vision of what you want to create.

WALK THE TALK PART ONE, WORK THE INNER GAME

THE PURPOSE OF CHAPTER 12 PART ONE:

In this chapter, you are going to see how you can apply some of the tools and principles in your own life so you can experience greater freedom and effectiveness.

Teach To Learn

You must begin to teach the processes that you want to master. Yeah, you have to practice these things regularly to be effective. Coaching, communicating, and collaboration depend on you integrating your wisdom and embodying your knowledge. Remember to "act by the good that you know."

If you are waiting for the day that you stop falling to start teaching, it will never happen. If that was the criteria, there wouldn't be anyone teaching anything!

All you need to do is practice, practice, practice and then you can teach other people how to practice as well. Let's take a look at what you can practice.

9 Steps To Turn Fear Into Fuel & Upsets Into Opportunities

I want you to be able to welcome upsetting situations. When you stop resisting life, your life experience flows much more beautifully. You can say YES to life. And in Chapter 5, you learned about a 9-step process to handle fear or other emotional upsets that you can use to live with more flow. Remember that courageous living isn't a matter of not feeling afraid, it is a matter of feeling fear and doing something with that energy.

The most significant obstacle to developing courage is the automatic, unconscious avoidance of hurt and pain. It's also the single biggest obstacle to using the tool. But it is not enough just to read about this, you need to practice. And even though it may seem difficult or even weird, mastering your emotions, and especially fear, will open up a whole new world of possibility to you.

Here is an example to help you grasp this.

How Emotional Skillfulness Leads to Achievement

I was working with a young, twenty-something professional. He was dealing with constant, aggravating tension at work. Fast paced and hyper-cognitive, the corporate culture was weighing on him physically and mentally and affecting his performance.

What follows is a coaching process incorporating the 9 Steps.

First we identified the issue, the outcome and the intention:
Issue: dissatisfied with job/not performing at capacity.
Outcome: unlock creative potential and have more creative fulfillment.
Intention: I want to be comfortable laying it all on the line on a daily basis.

Seth in Bold / Client in regular font

What is going on?

Something internal is preventing me from being who I am in creative expression.

Fear of expressing full potential.

What do you think is happening?

Self-confidence is lacking, fear of what other people will think. The amount of effort that I as a human put into work is out of balance with the expectations. I am trying to prove something.

Are you really ready to have a breakthrough with this?

YES!

Are you ready to unlock your creative potential?

Yes.

Are you ready to lay it on the line on a daily basis?

Yes.

What are you feeling now?

Tightness.

When did you feel this most at work?

During feedback on a project, when I hold back on my ideas. This is amplified when I am with people in power or large groups. I was at a meeting and so wanted to share what was on my mind, I felt sick to my stomach from holding it in.

What is the judgment or criticism that you may be avoiding?

I am not sure. *(Some struggle here to connect to what is under the frustration.)*

What does it mean about you that you hold back?

I am not confident in myself. *(Difficult to connect, beginning to make the correlation.)*

What would your judgment be about someone who was afraid to speak his or her ideas?

They don't love themselves.

And if that were true about them, what would it mean?

There is no way that they will be successful.

And if it were true about you?

I would be a failure and not loveable.

And if that were true, what would it mean about you in this work situation?

Not confident. I am a fraud.

Are you *willing* to feel the feeling under this issue?

Yes.

What are you feeling right now?

(Long pause) A lot of tension. Super relaxed at the same time, like this is the right thing to be doing.

Can you describe the sensations you are feeling?

(Long pause, a lot of time is elapsing in silence, just holding the space.) Tightness. Feel a little anxious. I'm fearful. There are risks. Feel a lot of uncomfortable things in my stomach and chest right now. Feel like I would in that situation that I am describing.

Does that feeling want to have expression in any way? Are you willing to feel that like a child, let it come fully?

(Long, LONG, pause; I felt the energy shift away from the process.)

What is happening for you now?

My mind locked up. It could not think anything at all. I didn't even know what we were talking about.

Notice how Automatic Unconscious Avoidance kicks In?

No. I am not sure.

Can you see that we were moving pretty quickly?

Yes.

And then, all of a sudden your mind went blank?

Yes. That is a trip. It was like a cloud came over me. I literally forgot what we were talking about. Oh my God! I totally spaced it.

So, this is a great opportunity to demonstrate how the automatic unconscious avoidance works. *(I was facilitating a conference call. This was a process piece in the middle. I used the teaching opportunity.)*

Feeling this, according to the ego, would mean that you are: Weak. Really a fraud and a failure, which is unacceptable. Going to drop into a black hole of despair. So the mind does everything it can to keep you safe, including a hard "power-down" of the frontal lobes and rational thought.

Yeah, I can see that! The whole fraud piece is big. So much of my life is fraudulent. I am not really in touch with what I really want and what I really care about. I have this preoccupation with how people see me going way back. So I am hyper-concerned about how I seem to people and I get disconnected from what my core values are.

OK, has resisting this experience of "fraud" or "failure" ever worked for you?

Has resisting this worked for me? From a survival standpoint, has this worked, yes, but it has not allowed me to love myself and it hasn't resolved anything. I still carry the tension around. So it is now a hindrance to peak performance.

Let's be clear. In the mind, if you are a success, you are a failure. If you are authentic, you have fraud. They are on a spectrum. But it is really the feeling underneath that is being resisted. Does that make sense?

I am starting to get what you mean.

Well, this is enough for our process this evening. Let's shift into integration.

At this point, we did integration questions. We had spent a LOT of time and pretty intense focus together and I sensed that we had reached the threshold for integration. Here are some interesting comments from a few participants on the call

Participant D:

For me, applying it to myself, I scribble when I listen; I drew a robot, hands up, and whoa, hold back…I can totally relate to the blockage thing, I shut down when I am creative and I don't know why. I go through the exact same thing.

Client:

Feels so direct to me. But not in an unhealthy way. I think that you ask the right questions. You put the right questions out there to get me moving in the right direction. That is what I really like about the process.

I like how you regularly had me going back to my feelings. It is always happening a million times a day and I am not paying attention to it. Slowly getting more in touch with that. Really appreciate going back to the feelings. Being more mindful in my life.

Participant B:

I am excited that we get to learn about this whole process and that we get to learn about what's going on inside when we are freaking out.

Client:

I am really excited for this process and all the really great skills that we are learning and how it is grounded in good theory. Two strong components in what you are teaching us. I wake up as a human when I can identify what I am feeling, and then have an outlet, so it isn't just twisting on itself.

The Real World Results

This client experienced several promotions at work since working through this issue in layers. Clearing this freed him up to be more of himself, which helped him to step into his power. By facing his fear of failure, accepting it as a possibility, and removing the resistance to that fear, he was able to devote more attention and energy to what he did want to create, and then he could take more intelligent steps toward the achievement of those goals.

The Automatic Unconscious Avoidance of Hurt and Pain

You can see how this *automatic unconscious avoidance* literally made his mind go blank. This happens to you too when you dive into fear. It is so easy to turn to compulsive behavior to distract the mind.

How do you stay with the process? In this instance, anger can be quite useful. It can provide the fuel to stay in it. Journaling is exceptional. Keep working the material in writing.

Your journal may look like this:

The idiot. Who does he think he is? Telling me what to do.

Hmmm…I must be triggered. Yep. Definitely.

Arrrgghh. That fucker.

(The more you can uncensor your mind, the quicker you can work with this, and though I do not recommend crude language in a professional setting, in some coaching situations, it is necessary to use accurate and powerful language to evoke what is really going on.)

I should not be angry. I am a leader. I should be over this.

That asshole made me angry!

Wow. I am angry. I want to be at peace. How can I handle this?

What does it mean about me?

It means that I am pissed at that asshole.

Who does he think he is?

Yep. I am really triggered. How can I stay with this?

What does this mean about me?

I know that I am afraid of being taken advantage of.

I know that I am being impatient, not accepting his behavior. Heck, it doesn't have anything to do with me. Why am I so upset?

OK, what does it mean about someone who gets angry when bossed around?

They are insecure. A confident person would shake it off.

What would it mean about me if I were insecure?

I am weak.

Ouch, that doesn't feel good.

Oh yeah, I see that big well of hurt and pain.

Let the tears come and go.

Am I willing to have the thing I fear most happen?

No way! That would mean that I would be taken advantage of. I have to stick up for myself!

But why? What am I trying to protect? Yes, sometimes I am weak. Sometimes I am strong too. I can accept that.

But if I were taken advantage of, that would mean that I was REALLY weak.

Ouch. IF that were REALLY true, not just in a process, I would be worthless. I hate that. That feels really bad. There is a ton of hurt there.

OK, I am going to go for it.

Got to feel it to heal it. Hurt and pain resisted is suffering; hurt and pain embraced is healing.

No way. This is a bunch of bull. Your problem is that you don't work hard enough. What are you doing here "processing" this? Don't be a crybaby. It is HIS fault. The jerk. Don't be weak. Fight for your pride.

Hmmm…I almost bought that. The automatic unconscious avoidance of hurt and pain again.

You Have to Practice Using the Tools That You Have

These tools have to be used. It is essential that you are using the Generating Resourceful States tool regularly.

Do you know anyone who has gone to a Tony Robbins seminar?

Millions of people have studied Tony Robbins' books and audio recordings and attended his seminars. But how many people come home and use all the techniques that Tony presents? I mean really…I know a LOT of people who have been to **Unleash the Power Within**, which is awesome, and these folks get home PSYCHED. They are writing goals and have plans and are giving advice to all their friends.

Then, six months later, the bottom falls out.

Now, of course, that is why you go to another seminar. You need to get those "power-ups." That is why I offer seminars. Nothing beats a weekend intensive and a follow-up integration program. The group energy is amazing, for sure.

But that momentum sticks when you practice what you learn.

IF YOU WANT TO TAKE YOUR LIFE TO THE NEXT LEVEL YOU HAVE TO PRACTICE THE TOOLS.

In the UNITY Church of Practical Christianity, they say, "Practice the Good That You Know."

How are you practicing *Generating Resourceful States?*

If you haven't yet tried the practice in Chapter 6, now is the time.

Music + Movement + Voice + Affirmative Statement = A Powerful State Change

Affirmative Invocation produces the physical, emotional, mental, and vibratory energy necessary to step up, take action, and produce results.

What is the biggest obstacle to practicing?

The biggest obstacle to doing this daily is…

Looking like a fool!

Which is part of the broader category of THE COMFORT ZONE.

The Comfort Zone

The comfort zone is not a place on your thermostat. It is a set point in your body-mind matrix.

Any major accomplishment requires that you expand your comfort zone. And these practices will take you to your edge. Embarrassment is good news: it means your ego is losing ground. The ego loves the comfort zone. If you fail, you will have to grow. If you are really inspired, you will have to grow. The ego dislikes both pain and inspiration, because it requires a kind of death and rebirth (remember the Hero's Journey). That is why both of these core inner practices can be challenging.

Make Sabotage or Distraction Hard and Success Easy

Both of these practices are destroyed by compulsive behavior. Distraction and overwhelm are the garden for growing self-sabotage.

So how do you manage distraction and overwhelm?

Well, Chapter 13 is dedicated to this dilemma, but here is an interesting observation.

All of the great wisdom traditions suggest a life of simplicity. And we can see that this advice from the sages though the ages is supremely helpful for minimizing distraction.

Make it hard to engage in your favorite distractions and compulsions. I do not own a TV. Why? Because I can't turn the damn thing off! I just stare at it for hours. Hotel rooms are torture for me.

Sugar. Alcohol. Pfuh. Easy.

I went through a phase where I did not have Internet access at my home. Same dealio. I had to make success easy and failure hard. YouTube. E-mail. Google. Wiki. Blogs. Facebook. Hours in my day were gone. That nagging feeling that I had a lot to do turned into a nagging feeling that I had wasted my day.

Eliminate Sabotage: *Handle Danger Zones*

How do you eliminate sabotage?

Well, there are facets to that gem of a question.
1. Make the behavior hard. If you are a carbohydrate addict, don't keep cookies in the house. During a training phase, I had to hook up my Internet access to use it, each and every time. While it took a minute or two and seemed like a hassle, it was just the right pause for me to ask, "*Do I want to waste my time or am I getting online with a clear intent?*"
2. Address and heal the underlying hurt that fuels the compulsion (outlined in detail in Chapter 5).
3. Learn to accept the best version of your life by consciously choosing to see yourself as a success, in the way that your ideal life looks.
   (Our behavior is consistent with our identity; if we believe that we don't deserve a good life, then our actions will always follow that.) You can use the Affirmative Invocation Process to shift the way that you see yourself.
4. Use the crowding out theory. Keep putting good things in. Good food. Good exercise. Good people. Good places.
5. Make small choices. Life is built on small choices, one day at a time. All you need to do is make the choice right now.
6. Forgive yourself quickly. Everybody, I mean, EVERYBODY makes mistakes sometimes. The faster you forgive yourself, the faster you move up the ladder of your personal energy.
7. Make the behavior hard to do. I know, I said this twice. It is so simple, but so often overlooked.

I'm not saying you need to go to the extreme of getting rid of your TV and Internet in your home like I did. But a life of simplicity is the classic path for self-development, not from moral or spiritual purity, but from practicality. It is not the possessions, the substances, or the experiences that are the problem, but the attachment to the possessions, substances, and experiences that can bring you down.

If you have a sweet tooth, make your home a temple of health. Get rid of your *danger zones*: cereal, crackers, ice cream, cookies, candy, and rolls. Make it easy to stay on target and hard to fail.

If you are tempted to spend more money than you have, get rid of your *danger zones*: credit cards. Don't go to outlets, malls, warehouses, or big box stores without a clear intent, and stick to it.

If you tend toward gossip, don't spend time with gossiping people in that *danger zone*.

Momentum Moves You

Practicing resourceful states is just like exercise. Once you get going, it is easy to maintain. But if you drop the ball for a few days, an innocent distraction on Facebook makes you miss your weightlifting session. Then suddenly, inertia, ugh.

When you eliminate these *danger zones*, the momentum that you built with the inner and outer game stays strong.

> *You've got to pay the dues if you want to play the blues and you know it don't come easy.*
>
> **Ringo Starr**

By Teaching, You Accelerate Growth and Integration

Are you a leader? A coach? A teacher? Can you teach this practice to someone else and help him or her achieve his or her goals in life? That will help you learn at an even deeper level. In fact, everyone reading this could benefit from this mentoring process by deciding on one person to whom they can teach these principles.

But you can't teach this unless you practice. Thank God! You have the added leverage to practice because you want to teach these things! Everything that you can stack as leverage will help you out.

The best way to teach these tools is through a series of classes. One-on-one session time is where you can use the tools. You can give them pointers, suggestions, and guidance on the tools. But you need space and time dedicated exclusively to teaching the tools. You can set up live classes or you can use teleclasses. Teleclasses are especially useful since you can get people from around the globe who are interested in the specific niche material you want to teach.

The Teleclass

I've had a tremendous amount of success with teleclasses. Here is what you do:

1. Get a free conference call number online.
2. Google "free audio conferencing."
3. Look for the service that offers the technology that you need.
4. Get a dial-in code and passcode.
5. Schedule out six calls, three on the Healing Upsets Process, three on Generating Resourceful States.
6. Give yourself two months or more to promote.
7. Tell your clients, customers, employees, or team members about the call series.
8. Make the first one irresistible.
9. Make the price and topic enticing.
10. Make registration easy.
11. Once they register, send the dial-in # and passcode.
12. Prepare like heck for the calls.
13. Knock their socks off!

You can do the same thing with in-person classes. The added challenge is that you have the overhead for space rental. Lots of folks have a contact that offers space when they are starting out.

If you already have a massive patient base, like a chiropractor with hundreds and hundreds of clients, then you will want to use your space (of course) and create a little more developed marketing plan.

The Significance of the Inner Game

Practicing the inner game is the foundation for teaching and serving your clients.

Dr. Daly, founder of 4 Gateways Coaching, would often say to me, "If you want to be a great coach, clean up and handle all of your issues with your parents. Then all of a sudden, you will discover that you are pretty clear to help others!"

Whatever the area of your life, take the time to get alignment within yourself. Get a coach. Trade if you need to. Do the inner work necessary for outer success and fulfillment.

Before you move on to walking the talk in the outer realms of achievement, I want to share a thrilling story of courage. Olga Aura, friend and colleague, shares this excerpt with me from her book, *12 Secrets of Highly Successful Women,* where you can read it in full.

How to Write and Live Your Own Fairytale Even if All the Odds are Against You

My team won an Olympic Gold Medal in the 1996 Olympics in Atlanta for rhythmic gymnastics. I came from Ukraine where I had been training since age 5. Arriving in America at the age of 14, I chose to not get back on the bus and return to my country.
Note: This was an incredibly brave and risky decision on my part. If I'd been caught, the consequences would have been dire.

Instead, I accepted an invitation from a family in North Carolina to stay in the United States to go to school, learn English and start a new life.

After finishing high school, I went to college and had the sort of crisis most of us reserve for midlife. After retiring from competitive gymnastics, I gained weight and began to question who I was if I wasn't on the mat. I struggled silently with depression for years and eventually attempted suicide.

While I was recovering in the hospital, I felt a weight lift off my shoulders and heard a voice say, "no matter what mistakes you think you have made, the truth about who you are is unchanged."

If I truly am unchanged and my slate is always clean, I may as well dream big and write a brand new story for my life. **And that's exactly what I did.**

I moved to Boulder, Colorado and attended a university founded by a renowned Tibetan monk. I began to establish a new self-image and an empowering belief system. As an Olympic-class gymnast, I worked extremely hard to wipe out the strict Olympic indoctrination so that I could learn to love myself as a woman and heal my soul.

Instead of spending hours sitting and meditating, I had been trained to work hard. It was such a flip-flop! The experience stretched my mind and my heart immeasurably - I moved from go, go, go to allowing, receiving and asking for help. Learning these skills was a tremendous challenge.

After graduating from this amazing university, I went to see an immigration attorney. **He told me that I could get a green card if I secured a job at a corporation or if I got married.**

I looked at my options: corporations were not hiring spiritual mentors at that time. The second road was equally scary, because I had never been in love. I had three months until my student visa expired.

There was a lot at stake. **I needed to crack my heart open and allow my beloved to enter my life and love me just as I am - or face being deported.**

And so began "the Summer of Love" in which I had five marriage proposals.

Eventually, I dreamed that I should go to California where I would find my beloved.

I traveled up and down the West Coast, meeting people, "kissing many frogs." My three months soon ran out and I hadn't met 'the one'. I headed south to San Francisco; I didn't have a job or know anyone there, but I'd been cast in a theatre production. I was terrified by the constant thought of being deported.

On my very first night arriving in San Francisco, I was walking through Union Square under a full moon at midnight. I stopped to admire a window display and noticed a tall handsome man in the reflection. When I turned around, he greeted me in Russian and my jaw dropped. We grabbed each other's hands and started spinning around like children, right there on Union Square, looking up at the stars and the full moon, overwhelmed with joy.

We haven't let go of our hands since. And I feel blessed with more fun, deep intimacy and creative passion than I ever thought was possible.

These days, I harness that same magic and joy to help other women create the life of their dreams. If you are ready to go for it, let's work on bringing your own fairytale to life. www.OlgaAura.com

Olga has many more equally unbelievable stories.

RECAP OF CHAPTER 12, PART ONE:

- Teaching helps you learn faster.
- Walking the talk is the basis for good teaching.
- Automatic unconscious avoidance of hurt and pain is a hidden block to achieving your goals.
- Practice the tools that you know.
- Generating resourceful states is like exercise: sometimes you need a kick-start to get going.
- Distraction can become a form of compulsion that keeps us from practicing.
- Be willing to look foolish and step out of your comfort zone.
- Anger is the energy to make change.
- Find a compelling reason why you want to practice these tools.
- When you practice developing courage, unbelievable events occur.

CHAPTER 12: PART 2

WALK THE TALK PART TWO, WORK THE OUTER GAME

THE PURPOSE OF CHAPTER 12 PART TWO:

Now you are going to learn what I believe to be the underlying qualities most essential to enacting the Dreams>Vision>Goals>Plans>Action sequence. Focus, Believe and Persist. You will get inspired to define success for yourself.

Work The Outer Game

We've covered the sequence of:
1. Vision/Dream
2. Plan
3. Action
4. Keep the tools sharp

Working the outer game boils down to two simple principles. Make it easy on yourself to remember, because making your dreams come true, well hell, it can be hard!

Here are the two rules to always come back to:
1. Know what YOUR definition of success is.
2. Focus, Believe, Persist.

Practically speaking, there are only a few human stories and they have all been enacted previously. This is a fact that you must never forget—there are people who have overcome every conceivable difficult situation, even the one in which you find yourself and which to you seems utterly hopeless.

Norman Vincent Peale, *The Power of Positive Thinking*

Rev. Peale is referring to the archetypal "Hero's Journey" that you experience when you commit with Focus, Faith and Follow Through.

What Does It Mean To Persist?

Persist: 1. To continue steadily or firmly in some state, purpose, course of action or the like, esp. in spite of opposition, remonstrance, etc.
(The Random House Dictionary of The English Language, College Edition)

Closely related to 'persevere'.

1. To persist in anything undertaken; maintain a purpose in spite of difficulty or obstacles; continue steadfastly

Persistence is when you have reached the end of your rope. The end of the day, the kids are screaming at each other, and you can't even think of anything but sleep. Yet, you stay in the game.

Persistence is when you feel totally lost and disconnected from your practice and your clients come to see you and you think, "What am I doing here?" but you make the choice that you are going to figure out how you can serve even though you don't feel inspired.

Persistence gives you broader reference points.

When you are confused, tired, or disconnected, that means you are on the verge of a form of transformation. Often it means that you are shedding an old belief and replacing it with a new one. Your ideas about who you are, what can be done, and what you are capable of melt down and you create a new identity. But you have to be willing to move in and through discomfort. That is persistence.

What Do You Mean by Focus?

Focus: 3. A central point, as of attraction, attention or activity, focal point
(The Random House Dictionary of The English Language, College Edition)

This means getting exceptionally, exceedingly clear on what you can be remarkably, outstandingly clear about.

Focus requires courage, because focus means the possibility of failure. If you really go for it and fail, what would it mean? That is a powerful question.

Imagine a magnifying glass. My dad had a giant magnifying lens that could melt soft metals. As a young boy, I thought it was cool. But it was dangerous. A powerful lens can concentrate the sunlight into a fine point of heat. I could get burned. I could burn someone else. I could (and did) start a lot of fires and kill a lot of grasshoppers.

Playing with fire and not getting burned, when applied to focus, means that you understand the power.

My friend and colleague Eli Buren gave it to me straight when he once asked me, "Seth, do you want to piss away your power, or do you want to use it?"

Do you want to get fit, eat better, and have a better life but complain about not having enough time? Ask yourself this: how much T.V., movies, and internet time are you engaged in? Do you find yourself hanging out with friends at the bar whining about your life? Be fierce about where you are wasting your focus.

Stop distracting yourself with what Stephen Covey calls, "the not urgent and not important." Sometimes not going for your goals has nothing to do with fear, upsets, the inner game, or lack of vision. Sometimes it is simply a matter of changing habits and behavior.

The bottom line is that we create in the direction of our focus. What you focus on expands. When you focus on the problem, you have more problems. When you focus on the solutions, you have more solutions.

Be a warrior with your focus. If your time, energy, and attention are caught up in interesting and nice things, drop them. Life is too precious. Invest yourself in what is critical.

What is it for you?
1. Family and Relationships – Are you a father, son, wife, friend, collaborator? What can you do to fully show up in this role?
2. Purpose – Are you here to teach, heal, create, lead? In which primary role do you embody your deepest purpose?
3. Steward – What are you responsible for? Creative genius? A large family? A business? Wealth? What can you do to step up in your stewardship roles?

If you gave it your all in these each week, then life is good. But you have to be a warrior to maintain the boundaries. Here is an example:

I have realized, that to have the level of success that I want to have, it is difficult to spread it out and do multiple things. It takes such an obsessive, desperate focus...with all of your heart and all of your fiber and all your creativity.
Will Smith

What Do You Mean by Believe?

Believe: 1. To have confidence in the truth or the reliability of something without absolute proof.
(The Random House Dictionary of The English Language, College Edition)

I mean believe in yourself, in your dream, in other people, and in a higher power. I mean have faith. Trust in life.

This is a choice. It is not something that happens to you.

Ryan Arsenault, a member of my 72-day Hurricane Island Outward Bound Wilderness Leadership Training program, said something that has stuck with me. "Faith is something active, that you have to generate, it is not something that falls from heaven or comes from some other place."

The first step, before anyone else in the world believes it, is you have to believe it.
Will Smith

Belief has to arise from your desire to:
- do what you enjoy,
- make a contribution,
- and be unique.

That is the essence of belief. You are not anyone else.

Owning It

Going through your Dreams into Action process is huge. But now you need to discover how you can really own this process for yourself. It has to become yours.

YOU need to be intimate with YOURSELF. *To Thine Own Self Be True.* Engage the power of your dream.

Nevertheless and notwithstanding, it is helpful to study success. If you study music, you learn that music theory came from studying great music. First came the music, and then came music theory to explain the beauty. Music theory is an imperfect system. Believe it or not, all of Western classical music is slightly out of tune! The theory is not the experience. The map is not the territory. But music theory has made it possible to accelerate the pace of growth for all musicians. A theoretical map of success accelerates your development even if it is not the territory.

You want to find the point where this material "clicks" for you. I mean the outer words and symbols link up with your own inner knowing. Success, like vision, is unearthed from within you. It is who you become. You are becoming more of what you are. When you recognize the truth, it resonates. One guitar string vibrating will cause a guitar similarly tuned beside it to vibrate as well. Resonance is the "aha" experience.

How do you make friends with these teachings?

How can you make this conceptual lattice your own?

What is your unique way of learning, remembering, and integrating material?

How do YOU educate yourself?

Success Theory

It makes sense to have a study of success that includes learning from mistakes (failures) and from achievement (success), both in our life and in history. Then we can develop our own success theory.

Success theory is just a framework that attempts to organize and classify the thoughts, attitudes, feelings, and behaviors of successful people, while also learning as much as possible from the mistakes in human history.

What Is Success?

Your definition of success may be significantly different than mine. It is critically important that your life vision is aligned with your values.

This gets deep.

Self-inquiry demonstrates that many of the greatest accomplishments in the world have come from people trying to prove their worth. "I'll show them" inspired a heck of a lot of amazing triumphs over difficulty.

But there is more to life than simple black-and-white statements.

It is up to you to decide whether you want to use your upsets to fuel achievement or if you would prefer to live a simple life and let go of the need to prove yourself. Both are sacred in their own way.

Fuel for Achievement

At age thirteen, soccer phenomenon David Beckham was told by his football teacher, *You'll never play for England because you're too small and not strong enough.*

Beckham states that, "As upset as I was at the time, it made me think, I'm going to prove I can play football professionally."

So you have to wonder, if he hadn't gotten pissed off from that experience, would he be the football superstar that he is today?

Would he have eliminated the burning desire to succeed if his coach hadn't upset him? Is he satisfied? Is he living the life that he wants?

I don't know, because I haven't asked him.

Good or bad, who is to say?

But as the *Men's Health* article states,

"DAVID BECKHAM IS THE MOST POPULAR PLAYER IN THE MOST POPULAR SPORT IN THE WORLD. YOU'RE NOT."

Harsh but true.

Here are a few key points summarized from the article (with my commentary):

You have to know what you aren't going to do.	(Focus)
Build and protect your focus.	(Persist/Focus)
Don't compare yourself to anyone else.	(Believe)
Make things very simple.	(Focus)
Be good at the inner game.	(Believe)

You decide. What is success for you? Whatever form of success you study, you always find some version of:

Focus, Believe, Persist.

These three are the foundation.

It doesn't matter what you call it.

Many people call it **Focus, Faith, Follow Through.**

But you have to decide. What do you want to focus on?

The point I want to make here is simple. If you are going for success just to prove something to someone else, your success is going to be empty. Obviously, David Beckham was motivated not only to prove his coach wrong, but also to do what he loved, to challenge himself, and to go for what HE loved.

> *"I think that there is a certain delusional quality that all successful people have to have. You have to believe that something different than what has happened over the last fifty million years of history, you have to believe that something different can happen.*
> **Will Smith**

But I Want To Do So Much!

You have so many opportunities, I know. It can be hard to choose.

My clients have consistently come to the table with pretty great problems. 'Should I choose my dream job or pitch this business to investors?' 'Should I focus on getting my PhD or making this neat little film?' 'Should I sell the catering business and focus on working with clients or spend a few more years increasing the valuation and then sell it for more financial security?' These are all real questions my clients have wanted support in addressing. This is part of feeling overwhelmed. It stems from intrapersonal values such as taking responsibility for our destiny, being self-initiating, developing mastery and to see life as a system, which we fit into. Although these are tremendous, they are a fairly new frontier for humanity as a whole and require a new level of sophistication in navigating.

Distraction and overwhelm are the major obstacles to focus. I'm going to address the issues of distraction and overwhelm in the next chapter. We are going to have to deal with more and more opportunity, more and more information, and more and more choice. This is a great problem to have!

I encourage you to come back to the "What do I know for sure?" question that was introduced in Chapter 1. You really can't make a wrong decision. You have to have faith that there is a higher order to life. There are techniques – morning pages, meditation, self-inquiry – that help us get clear. If you are still worried, "Am I on the right path, is this the right track for me," then let me share a story with you.

Good or Bad, Who Is To Say?

The origin of this story is unknown to me. I've heard this at many retreats, from a variety of people, and have never heard the source quoted.

A Taoist householder had to raise his son by himself after his wife had died. All of the townspeople said to him, "Ah, this is so bad, what bad luck." The householder simply looked up and replied, "Good or bad, who is to say?"

Later that year, a wealthy and revered sovereign traveled through that region and bestowed a great gift onto any widow or widower, a purebred stallion. This great stallion was a treasure to the householder, for now he could plow his fields. The townspeople all agreed, "This is fortuitous, you're a lucky man!" The Taoist only replied, "Good or bad, who is to say?"

The next spring, the stallion broke the gate and ran away, leaving half the fields unplowed, which the son, now getting to be a young man, had to plow with his father. In town, locals gathered around commiserating on the awful luck that the father and son had. The father only responded to a few of these remarks with, "I cannot say that this is good or bad, only that the horse is now gone. We will wait and see."

A week later, the stallion returned with two wild mares. Now, with three horses, the householder could create wealth with the work that he could do. The townspeople all agreed that this was an incredible turn of events and that surely the man must agree that it was a very lucky circumstance. The man only shook his head, finally offering a brief comment to their remarks, "I only know that I now have three horses. Good or bad, I can't say."

As the moon waxed into the full cycle, the son worked on breaking the horses, training them for riding. On one such morning, the son was bucked off and broke his collarbone. All the townspeople agreed that this was terrible. How would the old man manage his home and farm now that his son was convalescing? The old man, when questioned in town, replied only that, "This may have good or evil for me, but who am I to say that I know the way of the Tao?"

The following week, the state army passed through, recruiting most young men, but not the son, for he was bedridden for weeks and would be unable to march. This time, the mothers of the village all exclaimed the man's good fortune.

Your destiny will meet you on every path that you choose. You cannot avoid it. If you intend to live your purpose and you keep that alive in you each and every day, then everything you do brings you one step closer. You literally cannot fail, because failure is just a way that we learn to go for our life purpose with more wisdom.

Humility Is the Only Reasonable Position

Focus. Believe. Persist. But remain humble, or life will humble you! You did not create yourself. There are approximately 100 trillion cells (that is 100,000,000,000,000) in your body doing an unfathomable job of maintaining your life without any conscious effort on your part. The sun remains just the right distance from the earth to maintain a dazzling array of life. Rejoice in the opportunity to be alive and stay humble. It works better that way.

Don't Worry, Be Happy

I've paraphrased one of my favorite reminders about worry from the Sermon on the Mount, by Jesus the Christ, from the Gospel of Matthew, 6:25-28.

"Therefore, I say to you, do not worry about your life, what you need to eat or drink or what you need to survive and fit in. Life is more than the needs of your body.

Look at the birds of the air. They don't have a nine to five job, they don't have a to-do list, and they haven't got a retirement account. But Life (God) supplies them with everything that they need.

And aren't you vastly more developed and conscious than the birds? Do you think you could make yourself taller by worry, plans, or mental preoccupation? So why are you even the least bit worried about your clothes and home?

Look at the flowers of the field, how they grow without any tending. They don't work until two am. They are not freaking out about deadlines and due dates and project management. Yet, the truth remains, King Solomon's most glorious robes are not as gorgeous as these flowers. If God clothed the flowers this splendidly, which spring up and die within a season, how much more are you provided for?

Your worry shows a lack of faith in the inherent order of life. Stop! Don't worry about your survival. Don't worry about how things are going to work out.

Put your attention on the consciousness (the awareness) of the miraculous and awesome reality of Life. Devote your attention to Love, Life, and The Way Things Are. The Kingdom of God, which is within you, is the single most important place of focus.

But I Am Too Old to Do What I Really Want in My Work!

Julia Child is the most significant personality in the world of food and cooking. Her life made the way for the culture of food in America. She paved the way for the Food Network. With the first TV cooking show and the first accessible book on sophisticated French cooking, Child is the Queen of Cuisine, the first American chef to receive France's Legion of Honor award.

Yet, Julia didn't have an easy go of her career at first.

"I couldn't boil an egg," she says of herself before entering *Le Cordon Bleu*, the famed French culinary school.

- Child was thirty-two when she first began to cook.
- She was thirty-seven when she entered *Le Cordon Bleu*.
- She was the only woman in her class (three to five percent of culinary students were women).

- The head chef did not make it easy for her and they were often at odds.
- It took her ten years to write her first book.

Persist. Believe. Focus.

I love watching old shows. Child is not particularly camera friendly. In fact, she appears awkward and uncomfortable in the early shows. Yet her genuine love and appreciation for the material is thoroughly engaging.

Julia teaches me that there is no script that I have to follow. My past doesn't equal my future. And anything is possible, at any age, especially when following our passion.

The Consistent Principles of Success

Thanks to the TED talks online posting, the whole world can learn from the best and brightest in technology, entertainment, and design (and much, much more).

Make it a point to log on to http://www.TED.com.

Here is a summary of Richard St. John's TED presentation *8 Secrets of Success*.

Success Equation:
Passion: I love what I do and would pay for it; I am driven by it.
Hard Work: It is all hard work; nothing comes easily, but I have a lot of fun. (Rupert Murdoch)
Good: Get damn good at something by focusing on one thing; to be successful get your nose down in something and get damn good at it; there is no magic; practice, practice, practice. (Alex Garden)
Focus: I think it all has to do with focusing yourself to one thing. (Norman Jewison)
Push: Push yourself physically, mentally, you gotta push, push, push. (David Gallo, marine scientist)
Serve: Create something of value . It was a privilege to serve as a doctor. (Sherwin Nuland, Professor of Surgery, Yale)
Ideas: I had an idea, founding the first microcomputer software company. (Bill Gates)

Persist: Persistence is the number one reason for our success. You have got to persist through failure; you have got to persist through CRAP (Criticism, Rejection, Assholes, Pressure). (Joe Krauss, co-founder of Excite)

"Push yourself, through shyness and self-doubt, pain and discomfort."
From Richard St. John's three-minute presentation at TED, February 2005

Let's take a look at this list and compare it to the two main ideas of the chapter. First, you need to know your definition of success, and second, you focus, believe, persist.

1. Passion. You can't persist if you are not passionate. Your inspiration will wane. Passion is the first part of the context of your Dream, Vision, and Purpose. This is why you persist, believe, and focus. This is half of the heart of knowing your own definition of success.
2. Hard work. That is persistence.
3. Good. Good means skillful, which is a combination of focus and persistence.
4. Focus = Focus.
5. Push = Persist.
6. Service = Purpose. This is the reason that we Focus, Believe, and Persist.
7. Ideas = Believe in yourself enough to follow the idea. *You have to be unrealistically positive about your ability.*
8. Persist = Persist. (That explains it.)

Here are my success equations.
Joy + Service = Purpose
Purpose + Creativity = Your Dream
Focus + Persist + Believe = Your Best
Tools + Support + Direction = Preparation
Preparation + Doing Your Best + Your Dream = Achievement

That Is All Fine, But What if I Am Rejected Over and Over, I'm in Debt and Can't Pay my Bills?

Yes. That reminds me of the story of Norman Vincent Peale's first book. Of course, he was always confident, positive, and persistent. Except when he was not.

Rev. Peale's first manuscript was rejected enough times that he gave up. The guy who wrote *The Power of Positive Thinking* gave up! But guess what? He persisted. Well, actually, thanks to his wife; she persisted. Peale dumped the manuscript. His wife fished it out and sent it to one more publisher. BLING! That was *A Guide to Confident Living*. Peale went on to sell millions more of *The Power of Positive Thinking* and other titles.

Use your fear as a path to doing the inner work. Heal the hurt under the fear of failure and then begin to focus your mind toward the attainment of your goal. And, let it go while doing your best. This is called *letting go*. Life works better when you let go. It seems contradictory, but it's not. You can focus better when you feel free of the anxiety of forcing something to happen.

If you are doing what you are passionate about and you are fulfilling your life purpose, you would PAY to do these things! Your life is already rewarding. When you focus on contribution, the money will get handled. Yes, do bookkeeping and steward resources responsibly. But stay in the game.

Your success begins with you believing in you.

The first step, before anyone else in the world believes it, is you have to believe it. There is no reason to have a plan B because it distracts from plan A.

Will Smith

The Role of Luck

What is luck? Is there any relevance to believing in luck?

If you read Malcolm Gladwell's latest book, *Outliers: The Story of Success*, you find that success always blossoms in some well-tended ground. Everything that we have attributed to your focus, belief, and persistence is foiled without opportunity.

Opportunity comes in many forms. It could be a market trend in business. It could be social change. It could be a family legacy. It could be a technological breakthrough.

Gladwell articulates the powerful effect that family, culture, collective technological innovation, and the legacy of generations gone by exerts on our opportunity.

This is not a new idea, that we are the product of context in our success. Gladwell's work suggests the importance of humility in any successful endeavor.

For Olympic swimmer Michael Phelps, the difference between being an epic world champion, winning more gold medals in one Olympic games than anyone else, was 1/100th of a second.

You have to admit that at the level he is competing at there has to be the commitment to intense training, and the slightest edge from personal will can make the difference between an eternity of recognition and a short spotlight.

But Phelps would not have even had the opportunity if it were not for the choices that his parents made, and the fact that as a boy, he had a place to train nearby his home.

How Do I Make My Own Luck?

My friend and colleague Luke Entrup used the term "learning how to make my own luck." This intrigued me. Is this possible?

Entrup pointed out that luck is the opportunity. It is having the opening. Even if you have mad skill and tons of talent, without an opportunity, that talent and skill will never be funneled into fruition.

So, how can you put yourself in a place where your particular talents, skills, passions, and contributions are going to meet opportunity?

Use all of your resourcefulness to generate profound personal and professional effectiveness. Then, be a fierce advocate for yourself. You need to put yourself into places, meet with people, and engage in circumstances that can help you come face to face with opportunity.

Success is never a solo endeavor. Create your luck by being in the right place at the right time. Create your own luck by staying ready for opportunity and seeking it out.

Focus on What You Can

Focus. Persist. Believe.

Then, take action. The bottom line is that you have to take action, action, action. Dedicate your action to contribution. Then GO!

In *Good To Great*, Jim Collins calls this "the flywheel effect." You need to build the momentum of success. Do what you are naturally good at. Do what you love. Do something with a clear value to the world (an economic engine). Then act. Sometimes all you can do is call the next person or write the next sentence. Just do the one small thing.

All men dream; but not equally,
Those who dream by night in the dusty recesses of their minds
Awake to find that it was vanity;
But the dreamers of day are dangerous men,
That they may act their dreams with open eyes to make it possible.

T. E. Lawrence

RECAP OF CHAPTER 12 PART TWO:

- Know your definition of success.
- Persist – keep going. So many people give up at the last leg of therace. Breathe; you will get your second wind. Confusion and upset mean you are learning and growing.
- Believe – It starts with you, believing in you. If you can conceive it, then BELIEVE it, you can and will achieve it. Don't fret about other folks; just stay the course.
- Focus – Don't let distraction and overwhelm (the two top obstacles for most of y'all) stop your momentum.
- Own these processes for yourself.
- Study successful people.
- Setbacks are only setbacks if you decide they are. Good or bad, who is to say? Every experience can move you toward your destiny. In fact, it is inevitable!
- You are never too old.
- Follow the practices of the principles of success.
- Humble yourself. Acknowledge all the support that success arises from.
- Then create your own luck by placing yourself in the best situations with the right people.

SECTION D:

Walking the Path: Life and Work As Awareness Practice

CHAPTER 13

PRODUCTIVITY: MODERN TIMES, MODERN CHALLENGES

THE PURPOSE OF CHAPTER 13:

You will identify the sources of distraction and overwhelm and learn how to handle them so you can have more fun, more results and more balance. You will learn how the obstacle of modern information overload is an opportunity for training your mind.

This problem of modern knowledge workers is summed up in two words:

Distraction

&

Overwhelm

I've repeated these over and over throughout this book, for good reason. The number one challenge for most people today is not a lack of motivation. It is not a lack of good ideas. It is not a lack of intelligence. It is not for want of a vision (though it gets lost sometimes). The biggest challenge is carving out your authentic voice in the midst of distraction and overwhelm.

The Battle for Your Attention Part One: Advertising

You are constantly being pulled. Marketing is sophisticated. Billions of dollars are spent on the process of grabbing your attention, your money, your energy, and your time.

Have you ever had this happen? You get an unsolicited email. Wouldn't it be great if the response was, "wow, I can't imagine someone sending me an un-requested email, how rude!" But that isn't the world you live in. More likely you get something like this (I happened to receive this just before writing this section).

From: dell_epp@dellhome.usa.dell.com

Subject: Sweet Deals Starting at $279: Dell Systems, Wrapped Up & Ready to Go!

How did this e-mail get to me?

I never click the box that says, Yes, Please Send Me Your Ads! And when I tried to unsubscribe to this one, I received an error message. Granted, most of the time, I can unsubscribe, but there are those times when it is impossible. E-mail spam is so ubiquitous that we have complex systems to manage it and it is still an issue.

The good news though is that someone in Nigeria found my email online and chose me to be the beneficiary of a large estate. So, I can't complain too much. I just can't wait for that $5,000,000 to get here.

(*This is a joke, I hope you got it.*)

We are bombarded with marketing at every turn. We do not own our attention when in the marketplace. Billboards. Radio. TV. Internet. E-mail. Phone Calls. Flyers. Inserts. Grocery store receipts. Truck stop urinal poster ads…on and on and on.

This affects you. You need to counter the effects.

Free Your Mind

> *Emancipate yourself from mental slavery, none but ourselves can free our mind.*
> **Bob Marley**

Malcolm Gladwell clearly demonstrated the effect of even the slightest suggestions on our mind and body in his book *Blink*. Gladwell refers to a study that tracks participants through a word game and then studies how fast or slow they walk in and out of the office. When the word game has references to old age, people walk out slower.

In *Blink,* he describes the adaptive unconscious as mental workings that consciousness does not filter or choose but that influence our preferences, opinions, and actions. He makes compelling arguments that these adaptive unconscious mechanisms are at work along many lines of development and across social strata, affecting the price you pay for a car, the job you get, and for whom you vote.

Media in all its forms is the root source of influence and distraction.

Garbage In, Garbage Out

There is a classic saying in the self-help world, borrowed from the early years of computers:

Garbage In = Garbage Out

In the modern world, you have to be fiercely vigilant, committed to your purpose and mission, and you need to understand the power and influence of marketing to push and pull the mind.

Whose life are you living?

Are you doing what you think you should be doing?

Are you taking cues from the magazine you just read?

How does media affect the direction of your life?

The Battle for Your Mind, Part Two: Two Channels of Disruption

1. E-mail & social networks
2. Mobile technology

These are at the root of so much potential and so much trouble!

Let me just say that I am not a technophobe. I am on my mobile devices and e-mail every day for work. That's why I know how pernicious the problem of e-mail and mobile tech distraction can be.

E-mail Evils Will Not Be Televised

Often, when I work with a client, I can trace a problem in their business or health to a behavior or habit with e-mail or social networking, like Facebook.

This chapter assumes that the TV is seldom used in your household, and especially by you. If you haven't yet done so, get rid of your TV, or at least the cable or satellite 300-channel access.

You don't need it.

If you have a dream, then spend your free time going for that. If you want to relax and have some down time, then walk, read, rest, or play with your children.

I am not kidding. People think I am kidding. Seriously. If you want to go for your dreams, don't watch TV. I haven't owned a TV in my adult life. Nevertheless, this was one of the first "assignments" from one of my KEY mentors over the last few years.

Sure, movies are fine, in moderation.

Now, assuming that the TV is out of the picture, let's talk e-mail.

Get a Handle on E-mail

In his book *Getting Things Done,* David Allen outlines strategies for handling e-mail. His website, www.DavidCo.com has a free PDF titled "Getting E-mail Under Control."

The take-aways for me are:
- See e-mail as a big inbox of communication.
- Delete! If it is not relevant, then delete. Simple.
- The GTD system recommends files for emails that you might keep for reference. I don't. I keep reference material in Mac Mail. If I need a password or an invoice or something, I just do a keyword search in my inbox.
- Complete two minute or less responses. Just like offline inbox. In this case, you can fire off short responses. (I often answer questions in both the subject line and the body).
- Organize longer follow-up. For me, I either print (rare), schedule time to respond (rare too), or just keep it open in its own window for the next time I am at e-mail (kind of lame). I don't have this problem because I carve out thirty minutes, twice a day to handle all new e-mail tasks, about five days a week.

- Finally, don't leave an e-mail hanging in your mind. The "I need to send Bozo that e-mail" thought is robbing you. Find a way to clean and clear the inbox regularly and have a system that you can use to hold your actions for you, even if it is kind of lame, like keeping the e-mail window open on several e-mails at a time.

I have adapted these from my study of his book, which I recommend.

Digital Agitations

Here are some wake-up call statistics:

The average American is highly likely to check e-mail on vacations, on sick days, and in bed.

Tim Ferriss, in *The Four Hour Work Week*, shares stats from a 2005 AOL study that suggest that 40 percent of us are checking our e-mail first thing in the morning!

The average Facebook user spends 55 minutes per day on FB. The average mobile user is on 50 percent more. Psychologists have introduced the diagnosis FAD (Facebook Addiction Disorder) as a new kind of addiction disorder.

But you don't need stats to prove this to you. You've done these things!

Every time you check your e-mail, Facebook, or get online during your work sessions, you stop all creative momentum and need 10-20 minutes to get back into your groove. You need to beat *e-mail and social media addiction*. Get a routine. Check e-mail and use social media at predetermined intervals. Do not keep going back and checking it every five minutes and do not set up your e-mail to "ding!" every time a new message comes in. This robs your attention and creates a Pavlovian response.

Cell Phones Are Killing Us

But not from radiation. Well, maybe. I don't know. I am not planning on stopping my service. No, cell phones are killing our interactions, our creativity, our communication, our focus, and our priorities. Sadly, they are also a factor in actual deaths in traffic as well.

How many times have you see one of these situations:
- Texting while driving
- Talking while in line at the grocery store
- Emailing during a meeting
- Compulsively checking smart phones during a work session
- Parents ignoring their kids at the playground to take a call and saying, "shhhh, mommy is busy now, hold on."

I do not answer my cell phone when I am playing with my kids, eating dinner, or going on walks with my wife. When it comes to getting productive work done, I turn it off.

Clients come to me wondering why they are procrastinating. I find out that every ten minutes they are responding to a text message, an e-mail on the mobile device, or a phone call. They are not procrastinating! That is distraction and overwhelm.

It takes time to get into a project. It takes time to get into your tasks. Every time you check your e-mail, cell phone, or text messaging, you pull yourself out of that mind. Not only did you interrupt the forward momentum, but now you have to take the time to reorient yourself to the work at hand.

The Problem With Deodorant

Have you ever gone to the store to buy deodorant? There are easily over 30 types of deodorant. You can get men's deodorant, (spice must be more manly smelling) and women's deodorant that smells like powders and flowers. You can buy sports deodorant, endurance deodorant, and professional deodorant. You can get roll on, solid, spray and gel. And then you have antiperspirants and another 30 choices.

We are faced with more choices than ever before. The problem with more choice is that we have to use a certain faculty of mind for each one of these little things that never used to be a choice.

That is yet another reason why we need to train the mind.

Creativity and the Mind

You need to have time of low to moderate input.

What do I mean by that?

When you are stuck, it is because you are backed up.

If you are reading this, you are not stuck because you are lazy.

You are not stuck because you are out of good ideas.

You are not stuck because you are uninspired.

You are not in need of a calling in life.

You are stuck because you have too much going on in your life and in your head. All of your ideas and visions and plans and actions have become mashed together with some emotions and it is all backed up.

Sometimes you need to go through the 9 steps to get clear.

Another time, you need to let it out through Affirmative Invocation.

And still, there is the real need to create, speak, teach, and let out your wisdom and experience; the need to show up in the studio. But if you are constantly putting more and more in, then you are going to get backed up.

Pay attention to the effect that input from the Internet, e-mail, phone, texting, TV, movies, and overexposure of advertising (such as being in a mall for a few hours) has on your mind.

Do you feel more inspired or less?

Do you feel more connected or less?

More or less energized?

If you want to create a life of magnitude, then get a handle on the input lines. Spend more time creating. Spend less time inputting. Check out *The Artist's Way* by Julia Cameron. Her work provides an effective way to reclaim your creative flow. Creative flow is essential to effectiveness.

The Digital Sabbatical

Many of my peers have instituted digital sabbaticals. Anytime that you can go camping, hunting, fishing, hiking, swimming or walking in nature can be a digital sabbatical. Some people have to force themselves to leave their mobile devices at home. Other folks attempt to go where they can't get a signal.

I have been taking people down to Nosara, Costa Rica for retreats since 2007. Part of the game is to leave your device at home. It takes two to three days for the effect to sink in. But you can see it when it does. Ahhhh...

Mind Training

Now more than ever, the mind training practices of the great contemplative traditions offer great practical value. The great contemplative traditions include but are not limited to Buddhist, Christian, Jewish, Muslim, Hindu, and Shamanic. The practices that you may draw upon include:
- Shamatha Meditation
- Centering Prayer
- Vipassana Meditation
- Contemplative Prayer, "Vacare Deo"
- Zen Practice
- Transcendental Meditation
- Taoist Awareness Practice

There are many forms and practices of mind training, and it is best to follow a lineage with a historical context that provides credibility.

In his book *Turning The Mind Into an Ally,* Sakyong Mipham Rinpoche describes the mind as a wild horse that we learn to ride. He likens the development of mind to the development of muscles. At first, it is challenging to lift weights, but with dedication, your muscles get strong.

The opportunity inherent in the energy-information age is the full access to the global mind training traditions and the motivation to practice for practical sanity and productivity.

Warrior Artist

Your daily life offers you the opportunity to develop your focus, concentration and mindfulness. While meditative and contemplative practice provides a space and time to build the muscles of mind training, the real practice is to begin to live life as a contemplative practice. Consider the many distractions of hyper-connected technology as your sparring partner in mind training. The warrior artist is fiercely committed to living life as a creative act and practices adaptability to the situation at hand.

RECAP OF CHAPTER 13:

- Get out the distractions. Set up your time, energy, and attention on your terms, not the marketplace.
- Handle your e-mail and social networking. Set up a routine.
- Determine your own "digital hygiene."
- Get your cell phone and texting in service of your work, not vice versa.
- Cut out input channels and find ways to be creative or productive.
- Take a digital sabbatical.
- Access the world's great wisdom traditions for mind training techniques.
- Daily life is the training ground for contemplative practice.

SELF-STUDY EXERCISES:

- If you work at your computer a lot, try keeping your email closed while you are working and open it at appointed times during the day.
- Use a time tracking tool, or simply write down what you work on throughout the day and observe how much time is spent on social media.
- If you are new to meditation, check out local resources from Christian, Buddhist, Vedic or other reliable contemplative lineages.
- If you have experience with meditation, how can you spruce up your practice?
- Practice observing your thoughts, feelings and actions throughout the day through mindfulness of daily life.

CHAPTER 14

RELATIONSHIPS: FOUNDATIONS FOR SUCCESS

THE PURPOSE OF CHAPTER 14:

The purpose of this chapter is to give you the tools you need to have successful relationships. This is the foundation for lasting success in business and creative work because it makes life fulfilling.

You Can Have Success in any Relationship

Relationships are not complicated. In fact, the path to a peaceful, loving, connected, meaningful relationship with your spouse, friends, children, or coworkers is simple.

But it is not easy. Simple, but not easy.

Did you ever know at an intellectual level that being kind and loving was the right choice, but you still made a mean comment or acted in a way that was not loving?

We all do this. These are knee-jerk reactions, which spawn small jabs, cuts, and criticisms. Alas, a satisfying relationship is built on small things. It is the moment-to-moment expression of patience, kindness, and love that creates the fabric of your life with those closest to you.

By the way, if you are thinking, "*Well, I don't make mean comments or act in an unloving way,*" then you are fooling yourself and stretch the truth to fit the version of your identity in other areas of your life too. This is out of integrity and will rob your power.

You can use the principles from this book to:
- Handle upsets and turn them into opportunities in your relationship
- Generate resourceful states between you and the other person
- Have a plan for success in your relationship.

How Does This Relate To My Entrepreneurial or Creative Work?

Relationships are the foundation for your life. If your relationships aren't working, then no matter how successful you become, you are hard pressed to have fulfillment.

Executive Coach and mentor Brian Gast once stated, "You never sit down with a client and hear 'my life is going great, but my relationship is awful.' And you never hear 'my marriage is fantastic but my life is falling apart.'"

Intimate relationships are so primary as to be like food, water, and shelter.

Breakthrough with Relationships

I was in the parking lot of the Boulder Public Library. We were making one of those "pick up/drop off" sessions for the parenting plan visitation schedule.

As I saw my daughter into my ex-wife's Jeep, I felt a pain of regret. Why does it have to be this way? Then my ex-wife reminded me with a sideways dagger. I had asked to check in with her and instead got the silent treatment.

I felt anger rising in me. I took a deep breath and used the 9 Steps Process that I introduced you to in Chapter 5.

I got clear that I was angry. AnaVictoria drove away with the girls. I recognized that this feeling lived in me, not in the circumstance. I was responsible for what was happening in me.

I asked myself, "What is getting triggered inside my heart and mind?"

Then, an "aha!" moment occurred. I realized that I was afraid of being *not worth the time*. And every time my ex's behavior triggered that nerve, I lost my temper, thus fueling a cycle of conflict.

I looked inside and saw how much hurt was there, and I just wept.

Ten minutes later, I got a call from AnaVictoria. "Hi Seth. Look, I am sorry I ignored you, that wasn't right. I'll talk to you later. Bye."

Wow! This stuff works! Nothing like that had ever happened before. But when I allowed myself to drop the fighting and resistance to my wife's behavior, a circuit of conflict stopped.

Fast-forward a few years. In the summer of 2009, AnaVictoria and I remarried at St. Gabriel and All Angels Church in Fairfield, Iowa.

This was IMPOSSIBLE to my mind. This was IMPROBABLE according to the laws of the world.

Yet, through commitment to some difficult inner work, support from community, and the Grace of God, we were able to experience the MIRACULOUS.

The Fundamentals

Skill in handling your upsets in relationships is essential. If you feel like you are at the "effect" of the situation, then you are finished. You need to feel like you have power, like you have the ability to be the "cause."

Moving from the experience of "effect" to the experience of "cause" is the foundation for empowered relationships. It is easy to feel empowered when things are going well. The rubber meets the road when you get upset.

Handling upsets in relationship is simple, but as stated, it is not easy. Here is what you do when you are upset:
1. Be quiet.
2. Be wrong.
3. Go after what got triggered in you.
4. Take the high road.
5. Find and give love.
6. Communicate your needs.

If your spouse or partner yells at you when you both arrive home from work, you have two options. You can either:
1. Yell back, criticize, complain, or attack.
2. You can be quiet, take the high road, be loving, or go after what gets triggered in you.

Let's take a look at your options.

Be Quiet

Sometimes the most important thing you can do is to be quiet.

In the past, I wouldn't do this. My wife would get hot about something I said that may have been true, but was not communicated tactfully. I would get irritated that she got so triggered and then proceed to agitate her further by subtly criticizing her.

The solution that I have found is to be quiet. This means that I accept that she is triggered, angry, or disappointed. This means that I have to be loving and accepting.

Be Wrong

If you are angry, frustrated, hurt, or feeling let down, then you have made a mistake. It is that simple. You are not being loving, accepting, and present without criticism. That is the truth.

One of the people in the relationship has to make the choice. Would you rather be right or be happy? That is the meaning of forgiveness. It means giving up the need to be right about resentment.

Are you perfect? Do you expect the other person to be perfect? Then now is the opportunity for you to love and take the high road.

Any time that you are angry, frustrated, or feeling let down, then you are wrong. You shouldn't beat yourself up about it. But an honest evaluation makes clear that when you are upset at someone, you are not loving.

The other person's behavior may be entirely inappropriate. It may be vulgar, offensive, or mean. But it is your soul that you control, not theirs.

When are you going to love? When someone else is nice to you?

If this seems harsh, well, it feels that way to me sometimes too. But the truth is that you have to put your foot down and make the decision to *take the high road.*

When you want to lash out, react, kick back the crap that was sent toward you (CRAP = Criticism, Rejection, Assholes, Pressure), that is the time that you have to practice love. Sure, it is easy to feel love when things are going well.

The ultimate measure of a man is not where he stands in moments of comfort and convenience but in times of challenge and controversy.
Rev. Dr. Martin Luther King Jr.

So, be wrong. It will help you quickly turn the corner on blaming the other person. It will give you access to your power. It is not justifying the behavior of the other person. It does not mean that you don't take action. It means that you come from a clear place, an honest place. Maybe you are angry. Maybe that isn't going to change soon. Do your best, and use that insight to BE QUIET, find the hurt in you, or get support in returning to love.

Then, from this place you can set appropriate boundaries and express your communication. Take the time to be quiet, be wrong, find out what your needs are, and then communicate them.

Try these things out and see how they work. Don't take my word for it.

Go After What Got Triggered in You

Sometimes it is really hard to be quiet, take the high road, or to love. The obstacle could your own hurt, pain, or upset that got triggered. One solution is to use the 9 Steps Upsets Into Opportunities process:
1. Notice that I am triggered.
2. Identify the surface feeling (anger, frustration, disappointment).
3. What does it mean about me that I have been treated this way, or that I feel this way?
4. What is the feeling under the judgment?
5. Be willing to feel the feeling completely, like a child. Own that these feelings live in you and are not caused by the person outside you.
6. Be willing to have the thing you fear most happen. The other person will not change. Can I totally and 100 percent accept that? I may need to revisit steps three, four, and five.
7. Invite spirit into the situation. Ask for guidance and support, and affirm that this is so.

8. Forgive yourself for keeping the emotions stuck and the judgments up.
9. Take action to improve the relationship from the place of genuine openness.

Take the High Road

This does not mean that you assume moral superiority, because, well, that is not the high road. The high road is where you can recognize that both you and your partner have tendencies to defend and attack, and that despite the burn to attack, you choose not to.

On-Ramp to the High Road

Having unconditional love in your life means that it begins with you. It has to begin with you. You reap what you sow.

If you are waiting for the other person to provide love, listening, presence, and care, then you are putting yourself at the effect. If you want a life that works, that is full of respect, love, appreciation, and mutual trust, then you must begin to practice taking the high road every time, in every relationship.

I know that this is hard. But it is also thrilling. When you make the commitment in yourself to take the high road, forgive yourself when you don't, and then quickly come back, you create a kind of a momentum. It is like a tidal wave of inner power. It is Love-Force. This makes life more wonderful, and you begin to ride the wave of good feeling.

The opposite is bitterness, resentment, and criticism. These have momentum as well. Riding them is less fun.

What does it mean to take the high road?

How can you take the high road more consistently?

When do you get tripped up on taking the high road?

Find and Give Love

You can take the high road one step further by actually doing something extraordinary like helping your partner with something. If you know that he is trying to get the car cleaned up for a trip, you could go out and vacuum it. This act of simply being helpful is actually better for you than the other person, because when you choose to act in a thoughtful loving manner, you begin to feel love.

What if you feel angry, spiteful and just plain mean?

Then there you first need to feel love, and then you give love. Here are four ways:

1. Tell the truth about yourself to someone that can listen unconditionally. When you feel heard and seen and accepted by someone else, even when you are feeling mean and angry, then love comes in.

2. Connect to God's love through prayer and meditation. There is a source of unconditional love that is not dependent on the world of form.

3. Use the 9 Steps Process to create compassion and acceptance for yourself and generate the love through self-referral.

4. Be loving anyway. Amazing shifts can happen when you take actions that are fundamentally helpful and kind, even when you feel angry. The person you are helping feels loved and cared for and you begin to feel love too!

Communicate Your Needs

Chapter 11 ends with a four-part communication model that I will repeat here.

After you have taken the time to reconnect with love, you can share your needs with others. You do this by making a request with no expectation or demands.

1. I felt angry today when we spoke in the kitchen. I am still a little annoyed.

2. The story I have is that I was tired, and you were tired and I was wrong to lose my temper but that our agreements about who is making dinner are not clear.

3. What I want here is for you and I to feel connected and to have a life that works.

4. And my specific request is that you work with me to set up an agreement and a plan for dinners each week.

In this way, you communicate what you are feeling, what you are thinking, what you would like to experience and a specific request.

Fool's Gold or Real Gold?

Fool's gold (hematite, iron, and copper pyrite) got its name because inexperienced miners found it and thought they were suddenly rich beyond their dreams, only to realize that they were holding an imposter.

It is the same with fake love.

There is a lot of fake love lying around.
1. Pleasure (sex, companionship, attention, "you scratch my back, I'll scratch yours")
2. Power (control over, command of, force, push and pull, dominance)
3. Position (status, pecking order, alpha-male, title)
4. Protection (comfort, security, familiar, known)
5. Placation (pleasing, calm, appease, "to say things that make another less angry")
6. Praise (stroking the ego, compliments, niceness)

You can call these the six P's of fool's love.

We use this to fill a void when we are not experiencing the genuine love that we all need.

We often expect those closest to us or most familiar to us to treat us with respect and kindness, to provide us with Praise, a sense of Power, and to Placate us when we are angry. When they don't, we want to manipulate them to get them to give us what we think is going to fill the void. We then do the following:
- Attack
- Criticize
- Blame
- Engage in Passive-Aggressive Behavior
- Withhold
- Run Away
- Provoke
- Shame
- Barter
- Give False Praise
- Give with Conditions

Sometimes, we settle for some of the comfort and familiarity of this type of relationship. The trading of these self-serving and defensive gestures is fool's love.

There is nothing wrong with pleasure, power, position, protection, placations, and praise. These are healthy aspects of living. When you use them to get love, however, you end up with fake love.

True love has no conditions. There is no currency. There is no trading, no bartering, no "I'll scratch your back, you'll scratch mine." This can still happen in relationships. Give and take is healthy, but not when it is a substitute for genuine love.

The currency of fool's love, the six P's, and the means to get it are at the core of the evolutionary adaptation and survival mechanism of physical existence. It is how the ego works.

A Normal Part of the Human Experience

Throughout history, in the process of evolution, humanity has been playing "pin the tail on the donkey" with our human problems. We have been looking for simple answers. We have done pretty well with this. One way religions have done this is to label attack, the artificial love of pleasure, the use of power for a sense of identity, and all the other kinds of "fake love" as sin.

By labeling these things sin, these fundamental, unavoidable expressions of human existence had the smell of shame and guilt hanging on them. While it helped people to follow a moral code, it left that bad smell on something that is inherent to living. This drives aspects of our self into the shadow. The shadow is the part of ourselves that we do not consciously identify with. It becomes more difficult to see ourselves clearly and work with relating in a powerful way when fundamental aspects or ourselves are hidden.

The ego got its start with the earliest animal life forms. Bacteria can't use photosynthesis, so it has to get energy from outside itself. Evolution of form brought forth more advanced organisms that not only had to seek energy from outside themselves, but had to protect, guard, claim territory, join in packs, and establish orders of power.

As humans, we have sophisticated ways to establish our position, power, and protection. But it is still the simple permutation of "defending" and "acquiring" for our survival.

These are fundamental aspects to living. And yes, they are mistakes (sin) but the solution is to have greater acceptance for these fallibilities. Hating our flaws does not make them go away.

Be Honest, Be Clear, Be Aware

The more you can be aware of the way that you are using the ego mechanisms, the more power that you can exercise in making choices.

Often I don't want to change these behaviors. I want to have power. I want to have position, authority, and status. That is fine. But it is not love. And it is only love and its expressions that have the power to transcend the fallibility of the ego.

You see, the ego can indeed serve us a great deal. It can get us power and status. But as many popular books of the day suggest, after success, you begin to look for significance.

Success without fulfillment is depressing! Read about the biggest success moments in history and you will find a large percentage of the people share an experience of depression the day after they won the great sporting event, appeared on Oprah, or finished the political campaign.

After all of the external ups and downs, only love (or the absence of love) remains.

Be clear, then, with yourself, and do not *pretend* to be more evolved than you are. Better to acknowledge your *sin* (mistake) and then consider if it really serves you.

Sin is defined as an action, a thought, or a behavior that opposes religious teachings and offends moral and ethical statutes. It is also defined as an act that denies the Grace of God.

The more accurate meaning, in terms of spiritual growth, which is the realm of authentic love as well as relationships, is "missing the mark."

Sin is an archer's term, meaning, "to miss the mark of the target." Christ taught people to stop making mistakes that they knew would harm them and others. The problem that was addressed then, and is still relevant now, is one that Plato stated thus: *Men seek the good, the true, and the beautiful but cannot always determine what is genuinely good, true, and beautiful.*

This means that we are inherently unable to be sure if we are choosing what is good for ourselves or not. Thus, we see the role of spiritual and religious involvement in a successful life.

Love does not follow the laws of the ego. When Jesus said, *"Bless those who curse you, pray for them who despitefully use you"* in the sixth chapter of Luke, twenty-eighth verse, we see that it is outside of the "acquiring and defending" system of the six P's.

Practically speaking, when your spouse, boyfriend, boss, or colleague verbally attacks you, you do not attack back, nor do you feel insulted. You realize that they must feel lonely, scared, hurt, or disappointed and are trying to get you to give them some form of love or fake love, probably the fake stuff, because that is what they know.

When you are hurt, angry, and upset, you do the same thing. So you have to accept their humanity, because you know your own. You can only do this if your self-esteem is high, if you feel loved and accepted, and if you feel free from anger and fear yourself.

That is why it seems to me that spiritual truth is at the root of healthy relationships.

Fill Your Cup

Regular spiritual nourishment through meditation, prayer and practice in a recognized spiritual lineage is one way to fill yourself with the experience of love.

In addition to spiritual practice, there are three other ways to experience more love and each of these seems to be equally valuable and important.

Another way to experience more love is to receive love from another person. The way you do that is:
- Tell the truth about yourself, the good, the bad and the ugly
- Tell it to someone that can hear and see you without blaming, • shaming, criticizing or trying to fix you.

- When you are seen and heard for who you are, not who you pretend, you feel acceptance.
- When you feel acceptance, you feel love.

Many people do this in 12-Step programs, support groups, spiritual study groups or with close friends.

An alternate way is to use the 9 Step Process outlined in Chapter 5, or some other self-inquiry process like The Work of Byron Katie, The Sedona Method or 4 Gateways Coaching to create more self-acceptance. By cultivating a relationship with yourself, you build compassion. And once you have compassion for yourself, it can be easier to have compassion for another.

Finally, you can act in a loving way even if you don't feel like it. By choosing to be loving, you generate love. You benefit from this. The person you act towards benefits from this. You literally create love out of nothing.

And that is the great thing about love. There is an endless supply.

My kids sing a song about it:
Love is something when you give it away, give it away, give it away
Love is something when you give it away, you end up having more
Love is like a magic penny.
Hold it tight and you won't have any
Lend it, spend and you'll have so many, it'll roll all over the floor!

RECAP OF CHAPTER 14:

- You can have success in any relationship.
- Successful intimate relationships are the foundation for long-term success and fulfillment.
- You are the one responsible for success in your relationship.
- Take the high road.
- Fake love is not bad or wrong, but it isn't the same as unconditional love.
- There are four ways to experience love; spiritual practice, compassion for self through inquiry, telling the truth about yourself to people that care or just act in loving way.

SELF-STUDY EXERCISES:

- Practice being quiet when someone upsets you.
- Recognize that when you are angry or disappointed you are wrong. Don't beat yourself up. Just see the truth.
- Make the choice to be the person that is going to start loving.
- Go after what gets triggered in you and create compassion for yourself.
- Spend time with people that can accept you when you tell the truth.
- This week, at least once, when you don't feel like it, be loving anyway.

CHAPTER 15

MONEY, MATURITY, AND VALUES

THE PURPOSE OF CHAPTER 15:

You are getting introduced to the idea that money is a not only pathway to richer living but also a path to maturity. You will get introduced to some different perspectives on money and get the reminder that your values determine how you relate to money.

Making Mistakes

I was cleaning my office one day and I had to go through a huge pile of divorce papers. That was an enlightening experience. How did I get to the place that I am now? How did I turn my relationship around and find myself married to my ex-wife, more in love with her than ever? How did I arrive in the space of supportive, nurturing, intentional relationship that is beyond anything I could have imagined? And why did I have to go through that awful, painful divorce to get here?

If you are reading this book to learn how to never make a mistake, then you have the wrong book.

Going through that box of files, I also came across a file for J. O'Neil and Associates. Now, at one point, I was facing a wall of debt that approached tidal wave proportions. I was scared. And I was also afraid to really look at the inner and outer game for myself. How could I be responsible for my experience? I kept looking intensely for solutions external to myself.

One of those was brokering small business loans for a shady character.

He painted a get-rich-quick picture to me and I bit. Then, I slowly eroded my integrity by telling myself stories to justify actions that were not aligned with my values.

The whole business model was set up on the premise that I had information the client did not. This was counter to my mission in life, to educate. So, I was working this sales position, essentially getting a signed non-compete form, promising to pull some strings with banks, and suggesting that the client "play with the numbers" on their unsecured line of credit application.

These "no-doc" applications were the next big thing for the now tapped-out mortgage professionals who sold all those loans to people who really could not afford them. It was how the economic meltdown functioned at the micro level. My colleagues were moving to these unsecured, signature-only lines of credit for businesses as their next big commission opportunity.

At an average of $3,000 per loan, this could be a lucrative way to sell without a great deal of expertise. The sale was simple, or so I was told: "You are selling money; everyone wants that." But in reality, we were asked to prey on small business owners, almost always asking them to get into debt they could not realistically afford to keep over the next year or two. Sure, there are a few business owners that needed immediate capital, but they could have gone to their local banks in most cases and gotten the same loans without the extra three percent or more.

But I was scared and wanted to make money fast, so I got into it completely. I spent my own money, used my own resources, and after six months and a few thousand dollars, I made a total of $400.

Now, back to J. O'Neil and Associates.

When I was at the Institute for Integrative Nutrition, I spoke in a large group session about the fear of debt. After that, a fellow student came up to me and said that he had a friend he trusted who could help me with this.

That friend was a broker, with a job much like I had. So, I conned myself into trusting him, because I was conning myself every day.

I paid somewhere in the neighborhood of $2,000 to have this law firm dissolve my debt through legal loopholes. The whole thing was languaged as a "consumer advocacy" group. Granted, credit card companies do often apply for more government insurance, backing, and credit in the name of their clients, which is out of integrity; nevertheless, helping people get out of paying for things they bought does not solve that problem.

Would you believe that the $2,000 I spent disappeared while my debt remained! I was culpable for the bad choices I made.

As I threw out the papers from this file, I looked back on how stupid that whole experience was. But I had to go through it to learn.

One mentor said to me, "You have to go through at least one major financial blowout. Be glad yours wasn't worse."

The truth is, it was worse! Since the debt dissolving process promised by the broker only dissolved my $2,000, I had to find a way to handle the collections agencies!

Taking Inventory

It took me two years to come to terms with my financial situation. I went through a divorce and teetered on the brink of financial disaster repeatedly.

Finally, with the help of Bari Tessler, Joetta Johnson, and Conscious Bookkeeping, I spent a year and a half in financial therapy, coaching, training, and action. Next to divorce, it was the most arduous personal challenge of my adult life. I used the tools I have shared with you here, as well as the tools that Joetta and the Conscious Bookkeeping community practice, and I transformed my financial experience.

Of course, it is an ongoing process, but out of my commitment to handle my relationship with money, clean up the mess, and create a container for wealth, I found myself unexpectedly receiving $400,000.

Was the intense period of inner and outer work on money the "cause" of the unexpected income? I don't think so. But I do understand the wisdom of spontaneous co-arising. There was an evolutionary impulse working in me to meet the experience of receiving that sum of money, which to some folks might seem quite large and to others, just a drop in the bucket.

Was it a coincidence?
Did I manifest it?
Did I attract it through thought vibration?

Based on the work I had done to prepare the fields, I was able to sow the seeds of that windfall in fertile soil and put it to good use as an anchor for my career and family.

Mastery and Joy in Finances

Handling money is a matter of:
- Your beliefs about money
- Your experience of your true source of wealth as internal
- A practice of financial integrity
- A standard of behavior
- Alignment with values and spending

Your Beliefs About Money

Money is the root of all evil.

Filthy rich.

It takes money to make money.

Poor people are lazy.

Rich people are greedy.

Your beliefs about money are going to determine your experience with money. It is that simple.

Most of your beliefs about money came from your parents. The rest came from your social circle. This could be a church, work, school, or neighborhood context.

The only way to have choice in your financial house is to excavate and explore the inherited concepts you carry. You do this by taking the time to investigate the stories that you tell yourself about money. This will take time, attention, and consistency.

You can do this many ways; one way is to contemplate five questions for a thirty-day period.
1. What was your mom's message to you about money?
2. What was your dad's message about money?
3. What was your grandparents' legacy and message to you about money?

4. As a child, did I see myself as poor, rich, middle class? How did I know? How did I feel about it?
5. What are my judgments about poor people, rich people, and middle-class people?

The Source of Your Wealth

The truth is that you are connected to infinite wealth.

Your genius, your mind, your ideas, creativity, flexibility, passion, commitment, love, joy, and enthusiasm constitute your wealth.

It is your ability to handle challenge and controversy that makes you wealthy. It is your smile in the face of a problem that creates abundance. When you feel good, connected, and on fire for life, you make things happen. This is wealth.

Some say that it goes even further.

Some would say that when you feel connected and in the flow of life, that it actually works in the subtle energy realms to determine the experiences that you are drawn into, or out of, as the case may be.

I think there is some truth to that. Nevertheless, it is enough for you to know that generating that resourceful state of being will create more ability in you to create value in the world.

How Do I Connect to That Place of Source Within Me?

Through meditation and prayer.

Affirmative prayer on the ideas of Divine Abundance + the contemplation of the source of life as the Divine Spark within your soul = resourcefulness and confidence.

I have completed a variety of course work on the realization of abundance. The most resonant for me came from a colleague when she gave me a copy of John Randolph Price's book *The Abundance Book*.

The book consists of testimonials, a bit of theoretical explanation, some instruction on metaphysics, and a forty-day prosperity plan.

Here are three sample meditations that are used in the book.

- "Money is not my supply. No person, place, or condition is my supply. My awareness, understanding, and knowledge of the all-providing activity of the Divine Mind within me are my supply. My consciousness of this Truth is unlimited."
- "My inner supply instantly and constantly takes on form and experience according to my needs and desires, and as the principle of supply in action, it is impossible for me to have any needs or unfulfilled desires."
- "The Divine Consciousness that I am is forever expressing its true nature of Abundance. This is its responsibility, not mine. My only responsibility is to be aware of this Truth. Therefore, I am totally confident in letting go and letting God appear as the abundant all sufficiency in my life and affairs."

The whole program is aimed at producing a realization that your awareness of God, the source of life, as the activity of your mind, is the true source of all abundance. This is accomplished by fifteen minutes of meditation on the ideas for forty days.

You then begin to live in a place of fullness and decreased dependence on the world for validation or peace of mind, which fosters confidence and joy. It is a positive growth spiral.

A Practice of Financial Integrity

Are you dealing with any of these?

Overspending: Are you able to consistently spend less than you earn and invest or tithe a percentage of earnings?

Excessive and consistent debt: Have you carried debt that is twenty-five percent or more of what you make in a year for more than two years? Do you keep moving back in and out of debt?

Money buffer: Do you have enough reserve money for emergencies?

Compulsive spending: Do you make purchases without any planning or consideration of a flow and budget?

Unprofitable business: Are you earning gross with no net profit? Is your business corrupt financially?

Money messes: Do you have excessive bank charges? Do you know what is in your checking account? Is your wallet organized?

Under-earning: Are you making less than you should, need, or want to make?

To be in financial integrity, you need to handle these areas of your life. It may not be easy, but you have to create the determination to do it.

How Do I Handle Out of Integrity Areas?

Write down everything that you need to handle. Everything.

Make a decision that you are going to handle each area. You don't have to know how; you just need to know that you are going to do it. The willingness to do creates the ability to do.

You have to do this to create the integrity that then clears our container for wealth. You can't put wealth into a vessel full of junk. Write these down. Clean up the junk.

Then, use the tools from the Work Your Plan section to consistently take action on these areas of your life each week.

Live With the Behaviors of Wealth

There are three time-centered behaviors that you need to take to keep yourself on track:
- Yearly Financial Practice.
- Monthly Financial Practice.
- Weekly Financial Practice.

The yearly financial practice is pretty straightforward. You have to pay taxes. I meet with my accountant to discuss tax strategies for the year. The most fundamental choice I make is corporate structure. Do I need to stay locked into an S. Corp, keep my LLC, or function as a Sole Proprietor? How do I maximize the legal tax strategies for my bottom line?

You also need to set yearly goals. To set goals, you need to look back on the previous year to learn about yourself and your relationship with money. To do this, you need records. You need a clear financial trail.

A monthly bookkeeping practice gives you the material for the yearly practice. It gives you immediate information too. The monthly practice helps you stay on track with goals and intentions.

In your monthly practice, you reconcile your bank statements; you review your budget and see how your cash flow is moving.

Are you spending more in one area than you want?

Are you earning from the areas that you expect?

This practice is for business and personal cash flow. You need to crunch the numbers into an easy-to-read and review product. This can be done with Quicken, Excel, QuickBooks, or other financial management software.

The weekly practice is data entry. You enter in your expenses and your income. You may want to work with a bookkeeper or administrative assistant.

Every week, I take an hour to download my personal account information directly into Quicken. Then I place each transaction in a category. At the end of the month, I can review my money by category, which is a nice way to get a broad overview and determine if I am on the path I want to be on.

The first step that you can take right now is to make a list of the spending categories in your life. This is your list, so do not feel the need to conform this to a category in Quicken or for tax purposes. Here is an example:

- Health
- Food
- Exercise
- Retreat
- Health Care
- Home
- Mortgage or Rent
- Insurance
- Utilities
- Décor
- Personal Growth
- Books
- Seminars
- Audio

- Events
- Community
- Charitable Giving
- Donations
- Hosted Dinners

This is a short example. You would want to flesh it out for yourself.

Look at the way you spend your time. This can give you the start to how you spend your money. When you are doing a monthly practice, you then assign expenses to one of the categories.

Align Values and Spending

Money won't be a source of joy for you until you determine your values and then align your use of money accordingly.

What does that mean?

Let me give you an example. You are going to make two columns on a piece of paper, titled **Needs** and **Wants.** Then, you are going to list everything you think you need and everything that you want.

When I did this, I realized that I did not need a car. I was living in Boulder at the time. My wife and I were divorced. She had a Jeep; I had a RAV4. I was essentially making two car payments. I hated that.

It did not align with my values. Why was I working my so hard to pay for things that I did not value? This was the case in some other key areas of my work life as well. I spent a huge percentage of my revenue on staff, rent, and overhead.

Once I got clear on what I wanted and needed, I eliminated the things I did not need or want; then I was more at ease in earning money!

Now, take your lists and fill them out as completely as possible. Use your list of categories from the previous section to trigger the expenses that you have on a regular basis.

Back to the Inner Game

The more you act to clean up your financial life, the more inner work you will get to do. Heal any underlying hurt that may be triggering automatic unconscious avoidance of hurt and pain. Here is another opportunity for the *9 Step Turning Upsets into Opportunities Process.*

1. What aspects of your financial life upset or trigger you?
2. What is the prevailing feeling?
3. What judgments do you have about getting triggered, feeling upset, or being in the situation that triggered the feelings?
4. Find the hurt under the judgment. If you need to, take a moment to see that there are two realities, the inner and outer, and changing the external circumstance will not resolve the internal feelings.
5. Be willing to feel that feeling totally.
6. Next, find the willingness to accept the thing you fear most. Fear is simply the unresolved emotions of the present projected onto the imagined future circumstances.
7. Invite in Spirit to the circumstance, into your awareness, and open to be changed at depth.
8. Forgive yourself for thinking that you needed to be perfect to have a good life.
9. Take determined, committed, and powerful action on the life situation that you started with.

Likewise, use practices to generate resourceful states in regard to wealth.

I am creating financial abundance in all my undertakings. Expected and unexpected income is coming to me through streams of connections that value my time, my gifts, and my offering.

I now see financial integrity, joy, mastery, and excellence in every area of my financial house.

I decree Divine Order and command my subconscious mind to bring forth integrity of thought, action, and feeling in the expression of my full potential as master of my financial health.

I am the source of my financial integrity. I take responsibility and arise to meet the challenge with gratitude, faith, and determination, and I cannot fail.

Back to the Outer Game

Use your weekly action plans to integrate a consistent financial practice and flow. Always come back to action, action, and action.

RECAP OF CHAPTER 15:

- Have beliefs that support wealth.
- Get coaching, bookkeeping, credit counseling, or other support you need.
- Connect to the Divine as the true source of wealth.
- Get clean and clear in the financial house and build integrity.
- Get into good habits with money mindfulness.
- Align values and standards with your spending.
- Don't overspend.
- Heal the hurt that pushes compulsive spending.
- Generate resourceful states with your financial realm.

SELF-STUDY EXERCISES:

- Set up a rhythm and routine for handling your finances. Schedule time each week, month and year to stay current, forecast and evaluate.
- Check out the Conscious Bookkeeping Home Study Course at http://baritessler.com/programs/home-study-program.
- Spend 20 minutes with your journal and evaluate your beliefs about money
- Use the 9 Step Process from chapter 5 to begin to clear up stuck emotions around money and create an opening for new experience.
- Experiment with creating your own Affirmative Invocation statements that support confidence and energy around money.

CHAPTER 16

AUTHENTIC SALES AND TRANSPARENT MARKETING

THE PURPOSE OF CHAPTER 16:

The purpose of this chapter is to simplify marketing and give you tips on successfully selling your products, works, and services.

Marketing Is Simple

The best way to market your work is to:

1. Find a need, and find a way to fill it.
2. Get really good at what you do.
3. Tell people about what you do and ask them if they are interested.

Marketing is simply a matter of getting the word out about what you do to the people that need what you have.

If marketing seems overwhelming, make it simple.

- Find the specific group of people that needs what you have.
- Find a way that works for you so this group can:
    - Get acquainted with you.
    - Develop an affinity for you.
    - Build up confidence in you.
    - Then contact you for a solution to their problem.

It really is that simple. It is communication. And it is not rocket science.

The Foundations

- Know your value.
- Know your customer.
- Know your competition.
- Know your results (product).

To know your value, you need to know your sweet spot in the business world.

The Good to Great Hedgehog

In his book *Good to Great*, Jim Collins demonstrates clear characteristics of phenomenally successful businesses.

I have found one principle in particular, The Hedgehog Concept, to be indispensable in my life and for my clients. It's a way to uncover your sweet spot. This guides every step of your business and creative work. This is the directional signal that you use to keep you coming back to your true north goals. This is the principle that will guarantee success if you commit to doing the inner work necessary to discover the truth about yourself and your business. When you are marketing work that is aligned with these principles, then marketing can get traction.

What Is The Hedgehog Concept?

According to Collins, it consists of three elements:
1. Your passion
2. What you can be the best at
3. What is the economic engine

When you are aligned with these three elements, then you are poised to succeed. However, this generally doesn't appear out of thin air. It is something you have to discover through personal and organizational inquiry.

Why Hedgehogs?

Jim Collins describes the business world like a wild ecosystem. Many business methods have suggested that you have to be fast, fierce, and cunning, like a fox or a wolf. Collins asserts that many successful businesses are like the hedgehog. They are not flashy, fast, or ambitious. They have simple strategies for success that they use consistently. When attacked, they roll into a ball. When they are hungry, they scavenge for food. The lesson is that if you find your place in the ecosystem of the business world, you can have a simple, successful strategy as long as you are consistent. The way you find that place is with these three questions:

1. What are you passionate about?
2. What can you (or your business) be the best in the world at?
3. What is your economic engine (what value can you create)?

Hence, the term, "Hedgehog Concept."

Go to www.JimCollins.com and watch his video and listen to the audio on finding your personal Hedgehog Concept. Then buy the book *Good To Great* by Jim Collins and read it. It is an essential part of your business library.

I have been asking myself these questions since 2007, since one of my mentors told me in no uncertain terms that I must read Collins' book. My mentor knows Collins, and knew from firsthand experience in his own businesses and from his relationship that the book was a real gem.

Armed with this knowledge, I have kept track of what sparks my interest, what I love to do, and what I would love to do regardless of the money.

As you can see, this process is directly related to knowing your life purpose and indeed is complementary to and tied up with purpose. It runs parallel to the techniques from Chapter 1.

But it's more.

When you can get really clear on your passion, as well as your ability, and look at it in the context of an economic engine, then you are working with the principles of success. I see these as laws, like gravity. They are impersonal and objective.

Most of the people I know can usually get one or two of the three principles right off the bat.

Joan: "*I know what I am passionate about, helping women get empowered.*"

Allen: "*I know what I am good at, sitting down with people and looking at them eye to eye, making a heart connection.*"

Samantha: "*I know that I can do well financially running my business in a franchise model.*"

The trick however is to get all three lined up.

Why Does It Matter?

A lot of my clients got into their line of work because they are passionate about helping people. They are also passionate about some specific form of helping people. Let's use yoga as an example.

Elizabeth loves yoga. She also loves to help people. Therefore, she quits her job to do full-time yoga teaching and trains to be a Yoga Therapist with an internationally recognized training program. She immediately embraces the training and she is excited about what she finds. Elizabeth is passionate about yoga. So that checks out.

She has a private practice and teaches workshops, which provide her with an economic engine. She lives in a metropolitan area, which provides an abundant client base. So that works.

But Liz is an incredibly introverted person and likes, even needs, to spend abundant time alone. Therefore, working with a lot of clients and facilitating two workshops a month is taxing for her. She begins to compromise her forward momentum by showing up late and exhibiting other disorganized actions.

Liz discovers that she actually could be the best in the world at spending more time alone creating training materials for the teacher training organization, creating a DVD series, and writing a book as well as a blog on the training style that she loves and so enthusiastically embraced.

Over the next year, she maintains a smaller practice and creates a job for herself with the parent organization, creating the training materials. She produces a DVD that she sells to other practitioners and clients, and through her blog, which she loves to update and maintain and is read by a large community. She still does workshops, but twice a year instead of twice a month. She can market more and gather a larger audience. Since this is her passion and her gift, she tends to get a lot of referrals.

She combines her passion for yoga therapy and her passion for writing and creating content into a viable and even more profitable economic engine.

It took more time, and seemed riskier, but in the end, it produced better results.

Another Example of The Hedgehog

Don is a doctor of chiropractic medicine. He is extremely gifted as a clinician, especially with nutrition. He works with functional medicine testing, kinesiology, and metabolic typing. This is his "best in the world" gift.

His economic engine is simple: clients. He sees five patients an hour, with a pretty full schedule, seven hours a day, four days a week. He has about one hundred visits on a typical week. He charges an average of $50 per visit, which means that he brings in about $5,000 a week gross, plus sales of supplements, testing, and other products, an additional $2,500 gross a week. His practice grosses $30,000 a month. His overhead is well managed and he has two employees, an administrative hero and a health counselor to coach people on how to change their diet.

He owns the building. He is passionate about serving his clients and gladly goes above and beyond what is expected to make a difference in their lives.

But it wasn't always this way.

For three years, he was a researcher for a top nutraceutical company. Though he was well compensated, and he loved the theoretical world of functional medicine, his real passion was on the ground, working with people in the day-to-day fight for health. He was passionate about clinical work.

As a researcher, he almost lost his job because he was so morose. He started drifting off, losing concentration.

Fortunately, he went to a weekend professional training event and spent time with other DCs. In a lunch conversation, a colleague said to him, "Why don't you get back to a clinical practice?"

He spent the afternoon considering the pros and cons of shifting his career. It was a financial risk but a heart reward. Today, he can look back and say that it was an obvious choice. But it does not always seem obvious to us in the moment, does it?

Of course, Don made a lot of mistakes in setting up his practice. Don't let me suggest that it was easy. He flirted with bankruptcy and had a handful of terrible employees. That is how he learned to manage the cash flow and hire a rock-star assistant. He learned that he needed a health counselor to help patients create strategies for success and that he could earn more by focusing on the clinical testing and analysis (his passion and strength) while giving patients the support they needed.

Let's take these three questions and get even more specific about how you can meet the marketplace. After you know you have begun to get clear about your hedgehog, you can start to identify niches and specialties in your business. One of the best tools to do that is the value proposition.

Remember The Foundations

1. Know your value.
2. Know your customer.
3. Know your competition.
4. Know your results (product).

Keep working with the hedgehog concept and then begin to use the value proposition process as a tool to bridge that inner value assessment to your customer, your competition, and your results.

The Value Proposition

The value proposition is the DNA of your marketing message. This is the most important step in sharing your invitation as a business. With a good value proposition, you can turn it into:

- Sales Pitch
- Web Content
- Postcards
- E-mails
- Brochures
- Elevator Pitch

This value proposition is used to convey the tangible results that your clients get when they work with you. Let me say that again:

A simple statement that conveys tangible results that clients get from your service (or product if you are moving in that direction).

Check out the subtitle points of *The Discipline of Market Leaders*, by Michael Treacy and Fred Wiersema.

- **Choose Your Customers,**
- **Narrow Your Focus,**
- **Dominate Your Market.**

A value proposition helps you do this. It is really not that tough.

Here is a great template for your value proposition:

1. **For** (clearly defined group of potential clients)
2. **That/Who** (write the need, want or pain that you can solve)
3. **{Your Company Name}** is a (what service do you offer)
4. **That** (write the tangible benefits that your customer will get)
5. **Unlike** (description of weakness of competition)
6. **{Company / Service}** (differentiate yourself from competition, compelling strength, gift, or unique aspect that makes you better)
7. **Because of our** (some explained verification that you can bring, more unique aspects of what you offer)
8. **You will experience** (the results, outcomes, feelings of your client)

Here is an example:

For women ages 45 to 65, who love style and who want to look their best

who are sick of diets that limit instead of liberate,

Nutrition for Style is a health and fitness boutique service

that gives you freedom to enjoy food you love while keeping the body you like.

Unlike a nutritionist who delivers a one size fits all diet plan or a trainer who makes you eat egg whites,

Nutrition for Style delivers customized programs that help you look good without deprivation.

Because of our 5-year experience in fashion, health food, and skin care,

you will have the care, the customization, and the facts that make life a celebration again!

Here is another:

For lawyers in small to mid-size practices, **who** are ready to get organized and handle the overflowing files, **Attorney Pro-File** provides simple software **that** helps you save time, money and space b automating your client processing.

Unlike other organizational software for lawyers, **Attorney Pro-File** delivers simple systems with clear results, which include faster payment cycles, reduced error and enhanced customer service.

Because of our 15 years track record of service in the legal profession, **you will experience** the genuine satisfaction of cutting through the clutter to create concrete results.

And one more:

For endurance athletes in their 20's, 30's, 40's and 50's **who** want a competitive edge and strive to stay injury-free, **Fit-Town Acupuncture** offers health care **that** saves you lost time, delivers you from potential disaster, and speeds your recovery.

Unlike your run-of-the-mill physical therapy and ice pack, **Fit-Town Acupuncture** combines effective ancient and modern treatments that will surprise even the most seasoned competitor.

Because of our training with revered Master X of Taiwan and our 3-year residency at Big Prestigious Hospital, you can feel confident that you are getting the kind of results that meet your rigorous standards.

Writing a value proposition is not something that you do once. It is something that you must do when you feel your business shifting. This may happen a lot in the first three years.

The next step is to take your value proposition and use it as the foundation for your one-page marketing template. This will give you the seeds of content for every piece of marketing that you create. You will get clear and focused in the process while enjoying the passion and inspiration that accompany the clarity! Your one-page marketing template will help you connect your inspiration to the marketplace.

The 25 Minute One Page Marketing Template

A one-page marketing sheet is the next step after the value proposition. This is the structure of your marketing message. Often, people get stuck with writing their one page. So here is the solution.

Instructions:

Set a timer for 25 minutes.

For one minute, state your purpose for doing this, "My purpose for doing this is to create effective marketing, which helps me serve more people, earn more money, and live my dream."

For one minute, read the questions below.

For one minute move your body and speak what is occurring in your mind, " I love this!" "I hate this!" "I don't know how to do this."

For three minutes mind-map everything on your mind.

Then, write for three minutes on each of the following questions:

1. Describe your ideal client's pain, problem, need, or opportunity.
2. Show them how great it could be if they use your service and their problem is solved.
3. Tell them what you do to solve the problem. Keep it simple and cover as many facets as you can in three minutes. Build on your mission.
4. Articulate features and benefits of your service. Use the Value Proposition statement.
5. Tell them why they can trust you; use statistics, endorsements, testimonials, and credentials.
6. Invite the clients to take action on their problem by seeking out your service. Call. Visit. Click. Register. Act now.

Take one minute to review your answers.

Take a break and edit it later in the day or tomorrow. Share it with your coach, buddy, or mastermind group.

Caution: Do not think you need to do this perfectly. The key is just to do it. Get your ideas out. Then, be willing to hear feedback from people you trust. This will engage the co-creative intelligence and will become fun. With less effort, you will have your one-page-marketing plan. This is a work in process and you can update it quarterly.

Don't Waste Time With Marketing

This was one of the best pieces of advice that I received from Joshua Rosenthal, founder of the Institute for Integrative Nutrition. This was the secret to building a successful health coaching practice while I was still a student. I focused on talking to people, not distracting myself with accessories.

There are a lot of ways to waste time in marketing:
- Websites
- Social Media
- Business cards
- Brochures
- Flyers
- Newsletters

Don't get me wrong. I think you can use all of these. But keep your focus on people. That will build your business. More than ever, word of mouth will make or break a business.

How do you connect with people?
You connect with people by speaking.
You connect with people by networking.
You connect with people by calling them.
You connect with people through referrals.
You connect with people through radio and TV interviews.
You connect with people through audio and video media.

You can also connect with people through your e-mail, blog, website and on social networking sites, however, you had better be strategic and authentic to make these work. The most consistent way to reach people with your business message is through public speaking. So how can you speak more?

It Is Really All About People

If you provide a service, the best way to fill you practice is to get in front of someone you know could be interested in your work. Persistently speaking to people about what you do is the key. Calling. Meeting. Talks. Fairs. Booths. However you can get face or voice time. That is the best.

Public Speaking

Without a doubt, one of the the best way to build a business is through public speaking. In fact, it can become the thrust of your business if you love it.

Not everyone loves it, though. Did you know that public speaking ranks close to death as the number one fear of most people? No kidding. As a trained performer, I really love public speaking. I certainly paid my dues in the trial by fire of performing live with my music at age eighteen. The first time I performed, I almost shook myself off the stage I was so nervous and frightened of what people would think of me.

I am a member of Toastmasters. This is the world's largest organization for training leaders and communicators. I highly recommend checking it out. Our dues are only $8 a month. You can get a lot of value from the club for $8 a month. I have mentioned Toastmasters repeatedly throughout the book. This is intentional. It is a great resource.

You, too, can follow this powerful calling. You can educate, inspire, and lead people to take action and make important changes in their lives. By becoming a professional speaker, you can prosper at levels you may have never dreamed were possible in your life.
Dottie and Lily Walters, *Speak and Grow Rich*

Dottie is one of the founding members of the National Speakers Association. The NSA is another excellent resource for aspiring speakers. To join the NSA, you need to complete 20 paid speeches in 12 months and then fill out their application and pay the membership dues.

Speaking To The World

Video is an effective way to harness your speaking and send it out to a broad audience. Instead of blogs and newsletters, more and more people are promoting with video on Youtube and Vimeo.

However, with anything web and tech related, whatever I write about now, could easily be outdated. Therefore, focus on developing offline speaking gigs to hone your skills and if you are interested and passionate about recording video for the web, then jump in and study successful systems.

How Do I Develop Speaking Opportunities?

The key to speaking more is speaking more.

You have to get out and start speaking anywhere you can. Then, ask the people at your talks if they know other venues that would benefit from hearing you speak.

You can ask friends, colleagues, and even family.

One starting point for speakers is through NACA and APCA (the National Association for Campus Activities and the Association for the Promotion of Campus Activities). You have to be willing to pay and audition, but this opens the door to more experience. You can do it!

The Great Secret to a Speaking Career

Most speakers start their career by speaking to small groups. Civic clubs are an excellent resource and where many of the great speakers cut their teeth. Clubs include:

- Lions Clubs
- Rotary Clubs
- Kiwanis Clubs
- Jaycees Clubs
- Optimists Clubs

You can also approach:

- Chamber of Commerce
- YMCAs
- City Recreation Centers
- Support Groups
- MeetUp Groups
- Mom Groups
- Church Groups

Do you know the difference between the people who have excelled as speakers and those who remain dormant?

It is not talent.
It is not interest.
It is not even knowledge.
It is booking speaking engagements!

So if you are serious about speaking, get out there and start scheduling talks on a regular basis. That is the key.

If you are like me and everyone else I have interviewed, you will do a lot of talks to three people. You will probably feel like giving up. You will flop. You might even look like a fool.

Come back to the inner and outer game practices. They are called practices because, just like speaking, you have to practice the tools for developing yourself.

Don't overcomplicate this. If you want to develop a career built on public speaking, it is not hard. Get on the phone and ask people at clubs and venues what they need to have you show up as a speaker.

Here is a three-step process to get you out speaking more:

1. Join Toastmasters (public speaking and leadership clubs) and then ask if you can come and speak as a guest at other clubs within an hour's drive. Many Toastmasters clubs are eager for more speakers and you can pretty much count on having a spot.

To find other clubs, just get on Toastmasters.org and click "FIND a club near you", enter your zip code, and search in a 50-mile radius.

2. Call or e-mail civic clubs.

These venues are always looking for you, because they NEED speakers as part of their program. This is the launch ramp for most successful speakers and a great place to promote your business.

3. Know how to get your foot in the door.

Here is my secret sauce for getting booked. Be stupid! Don't try to act like you know what you are doing. You don't! Ask questions instead. Here is what you can do:

Phone Script for Booking Talks at Clubs:

Seth: "Hi, who do I talk to about speaking at your club/school/business?"
Mr. Civic Person: "That would be Janet H., here is her #."
Seth: "Thanks, what is your name?"
Mr. Person: "Don W."
Seth: "Thanks Don."

Next call:

Seth: "Hi, is this Janet?"

Civic Janet: "Yes it is, who is calling?"

Seth: "I just talked to Don W. about speaking at your club, my name is Seth Braun."

-wait - don't talk -

Civic Janet: "Yes, what do you want to speak about?"

Seth: "Well, I guess I would like to know what you need from me to book me as a speaker."

Then she tells you what you need, and you provide it.

If you follow these steps, you can gain valuable experience as well as contacts for paid speaking.

Do not underestimate the value of this advice. This could earn you tens of thousands of dollars in business and if you'd like, speaking fees, when you actually take this take this to heart and act on it for one whole year.

I dare you to join me in using this simple formula to book 12 or more speeches this year (at least one a month) at a venue to promote your business.

More Scripts for Success in Sales

In any sales situation, you want to have practiced a script for closing the deal. There are many scripts that you can purchase specific to your industry. Here is an example of a script that I worked out with a client for enrolling people into a retreat.

Owner: Hey John, when is a good time to talk about the retreat I mentioned to you?

Prospect: Right now is good. I've got some time.

Owner: Well, we are doing this program, (name or program) and I want you to be a part of it. What do you think? Is this something that you want to know more about?

Prospect Response Scenarios:

The Prospects Response:

Favorable

1. Yes, definitely, sign me up.
2. Sure, when is it?
3. I'm intrigued, but I don't really know anything about it.

Resistant

1. Sounds like pulling out my own fingernails, no, not interested.
2. Maybe, but I am pretty busy and don't have any money.
3. I don't know anything about it (apprehensive).

Your response

Favorable

1. Great, I'm excited that you are on board. This is a dream of mine and having you there helps me live my dreams and I know you will get a lot out of it. You can write your check out to _____.
2. Great, the retreat is _____ and is $_____ . It is about X, Y, & Z and as I said, I want you to be there, and frankly, it would really help me out for you to come. Since we are just beginning, I need people I trust to show up and step up. What can I do to help make this work for you?
3. Great, the program is X,Y, & Z and will be on the ___. It costs $ ___ . It is about connecting and living authentically. And as I said, I want you to be there, and frankly, it would really help me out for you to come. Since we are just beginning, I need people I trust to show up and step up. What can I do to help make this work for you?

Resistant

1. OK great, well thanks for checking in with me about it. *"I don't want to talk to you no more, you empty headed animal food trough wiper. I fart in your general direction. Your mother was a hamster and your father smelt of elderberries. Come back again and I will taunt you a second time."* (Excerpted from Monty Python's **Search For The Holy Grail**)
2. OK, you are busy and don't have any money. Does that mean you are not interested? Because if you are not interested, I don't want to try

to convince you. But if you are interested, do you think it could be helpful to create a venue where you can figure out how to have more time and money for what is important? Great, the program is X,Y, & Z and will be on the ___. It costs $ ___ . It is about connecting and living authentically. And as I said, I want you to be there, and frankly, it would really help me out for you to come. Since we are just beginning, I need people I trust to show up and step up. What can I do to help make this work for you?

3. Great, the program is X,Y & Z and will be on the ___. It costs $ ___ . It is about connecting and living authentically. And as I said, I want you to be there, and frankly, it would really help me out for you to come. Since we are just beginning, I need people I trust to show up and step up. What can I do to help make this work for you?

Role-playing your sales scenarios is essential business training for your sales team. It is worth the time up front for better results at the close. And no, I don't really think you should insult your potential clients but if you remember this the next time you are talking to a resistant individual, you will probably chuckle to yourself. You might even make rejection funny and that is priceless.

The Consultative Sell

You know what my friends tell me they never want to experience again? The sales strategy of trying to use some advanced tactics to "persuade, convince or close," a prospect. There was a time when sales books taught all sorts of advanced mental tricks to get a sale from a client. But do you like being "sold."

What seems to be more functional for both you and the potential client is the path of consultative selling. You can both enjoy the process more when you know that you want the best for the prospect. You don't want to sell her anything that she doesn't need and you are there to help her solve a problem.

From this perspective, you are simply building great relationships helping people that either needs your services or not. From this place, if you think the prospect needs you services, then you can be as persuasive as possible knowing that you are 100% coming from a place of service.

Sales in this way can be fun and functional.

Indestructible Success Inside Marketing Tip

The strategies that marketing gurus sell in workshops or books on marketing are often only effective when selling books or workshops on marketing.

People are willing to spend a lot more money if they think that the information is going to get them more money. These techniques don't always work for other markets. Therefore, before you spend $5,000 on a marketing course, make sure that it is relevant to your business and that a track record with your profession is established.

Successfully Using the Web

A colleague of mine focuses on social marketing, podcasts, e-mail blasts, and e-mail capture systems on a content-rich website. She uses affiliate e-mail product launch strategies, and when all these are combined, she is successful at increasing her coaching business.

Her seminars and live events are filled by her diligent work online, as well as by referrals. Her system in online work drives people to offline events and teleclasses as her economic engine. Of course, she is amazing at what she does.

Have a website to support your offline marketing. Make a place to send people or to refer friends. It is a great place to keep up information for groups, businesses, organizations, and individuals.

If you are going to dive into a web-based business, find a mentor who has done it successfully.

Examples of Newsletters and Websites That Work

Pure Nourishment

Angelina DeWeese, a St. Louis-based health coach, has used the combination of offline and online marketing as well as anyone I have seen. She does events, collects contact information, and keeps in touch with value-added content in her newsletter. She then makes offers to her contacts via the newsletter. Angelina has begun to use video segments to feed her fans fun and useful tips. As a result, she has a thriving practice.

Her clarity about her target market (busy, stressed out professional women) her personal hedgehog, and her courage are prerequisite to her success.

Her newsletter is professional looking and features great copywriting with value and a call to action.

Her website is defined and attractive to her target market. www.PureNourishment.com

Baltimore Health Coach

Lucas Seipp-Williams has done what many people talk about. He has successfully implemented an online program that delivers health training without his presence.

He has found a way to stop trading hours for dollars, which is the great potential with the web. He took the time, money, and energy, and invested in video production, website construction, and newsletter development.

As a result of Luke's tenacity and commitment, he has a powerful, effective program that reaches much larger groups of people. Luke collaborates with his partner Richelle to produce events for women while Luke focuses on coaching men. Luke and I partner on delivering a men's coaching program called The Men's Mastery Course. Luke taught me a lot about collaborating, and I feature a story about him in Chapter 11.

To sign up for his newsletter, check out his site, BaltimoreHealthCoach.com.

What About Branding?

This is really fun and pretty essential. Eventually, you need to have a logo, a font, and an overall sense of what you are projecting professionally. Put some intention behind it. Be deliberate.

This too, can be overly complicated. It does not need to be. Usually, you just need:

A logo
A type of font to use consistently
A tag line

Here are some of the logos I use for business projects:

The P3E Project. This is what I first called the Indestructible Success training.

My first coaching business in 2004, Dream Seeker Consulting, which I still use sometimes. I love it actually.

And for a non-profit I started at the same time, The Warrior Artist Project.

Then my first health and nutrition business logo, Real Simple Nutrition.

Then came the versions of High Energy Health, my upgraded business name and logo.

HighEnergyHealth

The book cover for Healthy, Fast and Cheap.

Then there is the Aspen Protocols logo we had for an online presence, with our supplement protocol, online store, video, and content-rich pages.

What Is in a Name?

Naming your venture is a key step in marketing. I have relied on my gut and my feel for what is right. Of course, I have tried sophisticated techniques, but my gut is usually what I go with.

I like the idea of three-word names, which most of my businesses align with. Here are some examples:

Healthy, Fast and Cheap

High Energy Health

Real Simple Nutrition

Aspen Surgery Protocols

Warrior Artist Project

Dream Seeker Consulting

The three-word approach follows this formula:

One word is an adjective = *High*

Another word receives the adjective, but it's also a descriptor that holds the central word = *Energy*

And there is the central root word = *Health*

Adjective = *Real*

Adjective + Receive + Hold = *Simple*

Root = *Nutrition*

Aspen Surgery Protocols was fun to come up with. We used the same idea, but turned it around. If I followed the formula it would be Aspen Protocols Surgery. But that does not make sense.

Aspen here is used to conjure up an image, a feeling, and an aesthetic. It is used as an adjective. Surgery takes the energy of Aspen, but Protocols defines it. Although it's a little different, we used the same thinking.

I like this formula. It is something to play with. Your name is important, so take the time analyze the response as you try new things.

Keep Coming Back to Basics

The fundamentals of marketing are:

- Be really good at what you do. Refine your skills so your services refer themselves through your clients.
- Tell people about what you do. The more you can do this directly, the better!
- Be consistent with your brand, words, font, and logo.
- Public speaking is the best way to build your practice. Build systems to support speaking.

Public speaking not only builds your pipeline, but also delivers the client to you in an open and receptive state. They know you. They see you as trustworthy. They see you as an expert. This is so much more effective than trying to convince someone of your great service.

The Triple Threat of Business

Keep coming back to the *Good to Great* Hedgehog Concept. Jim Collins clearly details how being the best at what you do + having a passion for what you are up to + having a clear economic engine = long-term financial success for a large business.

In the recent books by Seth Godin and Malcolm Gladwell, these authors hammer home the significance of being exceptional. You are exceptional when you do what you are uniquely qualified to do and what you are passionate about.

Remember the "What do I know for sure?" question from Chapter 1? Use that same mind in marketing. Stay in your power zone. Don't be pulled into good ideas for the sake of good ideas. Play to your strengths.

Stick with your skill, talent, passion, and economic engine.

For me, it is public speaking, writing, and working with groups. I love these. I am good at them, and there is a good economic engine there for me. This is my personal hedgehog concept.

What Resources Do I Have?

Appendix B is full of books and people from whom you can learn more about marketing.

The Best Quick & Effective Action You Can Take

A couple of times a year, get yourself some flip chart pages and put them up on the wall. This is a variation on the work we did to take your vision into a plan, but specifically for marketing.

Get some Sharpie permanent markers in assorted colors.

1. Draw a line across the middle of three flip chart sheets both horizontally and vertically. This will result in four boxes in each of the three flip charts.
2. Write each month of the year in one of the squares until you have each of the twelve squares labeled, in sequential order.
3. Now, decide what seasonal and yearly goals you have, and then work back to market them.
4. For me, I have seminars, so I write down the seminar date and work my way back three to six months in terms of marketing.
   a. When do I need to call the warm leads?
   b. When do I need to send the first, second, and third e-mail blasts?
   c. Social marketing notification?
   d. Video?
5. Then, after you have sketched out the major flow of the year, including the seasonal concepts of "back to school," "new year, new you," etc., you can fill in the major blocks of your month.
   a. When do you want to do talks?
   b. Is there a consistent time and venue for talks to schedule monthly?
   c. What marketing and/or events are regularly occurring, or could be regularly occurring as a consistent buzz builder?
6. I sketch this out by either dividing the monthly square into four parts again or by dividing the box with horizontal lines approximating each week of a month.

After I have fleshed out the year pretty well, I take out another couple of flip chart pages and I really dissect the month, week, and day.

I take the time to draw up the ideal monthly flow, weekly flow, and daily flow.

For example, a weekly flow could look something like this:

Monday:	Client Time
Tuesday:	Bookkeeping and Toastmasters Mtg.
Wednesday:	Immersion Clients or Writing Time
Thursday:	Client times, Teleclass in the Evening
Friday:	Writing or Preparing for Talks, Workshops, and Seminars
Saturday:	Family and Home Time, Occasional Events
Sunday:	Sabbath Time, Occasional Seminar or Workshop

I get very specific in my planning. I write down each day by the hour for my week during visioning and planning phases.

As you might have guessed, this is just a variation of the Dreams > Vision > Goals > Plans > Action sequence.

By the way, can you do your marketing program right alongside the overall vision and planning session with your business and personal life? Of course! It works better that way. I love to have my self-care, marketing, family, and each key aspect of my life represented in a yearly, monthly, weekly, and daily vision.

You can do this a few times a year and focus on making one time a mini-retreat just to get yourself lined up for success.

Review on Marketing

Marketing is simple. You are telling people that need what you do about what it is that you are doing.

Don't waste time.

To build a business online, content is king. Today, the way to get clients from your site is to give a way a ton of free stuff. Help people to trust you and then ask if they want what you are offering.

It is always about serving and contributing to people. So stay in contact with people in any way you can. Network, social clubs, etc.

Brand yourself with font, logo, biz name, and tagline. That is the foundation. It grows from there.

Keep studying the resources. Devote time regularly to improving your ability to communicate your message as an act of service.

Use a system of yearly, monthly, and weekly strategies to guide you.

RECAP OF CHAPTER 16:

- Be really good at what you do. Refine your skills so your services refer themselves through your clients.
- Tell people about what you do. The more you can do this directly, the better!
- Do the Value Proposition exercise. Don't just read it.
- Be consistent with your brand. Words. Font. Logo.
- Public speaking is the best way to build your practice.
- Build systems to support speaking.
- Vision and plan yearly, monthly, and weekly.

SELF-STUDY EXERCISES:

- Play with defining your "hedgehog concept."
- Write out your Value Proposition
- Take half an hour to write out your one-page marketing plan.
- Try role-playing key sales conversations with a partner.
- Stop trying to sell, and start being a valuable consultant to your clients.
- Have fun and keep it real

EPILOGUE: CREATIVITY AND LEADERSHIP

During the final week of editing, *Time*, *Bloomberg Businessweek*, and *The Economist* all arrived with a picture of Steve Jobs on the cover.

So I scrapped the conclusion I had written and decided to focus on what we can learn from Jobs life. Jobs wove together creativity, leadership, success, and going for his dreams and made the world a richer place as a result.

On creativity and innovation:

Jobs had over 300 patents in his name.
"I connect the dots." He discovered what was there and made it better.
He thought of himself as an artist and his design sense permeated everything.

On leadership:

Referred to as "the most celebrated business executive in the world."
He could get people to do things that they wouldn't normally do.
"Great companies have a noble cause. Then it is the leader's job to transform that noble cause into such an inspiring vision that it will attract the most talented people in the world to join it."
He was a detail-oriented perfectionist and a big picture visionary.
He has been called the greatest executive of our time.

On living your dreams:

"The only way to be satisfied is to do what you believe is great work."
"Remembering that you are going to die is the best way I know to avoid the trap of thinking that you have something to lose. You are already naked. There is no reason not to follow your heart."

On failure:

He dropped out of college.
He was fired from the company he created.
He started a business, NeXT, that never turned a profit.
He made many mistakes and learned from them.

On success:

He revolutionized six industries: digital publishing, music, tablets, phones, personal computers and animated movies.

Apple recently took the spot for most valuable company in the world.

"We do these not because we are control freaks. We do them because we want to make great products, because we care about the user and we want to take responsibility for the entire experience rather than turn out the crap that other people make."

On meditation and mind:

"That's been one of my mantras: focus and simplicity"

"It comes from saying no to 1,000 things to make sure we don't get on the wrong track or try to do too much."

"I believe life is an intelligent thing, that things aren't random"

Jobs was a student of Zen Buddhism and Kobun Chino Roshi.

Warrior Artist

Kobun Roshi came to Naropa University to preside as the World Wisdom Chair in 2001 and 2002. Roshi and I attended committee meetings together at Naropa. I attended lectures and sitting mediations with Kobun Roshi.

So in closing this book, I wonder about the role that meditation played in Jobs life. I imagine that it was central in some way. I am appreciating the way that he fused creativity and commerce together so magically. I'm appreciating that he identified as both artist and executive, that he embraced paradox. And I am appreciating the tiny thread that connects us on the warrior artists' path.

We are moving into a time when daily life requires that we train our minds. The next greatest version of our lives necessitates holding multiple perspectives, cultivating agility in our interior emotional and mental landscapes setting a new standard for inner and outer skillfulness.

Serve

I wrote this book to help you better serve the world, to help you connect to the Dream God has given you and to help you take that dream and share it. This is part of my dream. I have been nourished in the writing of this book and I sincerely hope that some part of Indestructible Success nourishes you too.

Yours in service,

Seth Dream Seeker Waxing Moon Braun

Learn to use the body for the purpose of service so long as it exists, so much so that service, and not bread, becomes with us the staff of life.
Mahatma Gandhi

The Four Pillars of Indestructible Success:

- ACTION: Take Action and Get Results with The Work Your Plan Process™
- VISION: Know Where You Are Going with the Dreams > Vision > Goals > Plans > Action Process™
- COURAGE: Turn Fear Into Fuel with the 9 Steps from Upsets into Opportunities Process
- CONFIDENCE: Create Unshakable Confidence with the 3 Part Affirmative Invocation Practice

The foundation is Love.
Love is the energy propelling us to give our gifts.
It will give you the enthusiasm for life that is infectious.

I am grateful for the opportunity to write this book.

Thank you for reading it.

REFERENCES

Introduction

Pink, D. (2005). *A Whole New Mind: Moving From The information Age to the Conceptual Age.* Riverhead Hardcover.

Agency, definition. (1968). The Random House Dictionary of the English Language, College Edition, Random House.

CHAPTER 1

Landis, J. *The Blues Brothers* (1980) Film.

Proverbs, 29:18, *King James Bible*

Campbell, J. (2008) *The Hero With A Thousand Faces,* New World Library.

Beckwith, M. B. (2008). *Life Visioning (Audio Program)* Sounds True.

Bolles, R. N. (2009). *What Color Is Your Parachute?* Ten Speed Press.

Braun, S. (2006). *Healthy, Fast and Cheap: The Ultimate College Cookbook.* Rockpool Productions.

Braun S. & Mindell R. (April, 2003). *Dreams of a Warrior Artist.* Naropa University Performing Arts Center Theatrical Production.

Shabalala J. (March 2003). "All Things Considered." Interview with Lynn Neering. National Public Radio.

Solomon. Proverbs 29:18. *New Marked Reference Bible.*

Winfrey, O. "What I Know For Sure." *The Oprah Magazine.*

Cameron, J. (2002). *The Artist's Way.* J.P Tarcher/Putnam.

CHAPTER 2

Allen, D. (2003). *Getting Things Done: The Art of Stress-free Productivity.* Diane Pub. Co.

Collins, J. (2001). *Good to Great.* HarperBusiness.

Covey, S. R. (2005). *The 7 Habits of Highly Effective People.* Simon & Schuster.

Marc, D. (1999). *Nourishing Wisdom.* Random House.

Douillard, J (2001). *The Three Season Diet: Body, Mind and Sport.* Three Rivers Press.

Gangé, S. (2008). *Food Energetics: The Spiritual, Emotional and Nutritional Power of What We Eat.* Inner Traditions.

Hurricane Island Outward Bound School (Fall, 1997). *Semester Wilderness Leadership Training.*

Schuller, R. (1982). Sermon at Crystal Cathedral. *Hour of Power Video Recording.* How to Put A Wow in Your Tomorrow.

CHAPTER 3

Aurelius, M. *Meditations. Internet Classics Archive* http://classics.mit.edu/Antoninus/meditations.html.

Pressfield, S. (2003). *The War of Art,* Warner Books

Maurer, R. (2004). *One Small Step Can Change Your Life.* Workman.

Lao-Tzu, L. (1972). *Tao Te Ching* (Witter Bynner Version), Lyrebird Press Ltd.

Stravinsky, I. (1936). *Igor Stravnisky An Autobiography.* Simon and Schuster

CHAPTER 4

Foundation for Inner Peace (1996). *A Course in Miracles,* Penguin Books.

Allen, D. (2003). *Getting Things Done: The Art of Stress-free Productivity.* Diane Pub. Co.

Braun S. Nutrition for Integral Life Practice, PDF download at http://sethbraun.com/blog/integral-nutrition-pdf/

Bronson, P. (2005). *What Should I Do With My Life?* Ballantine Books.

Cameron, J. (2002). *The Artist's Way.* J.P. Tarcher/Putnam.

Cameron, J. (1996). *The Vein of Gold: A Journey to Your Creative Heart.* Putnam.

Cameron, J. (2003). *Walking In This World: The Practical Art of Creativity.* J.P. Tarcher/Putnam

Chek, P. (2004). *How to Eat, Move and Be Healthy!* C.H.E.K. Institute, LLC.

Douillard J. (2001). *Body, Mind and Sport.* Three Rivers Press.

Godin, S. (1999). *Permission Marketing.* Simon & Schuster.

Godin, S. (2009). *Purple Cow: Transform Your Business by Being Remarkable.* Portfolio.

Godin, S. (2008). *Tribes: We Need You to Lead Us.* Portfolio

Lam, H. (2008). 3 Body Workout. *Integral Life Practice.* Integral Institute.

Mandino O. (2005). *The Greatest Salesman in the World.* Frederick Fell Publications, Inc.

Sohnen-Moe C. (1991). *Business Mastery.* Sohnen-Moe Associates.

Toastmasters International. *Competent Communicator Series.* Toastmasters International.

Wiley, T.S., Bent, P.H & Fomby D. (2002). *Lights Out: sleep, sugar and survival.* Simon & Schuster.

Cirillo, Francesco, The Pomodoro Technique, *http://www. pomodorotechnique.com/*

Ziglar, Z. *Secrets of Closing the Sale.* Audio Program.

CHAPTER 5

Jeffers, S. (1988). *Feel The Fear and Do It Anyways.* Ballantine Books

Lucas, G., *Star Wars* (1977). Film.

Daly, T. (2005-2010). *4 Gateways Training.* Live Events. Boulder, Colorado.

Ferguson, B. *Mastery of Life.* Audio Program.

Ferguson, R. (2008). LCA Project. *Live Seminar/Evening Meetings.* Littleton, Colorado.

Ford, D. (October, 2006). *Live Lecture.* Institute for Integrative Nutrition. New York City, New York

CHAPTER 6

Allen, J. (2009). *As A Man Thinketh*. Empitude Books, USA.

Anderson, U.S. (2008). *Three Magic Words*. www.Bnpublishing.com.

Aurelius, M. (1983). *The Meditations* (Book Two, Part One). Hackett Publishing Company, Inc., USA.

Foundation for Inner Peace (1996). *A Course in Miracles*. Penguin Books.

Mandino, O. (2005). *The Greatest Salesman in the World*. Frederick Fell Publishers, Inc.

Santana, C. (February 2003). *Performing Songwriter Magazine*.

Smiles, S. (1859). *Self Help*. Open Copyright. Ticknor and Fields, Boston.

St. Matthew. *The Bible* (16:21). King James Version.

Wilber, K. (2007). *A Theory of Everything*. Shambhala Publications, Inc., Massachusetts.

CHAPTER 7

Foundation for Inner Peace (1996). *A Course in Miracles*. Penguin Books. (Lesson 21)

Dass R. (1971). *Be Here Now, Remember*. Crown Publishing Group.

Attenborough, R., *Gandhi* (1982). Film.

Hawkins D. *Power vs. Force, Eye of The I, I: Reality and Subjectivity, Truth vs. Falsehood: How to Tell the Difference, Transcending the Levels of Consciousness, Discovery of the Presence of God, Spirituality, Reality and Modern Man*. Veritas Publishing.

Schroeder, A. (2008). *The Snowball: Warren Buffet and the Business of Life*. Bantam Books.

St. Luke. *The Bible*. The Gospel of St. Luke 17:33

St. Matthew. *New Marked Reference Bible*. Zondervan

Washington, J. M. (ed.) (1986). *A Testament of Hope: The Essential Writings of Rev. Dr. Martin Luther King Jr*. Harper and Row.

CHAPTER 8

Blake, W. (1909-14). "Auguries of Innocence." *English Poetry II: From Collins to Fitzgerald*. The Harvard Classics.

Carlos Santana: What's So Funny about Peace, Love & Understanding? (February, 2003). Interview.

Collins, J. (2001). *Good to Great*. HarperBusiness.

Frankl, V. (1997). *Man's Search for Meaning*. Pocket Paperback. Updated Version.

Fuhs, C. (2008). *Presentation of Integral Framework to Practitioners at Mandala Integrative Medicine Clinic, Boulder, Colorado*.

Hawkins D. *Spirituality, Reality and Modern Man*. Veritas Publishing.

Kennedy R. F. *Quote from Readings*. Hurricane Island Outward Bound School.

King M.L. Jr. (1963). *Strength to Love*. Collins

Lemish J. (1961, Ed.). *The Autobiography and Other Writings*. New American Library

Plato. The Apology of Socrates. The *Internet Classics Archive*. http://classics.mit.edu/Plato/apology.html

Santana, C. (January/February 2003). *Performing Songwriter Magazine*. Bill DeMain Issue 67.

Santana, C. (March-May, 2005). *What Is Enlightenment Magazine*. "The Uncompromising Spiritual Passion and Positivity of Carlos Santana." An interview with Carlos Santana by Craig Hamilton and Jessica Roemischer.

Thoreau H. D. Quote from *Readings*. The Hurricane Island Outward Bound School.

Tutu, D. Live Lecture. University of Colorado.

Von Franz M. (1981). *Puer Aeternus*. Sigo Press.

Wilber K., Patten T., Leonard A.& Morelli, M. (2008). *Integral Life Practice*. Integral Books.

Ziglar Z. Secrets of Closing the Sale. *Audio Program*.

CHAPTER 9

Arrien A. (1993). *The Four-Fold Way.* Harper SanFrancisco.

Daly, T. (2007). *4 Gateways Coaching: Evoking Soul Wisdom (9ᵗʰ edition).* Living Arts Press.

Dwoskin, H. (2005). *The Sedona Method: how to get rid of your emotional baggage and live the life you want.* Element.

Ferguson, B. *Mastery of Life Audio Program*, Self-Published.

Gilligan, S. G. (1997). *The Courage to Love.* W.W. Norton.

Hawkins, D.R. (2006). *Transcending the Levels of Consciousness.* Veritas Publishing.

Moore, R. & Gillette, D. (1990). *King, Warrior, Magician, Lover.* Harper SanFrancisco.

Myss, C. (2003). *Sacred Contracts: Awakening Your Divine Potential.* Three Rivers Press.

Pearson, C. (1989). *The Hero Within: Six Archetypes We Live By.* Harper and Row.

Robbins T., Madanes, C. (2004). *Negotiating Conflict: Leadership In Times of Crisis.* (DVD) Inner Strength Series, Robbins Madanes Center for Strategic Intervention

Robbins T. (October, 2008). Unleash The Power Within. *Live Event.*

Warner, J. (2002). *Aspirations for Greatness.* Wiley.

CHAPTER 10

Cameron, J. (2002). *The Artist's Way.* J.P. Tarcher/Putnam.

Covey, S. *Audio Program.* First Things First.

Epictetus. The Discourses. *The Internet Classics Archive.* http://classics.mit.edu/Epictetus/discourses.html.

Golden Speakers Toastmasters. Club # 7515. 1st Presidential Distinguished Club Program in the State of Iowa, 2005, 2006, 2007, 2008, 2009, 2010, 2011.

History Channel (2009). *Secrets of Body Language.* A&E Home Video.

Hurricane Island Outward Bound School (Fall, 1997). *Semester Wilderness Leadership Training Program.*

Molloy, J.T. (1978). *Dress for Success.* Warner Books.

Ortell, P. (2001-2003).*Classroom Teaching.* Naropa University.

Rosenthal, J. (2005-2006). *Live Lecture.* Institute for Integrative Nutrition.

Trungpa, C.T. & Lief J.L. (1996). *Dharma Art.* Shambhala

Lao-Tzu, L. (2009). *Tao Te Ching.* Witter Bynner Translation. BiblioBazaar

Wenger, W. (2003) *Brain Boosters. Audio Program.* Nightingale-Conant

Worley L. (2002). *Classroom Teaching.* Naropa University.

CHAPTER 11

Naughton, J. (2009) *Face Facts: where Britannica ruled, Wikipedia conquered,* http://www.guardian.co.uk/media/2009/apr/05/digital-media-referenceandlanguages

Kirkpatrick, D. (September 26th, 2011). *Forbes.* "Social Power and The Coming Corporate Revolution" Volume 188 Number 5.

Tapscott, D. & Williams, A. (2006). *Wikinomics.* Portfolio Hardcover

Tapscott, D. & Williams, A. (2010). *MacroWikinomics.* Portfolio Hardcover

Szollose, B. (2010). *Liquid Leadership,* Advanced Reader's Copy

Semlar, R. (1995). *Maverick: The Success Story Behind the World's Most Unusual Workplace.* Grand Central Publishing

Drucker, P. (1959). *Landmarks of Tomorrow.* Harper and Brothers.

Sivers, D. (2011). *Anything You Want.* The Domino Project.

Covey, S. (2010). Live Lecture, Fairfield, Iowa.

Adizes, I. (1992). *Mastering Change.* The Adizes Institute.

LaChapelle, N. *The Structure of Concern: A Challenge for Thinkers.* Lulu.com.

LaChapelle, N. *Adizes Methodology (PAEI)* http://paei.wikidot.com/adizes-methodology

Ackerman, J. (2010). Comments on the Manuscript. *Indestructible Success.*

Findhorn Foundation Members (1999-2005). *Personal Communications.*

Williams, L. S. (September, 2009). *Conversation.* http://monkeybusinessretreats.com/.

CHAPTER 12

Brown, L. (2005). *Increasing Your Presentation Power.* (Vols I & II). Les Brown Enterprises, Inc.

Buren, E. (2005). *Workshop on Masculine Energy.* Boulder, Colorado.

Childs, J. (2004). *America's Favorite Chef.* WGBH Boston PBS.

Collins, J. (2001). *Good to Great.* HarperBusiness.

Coaching Session (2009). *Men's Mastery Course.*

Covey S., Merill, R.A. & Merill R.R. (2001). *First Things First.* Covey.

Gladwell, M. (2008). *Outliers.* Little, Brown and Company

Entrup, L. (2009). *Conversation between author and Luke Entrup.*

Lawrence, T. M. Quote from *Readings from the Hurricane Island Outward Bound School,* Hurricane Island Outward Bound School.

Peale, N. V. (2003). *The Power of Positive Thinking.* Simon & Schuster.

St. John, R. (2005). *Secrets of success in 8 words, 3 minutes* Richard St. John's TED presentation, http://www.ted.com/talks/lang/eng/richard_st_john_s_8_secrets_of_success.html.

St. Matthew (adapted and paraphrased from the Gospel of St. Matthew 6:25-34). *The Holy Bible.*

Starkey R. & Harrison G. (1971). *It Don't Come Easy.* Apple Records.

Fairmont, K., *Taoist Farmer Story,* as told at 2004 Art of Leadership Training, Eldora, Colorado.

Will Smith Interview with Jonathan Ross. *Friday Night with Jonathan Ross*. Unknown Date. *YouTube Video from TheMindGuru*. http://www.youtube.com/watch?v=OLN2k0b3g70.

Will Smith Interview with Harry Smith, *The Early Show*. CBS. Unknown Date. *YouTube Video from TheMindGuru*.   http://www.youtube.com/watch?v=OLN2k0b3g70.

Will Smith Interview with Charlie Rose, *The Charlie Rose Show*. Unknown Date. *YouTube Video from TheMindGuru*. http://www.youtube.com/watch?v=OLN2k0b3g70.

Zimmerman M. (September, 2008). "Live It Like Beckham." *Men's Health*.

CHAPTER 13

Allen, D. (2003). *Getting Things Done: The Art of Stress-free Productivity*. Diane Pub. Co.

Cameron, J. (2002). *The Artist's Way*. J.P. Tarcher/Putnam.

Ferris, T. *4-Hour Workweek*, www.fourhourworkweek.com

Getting_E-mail_Under_Control, https://secure.davidco.com/store/catalog/GETTING-E-MAIL-UNDER-CONTROL--p-16377.php.

34 Interesting Facebook Statistics And Facts, http://www.penn-olson.com/2009/12/02/25-interesting-facebook-statistics-and-facts/

Gladwell, M. (2007). *Blink: the power of thinking without thinking*. Back Bay Books.

Marley, B. (1980). Redemption Song. *Uprising Album*. Island/Tuff Gong Records.

Mipham, J. (2003), *Turning the Mind Into An Ally*. Riverhead Hardcover

CHAPTER 14

Baer, G. (2004). *Real Love*. Penguin Group (USA), Inc.

Ferguson, R. (2005). *Outrageously Fulfilling Relationships*. Heart Centered Communications, Inc.

King, M.L. Jr. Quote from *Readings*. The Hurricane Island Outward Bound School

St. Luke, *The Holy Bible, Luke 6:28.* King James Edition.

Plato. *The Apology of Socrates.* The Internet Classics Archive. http://classics.mit.edu/Plato/apology.html.

CHAPTER 15

Conscious Bookkeeping. *Private Coaching Sessions with Joetta Johnson.*

Price, J. R. (2005). *The Abundance Book.* Hay House.

CHAPTER 16

Treacy, M. & Wiersema, F. (1994) *The Discipline of Market Leaders,* Addison-Wesley

Collins, J. (2001). *Good to Great.* HarperBusiness.

Constant Contact. http://www.constantcontact.com/index.jsp

Dr. Mercola website, http://www.mercola.com/

InfusionSoft. http://www.infusionsoft.com/

SBI. http://www.sitesell.com/

Walters, D. & Walters, L. (2002). *Speak and Grow Rich.* Prentice Hall Press.

Collins, J. (2001). *Good to Great.* HarperBusiness.

Gladwell, M. (2002) *The Tipping Point.* Back Bay Books.

Gladwell, M. (2007). *Blink: the power of thinking without thinking.* Back Bay Books

Gladwell, M. (2008). *Outliers.* Little, Brown and Company.

Godin, S. (1999). *Permission Marketing.* Simon & Schuster.

Godin, S. (2009). *Purple Cow: Transform Your Business by Being Remarkable.* Portfolio.

Godin, S. (2008). *Tribes: We Need You to Lead Us.* Portfolio.

Gandhi, M.K. (1995). *From Yeravda Mandir: Ashram Observances.* Bombay.

EPILOGUE: CONCLUSION

Alley, J. (October 10th, 2011). *Bloomberg Businessweek: Steve Jobs Special Issue* "The Beginning" Issue # 4249.

Burrows, P. (October 10th, 2011). *Bloomberg Businessweek: Steve Jobs Special Issue.* "The Wilderness" Issue # 4249.

Stone, B. (October 10th, 2011). *Bloomberg Businessweek: Steve Jobs Special Issue.* "The Return" Issue # 4249.

Wisley, S. (October 10th, 2011). *Bloomberg Businessweek: Steve Jobs Special Issue.* "The Products" Issue # 4249.

Leaders. (October 8th, 2011). *The Economist.* "The Magician" Volume 401 Number 8754.

London and San Francisco. (October 8th, 2011). *The Economist.* "A genius departs" Volume 401 Number 8754.

Isaacson, W. (October 17th, 2011). *Time.* "American Icon" Volume 178 Number 15.

Grossman, L. & McCracken, H. (October 17th, 2011). *Time.* "The Inventor of The Future" Volume 178 Number 15.

Milian, M. (October 6th, 2011) *The spiritual side of Steve Jobs.* http://www.cnn.com/2011/10/05/tech/innovation/steve-jobs-philosophy/index.html

Gandhi, M.K., (1995). *My Religion,* edited by Bharatan Kumarappa, Navajivan Publishing House.

APPENDIX A: RESOURCES FOR PERSONAL AND PROFESSIONAL EFFECTIVENESS

The Master Mind Group

There are two forms of a Master Mind Group.

The first is a collection of people committed to each other's success and function as one part networking and one part motivation.

The second form is similar but has a concise system for shifting the mind into forward focused action and expectation. This group uses the Master Mind Process designed by Rev. Jack Boland. Jack was the minister at UNITY Church of Today near Detroit, Michigan.

This second form is usually done without anything but a formal process. There is very little networking or brainstorming.

For more information about Master Mind groups, check out Napoleon Hill's *Think and Grow Rich* and Jack Boland's *The Master Mind Principle*.

I personally enjoy a combination of these two forms. A formal process of directing the mind is powerful with a group. Then the members of that same group actively help each other to connect with resources, to think outside the box.

APPENDIX B: RESOURCE LIST BY SUBJECT MATTER

(There is repetition here, which means repeated material is really good.)

STUFF I THINK IS REALLY COOL

Anything You Want, Derek Sivers – entrepreneurs, buy this book.

Music by *Seth Bernard*... this is the real deal. www.samuelsethbernard.com

The Art of War, Stephen Pressfield

The Blind Café... a nationally touring performance experience. Check it out at www.theblindcafe.com

The Artists Way, Julia Cameron

The Alchemist, Paulo Coelho

American Meat, documentary by Graham Meriwether, solutions focused for health, quality of life and food production

The Blues Brothers, a film by John Landis, which will teach you about how to have a mission from God.

Integral Life, Provider of educational media on the emerging integral worldview

Stagen, A leadership and consulting firm that specializes in helping mid-size businesses scale, using integral theory framework

Prezi, 3 dimensional presentations, www.Prezi.com

God Grew Tired of Us, this documentary tells the story of John Bul Dau, and other "Lost Boys of Sudan." What starts in Sudan, ends in America. It is both heart breaking and uplifting.

Buck is the documentary of the life and work of the real "horse whisperer." His work shows you how real love can transform animals and people.

SUCCESS PRINCIPLE RESOURCES

The Success Principles, Jack Canfield

As a Man Thinketh, James Allen

Success Through a Positive Mental Attitude, Napoleon Hill and W. Clement Stone.

The 12 Universal Laws of Success, Herbert Harris

Making Your Dreams Come True, Marcia Wieder

Your Greatest Power, J. Martin Kohe

The Power of Positive Thinking, Norman Vincent Peale

Outliers, Malcolm Gladwell

The Power of Possibility Thinking; Life Is Not Fair, But God Is Good!; Be an Extraordinary Person in an Ordinary World; If It's Going to Be, It Is Up to Me; all and more by Rev. Robert H. Schuller

The 5 Principles of Success, Newt and Carrie Gingrich

Start With Why, Simon Sinek

Doing Less and Having More, Marcia Wieder

The Art of Non-Conformity, Chris Guillebeau. He also runs the World Domination Summit, www.worlddominationsummit.com, which I would love to attend soon.

The Four Hour Work-Week, Timothy Ferris

CHARACTER DEVELOPMENT RESOURCES

The 7 Habits of Highly of Highly Effective People, Dr. Stephen Covey

Men's Leadership Alliance, *The Art of Leadership Training and other trainings,* www.mensleadershipalliance.org, how to be a man.

Men, Meaning and Prayer, by Jeffrey Duvall with James Churches

The 8th Habit, Dr. Stephen Covey

First Things First, Dr. Stephen Covey

Truth vs. Falsehood: How To Tell The Difference, Dr. David R. Hawkins

Benjamin Franklin: The Autobiography and Other Writings

I Dare You, William H. Danforth

Uncommon, Tony Dungy (outlines powerful principles to step up to the plate as a man)

Way of The Spiritual Warrior, Dan Millman

A Woman's Worth, Marianne Williamson

CREATIVITY AND HUMAN PERFORMANCE RESOURCES

Naropa University – Programs in visual arts, music, dance, and writing and poetics. "Where east and west collide, sparks will fly." A laboratory for experimental creative work and personal development for close to 30 years.

The Artist's Way, Julia Cameron

Awaken the Giant Within, Anthony Robbins (one of the most tagged, dog-eared, highlighted books that I own)

Walking In This World, Julia Cameron

The War of Art, Stephen Pressfield

Power vs. Force, Dr. David R. Hawkins

Creating Minds, Howard Gardner

Intelligence Reframed, Howard Gardner

Switch: How To Change Things When Change Is Hard, Chip and Dan Heath

The Three Laws of Performance, Steve Zaffrron & Dave Logan (an excellent, straightforward guide to creating possibilities in your life, family, and organization)

Made to Stick, Chip and Dan Heath

Six Thinking Hats, Edward De Bono

A Mythic Life, Jean Houston

George Washington Carver, Rackham Holt

Drive: The Surprising Truth About What Motivates Us, Daniel Pink

MARKETING AND SALES RESOURCES

Instant Income, Janet Switzer. A virtual storm of information that you can come back to again and again to build a business.

The Ultimate Sales Machine, Chet Holmes is another tsunami of sales and marketing content. His intensity comes through the page and is a great motivation to action.

The Greatest Salesman in the World, Og Mandino

Permission Marketing, Tribes, Purple Cow, and other books and lectures from Seth Godin.

InfusionSoft, http://www.infusionsoft.com/ E-mail and contact management with useful follow up, web form, tracking, and customization features.

Power Up Productions, Ryan Oelke is a Word Press Boss and specializes in getting blog websites up for small businesses. http://www.powerupproductions.tv/

Site Build It, http://www.sitesell.com/ A simple and effective system for setting up an income producing website. The designs are plain. The training is the best in its class. Note that this type of site may or may not be relevant to actually represent your practice but it is a great platform for a web-based business, adjunct to your practice.

Constant Contact, www.constantcontact.com, a standard in newsletter systems.

1ShoppingCart.com, one of the main platforms for web commerce.

Eben Pagan, Info-marketing online. Google him.

Rich Sheffren, More info marketing online.

Robert Notter, A consistent provider of solid and effective marketing training for holistic health professionals, http://www.bookclientsnow.com/. Here is what Robert has to say: *I love supporting others to claim abundance and freedom in their finances, doing work they love. And having the ability, through this work, to create the same for myself.*

Stacey Morgenstern and **Carey Peters** of **Holistic MBA** have made marketing their focal point. Friends and colleagues have benefited from their offerings. I have collaborated with Stacey and can see that she is thorough and committed to creating value for her clients. Check her out at www.HolisticMBA.com

Mark Silver, http://www.heartofbusiness.com/ The Heart of Business, sales, marketing, and business advice especially for introverts and people in the healing arts that don't like the "over-the-top" marketing styles of other business/sales coaches.

The Shef, http://www.theshef.com/ sales and marketing trainer and speaker.

Book Yourself Solid, Michael Port, www.bookyourselfsolid.com.

Attracting Perfect Customers, Stacey Hall & Jan Grogniez

Get Clients Now!, C. J. Hayden

BUSINESS RESOURCES

Business Mastery Training, A Tony Robbins and Chet Holmes business boot camp with live event, coaching, and media.

The Three Laws Of Performance, Steve Zaffron and Dave Logan

Good to Great, Jim Collins. Although it was written as an analysis of big companies, the lessons apply to anyone in business, including private practice. I have come back to this book over and over again and it keeps bearing fruit.

The Tipping Point, Malcolm Gladwell

The 5th Discipline, Peter Senge

Conscious Business, Fred Kaufman

Knockout Entrepreneur, George Foreman

Business Mastery, Cherie Sonan-Moe offers a great fundamentals book for health professionals.

The Discipline of Market Leaders, Michael Treacy & Fred Wiersema

Getting Things Done, David Allen

Making It All Work, David Allen

SBDC The Small Business Development Center offers FREE business consulting to you. All you need to do is locate the SBDC closest to you and schedule an appointment.

SBA The Small Business Association funds the SBDC and also offers other support, including assistance with some types up start of funding.

Integral Incubator, at Boulder Integral, a 5-day immersion in your business and life with amazing people from around the world. www. IntegralIncubator.com

PUBLIC SPEAKING RESOURCES

Toastmasters International is the world's largest organization dedicated to training competent communicators. The mission of a Toastmasters club is to provide a mutually supportive and positive learning environment in which every individual member has the opportunity to develop oral communication and leadership skills, which in turn foster self-confidence and personal growth.

National Speakers Association is the largest professional organization for professional speakers.

Confessions of a Public Speaker, Scott Berkun

Slide:ology: The Art and Science of Great Presentations, Nancy Duarte

Increasing Your Presentation Power, Les Brown

Speak and Grow Rich, Alice and Dottie Walters

Motivating Your Audience, Hanoch McCarty

Speaking Your Way to the Top, Marjorie Brody

Speaking for Profit and Pleasure, William D. Thompson

Speaker's Edge: Secrets and Strategies For Connecting With Any Audience, Mark Brown, Darren LaCroix, Patricia Fripp, Ed Tate, Craig Valentine

Ted Talks, www.Ted.com, The 18 minute talks have changed the standard for public speaking.

MONEY RESOURCES

The Conscious Bookkeeping Home Study Course, Coaching and Programs, Bari Tessler & Staff, http://www.consciousbookkeeping.com

The Soul of Money, Lynn Twist

Think and Grow Rich, Napoleon Hill

Your Money or Your Life, Joe Dominguez and Vicki Robin

The Courage to Be Rich, Suze Orman

Rich Dad, Poor Dad (and series), Robert Kyosaki

Acres of Diamonds, Russell Conwell

Andrew Carnegie, David Nasaw

The Education of Millionaires, Michael Ellsberg

Overcoming Underearning, Barbara Stanny

The Economist, get a subscription.

*my***Local,** www.mylocal.coop, novel platform for keeping money in a community and building robust local economies that can weather national fluctuations

PRODUCTIVITY AND EFFECTIVENESS

Getting Things Done, David Allen. You have to read this. Period.

Making Things Work, David Allen. A follow up to *Getting Things Done.* Worth reading on its own and a great follow up to GTD.

7 Habits of Highly Effective People, Stephen Covey

The 8th Habit, Stephen Covey

The Pomodoro Technique, Francisco Cirillo, great site, www. pomodorotechnique.com, plus many apps online for timers, here is one I use http://tomatoi.st/avkk

COACHING SYSTEMS / CONSULTING TOOLS

4 Gateways Coaching. This is the first form of coaching that I practiced diligently for many years. The founder, Dr. Tom Daly, is a master trainer. I highly recommend completing his training program. The Indestructible Coach training that we offer qualifies for Weekend One of the 4 Gateways certification program. For more information, check out: www.4GatewaysCoaching.com.

Shadow Work Seminars, a wealth of resources on human transformation including Shadow Work Facilitation trainings, founded by Cliff Berry and Mary Ellen Whalen. Similar in many ways to 4 Gateways Coaching, Cliff is a close friend of Dr. Tom Daly.

Tony Robbins could go under any of these categories because he has created information products on every aspect of life. He is the guy that deserves credit for creating the "coaching" industry. His book *Awaken the Giant Within* and *Unlimited Power* are classics already. My copy of *Awaken the Giant Within* is so worn, tagged, highlighted, and marked up, it's unbelievable. I have repeatedly gone through his audio programs over the last fifteen years and I have attended live programs. He is a big inspiration to me.

Institute for Integrative Nutrition – Health Coaching program for the next generation of leaders in whole person health care.

The Sedona Method – Hale Dwoskin's work based on emotional release techniques for greater freedom.

Mastery of Life, Bill Ferguson

Miracles are Guaranteed, Bill Ferguson

Love, Courage and Achievement Project (LCA), Randy Ferguson, www.LCAProject.com

Olga Aura, Coach for women around relationships and money, walks her talk, www.IAmFullyAlive.com

Finding Your Own North Star: Claiming the Life You Were Meant to Live, Martha Beck

The Power of TED* The Empowerment Dynamic, David Emerald

Why Good People Do Bad Things, Debbie Ford

Immunity to Change, Robert Kegan, Lisa Laskow Lahey

SuperCoach, Michael Neil

Executive Coaching With Backbone and Heart, Mary Beth O'Neil

Power in The Helping Professions, Adolf Guggenbühl-Craig

Right Use of Power, Cedar Barstow

RELATIONSHIP AND COMMUNICATION RESOURCES

Outrageously Fulfilling Relationships, Randy Ferguson

Real Love, Dr. Greg Baer

Real Love in Marriage, Dr. Greg Baer

How To Heal A Painful Relationship, Bill Ferguson

Non-Violent Communication, Marshall Rosenberg

The Soulful Communication Process, created by Taber Shadburne

7 Habits of Highly Effective People, Dr. Stephen Covey

The Relationship Cure, Dr. John Gottman

The Living Arts Foundation, Dr. Tom Daly and Jude Blitz offer powerful family systems facilitation and relationship coaching.

Family Systems Constellation Work of Burt Hellinger

CONSCIOUSNESS AND SPIRITUALITY RESOURCES

A Course In Miracles, The Foundation for Inner Peace

The Holy Bible (especially the New Testament, Psalms, and Proverbs)

The Bhagavad Gita, translated by Ecknath Eswaran or Mohandas K. Gandhi (There are many translations; these two are personal preferences.)

My Religion, Mohandas K. Gandhi

Anatomy of The Spirit, Caroline Myss

Integral Yoga, Sri Auribindo

Grace and Grit, Ken Wilber

Sex, Ecology, Spirituality, Ken Wilber

The Way of The Peaceful Warrior, Dan Millman

Eye of the I, Dr. David Hawkins

I: Reality and Subjectivity, Dr. David R. Hawkins

Transcending the Levels of Consciousness, Dr. David R. Hawkins

Discovery of the Presence of God, Dr. David R. Hawkins

Reality, Spirituality and Modern Man, Dr. David R. Hawkins

Call Me By My True Names: The Collected Poems of Tich Nhat Hanh, Tich Nhat Hanh

Going Home, Jesus and Buddha as Brothers, Tich Nhat Hanh

Cutting Through Spiritual Materialism, Chogyam Trungpa Rinpoche

Shambhala: Sacred Path of the Warrior, Chogyam Trungpa Rinpoche

Transcendental Meditation, www.TM.org, and consciousness-based education, www.MUM.edu

Lessons In Truth, H. Emilie Cady

How to Know God: The Yoga Aphorisms of Patanjali, translated by Swami Prabhavananda & Christopher Isherwood

Soul Survivor: How Thirteen Unlikely Mentors Helped My Faith Survive the Church, Phillip Yancey, WaterBrook Press, 2003

UNITY Worldwide Ministries, "Unity is a positive, practical, progressive approach to Christianity based on the teachings of Jesus and the power of prayer. Unity honors the universal truths in all religions and respects each individual's right to choose a spiritual path." www.UNITY.org

INTEGRAL THEORY

The Integral Vision, Ken Wilber

A Brief History of Everyting, Ken Wilber

Sex, Ecology, Spirituality, Ken Wilber

Integral Life Practice, Ken Wilber, Terry Patten, Adam Leonard, Marco Morelli

The ILP Kit, The Integral Institute

Integral Life, www.IntegralLife.com

Core Integral, www.CoreIntegral.com

Integral Coaching Canada, www.integralcoachingcanada.com

Spiral Dynamics: Mastering Values, Leadership and Change, Don Beck

Susanne Cook-Greuter shares exceptional materials, including papers and reviews at her site, www.cook-greuter.com

In Over Our Heads: The Mental Demands of Modern Life, Robert Keagan

Integral Health, Elliot Dacher

Stagen, www.Stagen.com, applied integral theory for executives and mid-market companies

HEALTH AND WELLNESS

Corporate Health Programs that work, www.transformationone.com

Institute for Integrative Nutrition – teaching cutting edge nutrition and health curriculum worldwide.

Weston A Price Foundation – Unique and refreshing perspectives on health and nutrition, publisher of *Nourishing Traditions.*

Metabolic Typing – Dr. William Walcott's book *Metabolic Typing* and the parent organization, **Health Excel** can help you discover what foods work for you and connect you with a Metabolic Typing professional.

Healing With Whole Foods, Paul Pitchford, the encyclopedia of nutrition

Lifespa – Dr. John Douillard, author of *The Three-Season Diet, Body, Mind and Sport,* www.LifeSpa.com.

Health Coaches – Two of the best nationally recognized health coaches, for women, Angelina Deweese at www.PureNourishment.com, and for men, Lucas Seipp-Williams at www.BaltimoreHealthCoach.com, or for a directory, www.integrativenutrition.com/alumni/findahealthcoach

Boulder Nutrition – Sue Van Raes, MS in nutrition offers clinical and whole food nutrition.

Mandala Integrative Medicine Clinic – offers acupuncture, bodywork, and many other forms of whole person healing in Boulder, Colorado.

Jingui Golden Shield Qi Gong, www.Jingui.com

APPENDIX C: THE INDESTRUCTIBLE SUCCESS FORMULA FOR SETTING GOALS

1. Write down the goal.

2. Put a date on it.

3. Ask yourself why you want to achieve this? What burning desire do you have for this?

4. List the obstacles that you need to overcome.

5. Identify the people, groups, or organizations that you need to work with. Establish a Mastermind Group if appropriate.

6. Make a list of skills & qualities you have that contribute to your goal.

7. Make a list of skills & qualities you will need to develop to reach your goal.

8. Spell out a plan of action with a mind map. Identify everything that you think you will need to do.

9. Set the time limit in the plan. Put it into a linear timeline with milestones in a twelve-month period.

10. Identify all the benefits that you will receive from achieving the goal and all of the loss that you will have if you fail to reach the goal.

11. Define the time you can take each week in your Work Your Plan process.

12. Put the timeline in a schedule on your calendar, in a mind map on the wall, or some other referential system.

13. Determine who will hold you accountable in a supportive way (if applicable).

14. See and feel your goal totally complete. Every morning and evening, visualize yourself successful.

That is the process. If you commit to this and persist despite the sure presence of obstacles, stay focused, and believe in yourself, you will experience tremendous results!

APPENDIX D: CHECKLIST FOR ACHIEVEMENT

1. Heal and address the habitual unconscious evading of hurt and pain that is driving the fear-driven, tunnel vision, compulsive behavior, and self-sabotage that prevent you from having 100 percent of your resources available. Be willing to have the thing you fear most happen, not intending it, not creating it, not wanting it, just remove the resistance (the fear) to it happening and address the unresolved emotional issue that is fueling projection of the unresolved situation into an imagined future.

2. Focus on what you want to create. Imagine it is done already. Act as if this was reality now. Use affirmative invocation to bring out your best each day.

3. Make sure your goal aligns with your core values, skills, talents, desires, and dreams.

4. Paradoxically, get clear on all that you will lose if you do not follow this goal as a way to condition the nervous system away from procrastination. NOTE: This may seem opposite to the instructions in number one, which address core issues. Step five deals directly with decisions directing behavior, not with core issues as hidden determinants. Both are essential.

5. Constantly cultivate your own character, integrity, dignity, industriousness, speech, manners, and sobriety for the sake of becoming a person who can contain the higher bandwidth of energy that will come from having your goal. After all, it is not really something that we want to get; it is who we want to *become* that we seek.

6. Have a clear and definite purpose in your life and make sure your goal is in direct alignment with your purpose.

7. Have faith that there is a power that supports you in your life. Whatever that faith is, is up to you, but you must have faith. The Great Creator gives us goals that are just outside of our reach so that we are forced to call forth faith in something greater than ourselves, which stretches us always further and further than we thought we could go!

8. Know that happiness and fulfillment do not come from the world of form. We do not have goals to get something or to gain happiness. We have goals to express something and to direct our own nature, which is happiness and creativity.

9. Stay away from *Danger Zones*.

ACKNOWLEDGEMENTS AND SHOUT OUTS

Thanks to my wife, AnaVictoria, and daughters, Paloma and Marisol, the most important people in the world to me. Thanks for putting up with my grumpiness while putting in the late nights writing.

A special heartfelt thanks to Randy Ferguson and the Love Courage & Achievement (LCA) Project. Randy Ferguson's LCA Project inspired me to create the format of our live trainings. He masterfully facilitates growth experiences for people. For more information on Randy's work, visit www.LCAProject.com.

Thanks to all the Integral pioneers, especially Jeff Salzman, Nomali Perera, and the staff at Boulder Integral, Robert MacNaughton at Integral Life and all of the other Integral friends too numerous to name here.

Thank you to the emerging Integral community in Fairfield, Iowa: Steve Cooperman, Robbie Gongwer, Ashley Smith, Andrew Perry and all of the rest of you at the Bonnell Building, The Beauty Shop, and the St. Mary's project.

Deep bow to Men's Leadership Alliance, Dr. Tom Daly, Jeffrey Duvall, Keith Fairmont, and the Moon Belly men's group for all you taught me about being a man. www.MensLeadershipAlliance.com

Thanks to Jason Digges for constantly providing peer-to-peer review of my work. You have helped me get clearer about how to serve.

Thanks to Steven McCugh at Unison Business Consultants for the great business coaching that helped me further clarify and distill this work for maximum service to others.

Thanks to Morella Devost for the content and editorial support. The self-study portions are essential.

Thanks to Olga Aura for the feedback on illustrations and content and for the peer mentoring we have shared. www.IAmFullyAlive.com

Thanks to Marco Lam for the critical feedback and for encouraging me to share some of my successes in the book and for sharing the Mandala Integrative Medicine Clinic with me.

Thanks to Jack Ackerman and Christine LePorte Editorial Services and Steve Cooperman for proofreading.

Lauryn Shapter and Steve Cooperman came in at the end to bring the material the final professional touch. Thank you for the tough feedback and very thorough editing.

Thanks to Nicole Didio Johnson for a magnificent cover. www.TheHealthyDesign.com

Sylvie Abecassis is a creative genius. She did the design for this book as well as the cover and design of my first book, *Healthy, Fast and Cheap*. Thank you.

Thanks to Joshua Rosenthal, founder of the Institute for Integrative Nutrition, the Institute for Integrative Nutrition alumni, the IIN Immersion program, my student coaching clients, and for the many opportunities to teach this material, and a very special thanks to all of my immersion and student clients that reviewed this manuscript.

Thanks to mentors Sina Simantob and Dr. Mark Belford for many conversations about life and work.

Thanks to my Dream Team peers and Master Mind team.

Thanks to the participants in the Men's Mastery Course, especially Lucas Seipp-Williams, for helping me create an amazing program where we tested these concepts.

Thanks to the foundational P3E Project Alumni (the precursor to Indestructible Success) for being the test subjects for this material (Ondrea Lynn, Jeanne Cooper, Megan Gelber, Morella Devost, Slavka Benova, Beata Andreone, Rose Soto, Brandon Redlinger).

Thanks to Jonathan Hefter and Lucas Seipp-Williams for co-coaching.

Thanks to the all the Awakened Life project participants for helping me fine-tune these techniques and principles in real time facilitation.

I am grateful for all of the Golden Speakers, Speakers Trust, Area 92, Division E and District 19 and International Toastmasters with whom I have worked, supporting each other to grow and develop as leaders and communicators. What a wonderful group of people.

ABOUT INDESTRUCTIBLE SUCCESS PROGRAMS:

We offer training programs for the next step in your journey of personal and professional effectiveness.

Indestructible Success Group – Contact us through www.SethBraun.com
- **Speaking** – We represent excellent speakers. If we take you on as a client, we guarantee that our message will be well received by your audience.
- **Consulting** – Our team is available for strategy to a limited number of clients each year. We like to work for businesses we like.
- **Training** – If you need custom training on the topics covered in the book, contact to see if there is a match with our trainers.
- **Facilitation** – Customized application of the Indestructible Success model to lead businesses and departments to greater communication, sharper vision, and results-oriented teamwork.

The Indestructible Success Training – Go through the Dreams > Vision > Goals > Plans > Action sequence with the support of our skilled facilitators. Work through inner obstacles and create courage and confidence to live the life of your dreams.

Indestructible Business – Use the Indestructible Success model to achieve better results in your business. Includes training in authentic sales and marketing, public speaking, and sustainable business practices.

Indestructible Success: Men's Mastery Course – A variety of retreats and programs culminating with the MMC 'Best Year of Your Life,' 52-week program. This high level-coaching program for men is comprehensive and terrifically effective at producing results for committed men, ages 24-42. Previous experience with coaching or personal growth is required.

More information at www.SethBraun.com.

Have fun and keep it real.

Did you just read this book like it was a hot meal,
all nourishing and satisfying?

Does this material light you up?

Are you ready to play full out with like-minded people?

If so, you may be part of the Indie Success tribe!

Come get some more!

If you haven't done so, sign up for the FREE twenty-eight video Business
Accelerator Course at SethBraun.com.

Hey, if you already watched the video series and that is how you discovered
this book, go ahead and head over to SethBraun.com and sign up for our
blog updates and newsletter where we send out new videos, interviews,
speaking dates, and heads up on cool stuff.

Join the Facebook group by searching "Indestructible Success".

Follow us on Twitter for resourceful state reminders and other updates.

Welcome to our world!